Identity and Inner-City Youth

Beyond Ethnicity and Gender

Identity and Inner-City Youth

Beyond Ethnicity and Gender

Edited by

Shirley Brice Heath and Milbrey W. McLaughlin

TEACHERS
COLLEGE
PRESS

Teachers College, Columbia University
New York and London

Published by Teachers College Press, 1234 Amsterdam Avenue, New York, N.Y. 10027

Copyright © 1993 by Teachers College, Columbia University

Library of Congress Cataloging-in-Publication Data

Identity and inner-city youth: beyond ethnicity and
    gender/edited by Shirley Brice Heath and Milbrey McLaughlin.
        p.   cm.
    Includes bibliographical references and index.
    ISBN 0-8077-3253-2 (alk. paper).—ISBN 0-8077-3252-4 (pbk.:
alk. paper)
        1. Urban youth—United States—Attitudes. 2. Youth—United
States—Societies and clubs. 3. Social work with youth—United
States. 4. Self-esteem in adolescence—United States. I. Heath,
Shirley Brice. II. McLaughlin, Milbrey Wallin.
    HQ796.B788   1993
    305.23'5'0973—dc20   92-45696

ISBN 0-8077-3253-2
ISBN 0-8077-3252-4 (pbk)

Printed on acid-free paper
Manufactured in the United States of America
99 98 97 96 95 94 93   8 7 6 5 4 3 2 1

Contents

Chapter 8 — 196

Misperceptions of Gender and Youth: Learning Together,
    Learning Apart
Elisabeth Hansot

Chapter 9 — 210

Casting the Self: Frames for Identity and Dilemmas for Policy
Milbrey W. McLaughlin and Shirley Brice Heath

Index — 241

About the Contributors — 249

Introduction

Identity and Inner-City Youth

Shirley Brice Heath
Milbrey W. McLaughlin

The universe, which is not merely the stars and the moon and the planets, flowers, grass, and trees, but *other people*, has evolved no terms for your existence, has made no room for you. . . .

James Baldwin
The Fire Next Time

Politicians thrive on having problems to solve and prefer those that are dramatic, short term, and distant. By the final decades of the 20th century, it was clear that the problems of inner-city youth would receive little direct and sympathetic attention from policymakers, for the problems of urban life are repetitive, enduring, and too close to home. For more than a century, public institutions, ranging from settlement houses to schools to social agencies, had been expected to take care of the problems of youth in the ghettos. And they failed to do so, leaving urban areas with the continuing dangers represented by gangs, poverty, crime, and—by the 1980s—teenage parenthood, drugs, and AIDS. Policymakers and the general public blamed institutions for offering an inadequate approach to these problems: Law enforcement agencies, schools, and, finally, families had not kept urban youngsters in line and successfully prepared them to become effective citizens, workers, and parents.

It was this policy situation that we entered in the late 1980s—McLaughlin as a policy analyst and Heath as a linguistic anthropologist. Both of us had long-term experience in studying schools, subordinated populations, and policy-making and implementation designed to solve "the problem of inner-city youth." And both of us puzzled over a similar observation. Our work in schools had revealed to us cases of successful youngsters whose home and community lives should have foretold disaster but who had somehow survived—who had not been destroyed by their environments. We asked the simple question: Is there anything these young people have in common?

Dimensions of Selfhood

When we discussed this question with our colleagues in education and youth policy, expressions such as "self-esteem," "ethnic pride," and "a sense of self" occurred again and again in their answers. We always emerged dissatisfied from these conversations, for aside from individual case histories and anecdotes, our colleagues offered us little that could be of practical use, either to policymakers or to youth workers. Only the barest hint of anything resembling an "answer" was contained in these discussions: Youngsters whose inner strength got them through the toughest of community, home, and school situations were often linked in some way with neighborhood-based organizations. We decided to take this slim lead and follow it. McLaughlin wanted to know what makes it possible to construct an environment for youth that creates a strong sense of self. Heath wanted data on the everyday life—the speech, behavior, and beliefs—of youngsters who found their way into environments of learning that enabled them to develop a sense of self, of empowerment, and of persistence.

These questions led to 5 years of fieldwork in youth organizations of inner cities. We worked with a team of ethnographers in some of the most troubled neighborhoods of three major metropolitan areas of the United States, referred to here as River City, Lakeside, and Big Valley. Each of these urban areas had made concerted efforts to identify and support effective programs for urban youth; all had strong philanthropic support and had initiated efforts at collaboration among diverse policy groups and youth organizations in their cities. In addition, all were significantly involved in major school reform efforts they had begun in the 1980s. Although all of these metropolitan areas had strong traditions of ethnic identity and separation, each had also pursued efforts since the 1960s to relieve ethnic tensions and to offer places of leadership to the growing number of middle-class African-Americans and Latinos. But each urban area continued to suffer from what local officials regarded as severe problems of dissent: pockets of poverty; increased drug, gang, and criminal activities by youngsters; and frightening levels of school attrition and unemployment among young people of color.

In each of these metropolitan areas, in organizations ranging from the Boy Scouts to Boys and Girls Clubs to church youth choirs and sports teams of community centers, McLaughlin pursued questions related to these organizations' history, rationale, leadership, networking, and governance. McLaughlin was curious about the ecology of youth organizations and about the ways that city politics, local leadership, and financial possibilities affected these institutions. She spent long hours with city and county officials, philanthropists, and administrators of national and local youth organizations to gain an understanding of their views on youth and on the programs that served them. She wanted to know how the layers that embedded youth—from their local neighborhoods to city politics—shaped their institutional and individual identities and how the diverse conceptions of youth expressed at various locations within a community joined together—or did not join together—to produce policies and programs for youth.

Heath focused on discovering how youth organizations strengthened and empowered disenfranchised youngsters who found their way to the groups they believed could help them to survive the streets. Heath believed that the catch phrases of "self-esteem" or "making kids feel good about themselves" operated through highly specific ways of speaking, using space, and forming relationships in the work and play of organizations. Documenting these patterns could reveal much about how young people build a sense of themselves.

Use of space, the shape and content of narratives, the pace and type of activities, and the ways in which youth leaders gave directions all emerged as the "stuff" with which youngsters constructed their views of their own lives and of their potential. "Junior ethnographers" from within these organizations worked with trained ethnographers to document—through field notes, audiotapes, and videotapes—the speech, activities, and reflections on life of these young people in their neighborhood-based organizations.

We all adopted a particular youth-based notion of effectiveness in choosing organizations to study. Effective youth organizations were those judged as such by community young people who wanted to be members of these groups, choose their friends from members, and identify their free time, away from schools and households, with those organizations. Although these groups were often not those highlighted as the most successful ones in the eyes of city officials, local educators, or regional politicians, they were the ones that the youth of the neighborhoods considered good places to be. This judgment was reflected in their oversubscriptions, waiting lists, and high positive visibility across all segments of the local communities.[1]

The primary audience for this book consists of those who both shape youth policy and work directly with young people in urban areas. Included in these categories are not only those who are professional social workers, recreation therapists, administrators, and educators in community centers run by city parks and recreation units, but also volunteers, such as Girl Scout leaders, church choir directors, and administrators of independent community centers. Many of those who sustain youth organizations are either part-time or unpaid workers—people who have other careers and who work in these groups because of their commitment to youth in general or their desire to be involved with their own children's activities in such groups. A large portion of these individuals dedicate their time because of their conviction of the value of their work to other causes, such as organized religion or community cohesion.

Yet another audience for this book is educators, especially those who increasingly feel that families and other community institutions, such as churches, no longer support the education of youth as they did in the past. Some of these educators find it possible to turn to community youth organizations as partners in their effort to help meet students' mental and physical health needs, as well as to give educational support through tutoring and scholarship programs. Such educators may find much within this book about learning, discipline, and group cohesion that will be useful as they consider potential collaborations with youth organizations.

In late 1992, the Carnegie Council on Adolescent Development urged that the public and private sectors give special attention to the out-of-school experiences of young people. In their study of the nonschool hours of youth, they found that unscheduled, unstructured, and unsupervised time spelled trouble for young people. The report recommended that communities build networks of youth organizations that incorporated the interests, energies, and ideas of young people, and that they be given roles of responsibility within these organizations—teaching others, caring for facilities, and planning activities, finances, and governance of the youth groups. Such organizations must proceed, however, not as mere adjuncts to school or as "youth-servicing" agencies, but as groups that establish young people at their center—as resources.

Currently, those youth leaders and organizations judged most effective by young people do not define themselves with reference to schools. Most exist with relatively little recognition from or similarity to schools; most of the young who come to these organizations, in fact, regard school as a place that has rejected and labeled them by *what they are not* rather than by *what they are.* Young people resent, for example, labels such as "*non*–college bound" for those whose academic achievement is interpreted by schools as insufficient for further education.

Inner-city youth see themselves excluded from school life in other ways as well. They find few connections between their lives and those of young-sters who populate ethnicity-based clubs. Their academic records often exclude them from student councils, cheerleading, or athletic teams. Hence, they find no groups that they can join for sustained activities and team membership within schools. In addition, they often hear themselves labeled ethnically as "those blacks," "those Hispanics," or "those Asians." They have little sense of why or how such terms might bear any relation to their daily interactions with their neighborhood friends or street connections. Their public housing units and neighborhood shopping areas are populated with families that include members of many different national, ethnic, racial, and linguistic groups, as well as families with widely varying amounts and types of experience with life in the United States.

Beyond Ethnicity and Gender in Youth Organizations

What do effective youth organizations offer inner-city youngsters that schools do not?

In our 5 years spent studying 60 different organizations engaging in a total of approximately 24,000 youngsters, we found that over 90% of these groups were located in communities described by local city officials as "the projects," "the barrio," or, alternately, "communities suffering from poverty, crime, severe ethnic tensions, teenage pregnancies, and broken families." Public officials characterized these neighborhood-based organizations—casting them in a variety of prevention, intervention, or reform roles—as rehabilitation opportunities for young people who wanted "a way out" and as alternatives to the crime, violence, and drugs in the young people's own homes and on the streets of their communities. Approximately 10% of the groups were institutions that catered to youngsters from neighborhoods scattered all over the city, brought together by a specific focus on national heritage, often with the goal of practicing for particular activities planned for local folk festivals.

Many local public officials, often only indirectly connected to the inner-city youth for whom they set policies and programs, believed that most neighborhood youth organizations had to be centered around ethnic inter-ests to build a sense of ethnic or racial pride. The assumptions of policy-makers who retained images from the 1960s of proud, protesting, largely homogeneous urban ghetto communities rarely met dissent in board meet-ings or planning committees. Within a year or so into our study, however, we began to question just how central ethnic identity was to inner-city youth in the 1990s.

We convened a small conference of youth workers and social scientists to consider this and other related issues, as well as the question of gender roles and ways that gender identity played out in building the self-conceptions of inner-city youth. Several individuals who attended that conference have contributed chapters here to help answer the question of how *ethnicity* and *gender* figure in building the embedded identities of youth in different contexts.[2]

Ethnicity seemed, from the youth perspective, to be more often a label assigned to them by outsiders than an indication of their real sense of self.[3] Many young people told us repeatedly, "Ethnicity ain't what it's really all about." To them, ethnic labels could mean something only later on; achieving a sense of belonging and of knowing that they could *do* something and *be* someone in the eyes of others had to come first. Ethnicity came to carry import only as it functioned within a host of embedded identities that could get a young person somewhere in the immediate community. Being the local tough kid's younger brother, the girlfriend of a prominent gang member, or a player on a winning local ball team counted more heavily in daily street life than one's label of ethnic membership. Many young people pointed out that at one time their communities may have been identified with a single ethnic group but that what they see today are different groups continually moving in and out of their housing projects and neighborhoods. They have learned to "hang with all kinds," to "be local," to get along, and to survive. They acknowledged that they had heard of inner cities where "everybody looks and talks alike" but said that they see their daily world as a place filled with diversity and unpredictable changes. "Flav," meaning flavor of the month, entered the jargon of young people as a term for the rapid changes they saw in their communities, their homes, and their social environments.[4]

Gender, on the other hand, was a concept that policymakers usually addressed in the context of age, generally confusing gender and sex when offering opinions such as "sex [is] a problem as kids get older." As long as policymakers could make decisions in terms of the traditional expectations of certain groups (such as the Boy Scouts or Girls Clubs), they felt comfortable. But with the creation of groups such as the Boys and Girls Clubs, national boards in particular found it difficult to reconcile the different types of responses from local communities.[5] Some community members wanted to keep boys and girls separated; others argued that more equitable opportunities would be offered to girls if they joined with boys. Views of appropriate gender behavior were expressed by specific ethnic groups, such as Latino parents, who often wanted activities that were designed just for girls and others that were designed just for boys. African American community leaders were more likely to want young males to have intensive opportunities for sustained engagement with adult male leaders of scout troops, athletic teams, and leadership clubs and to give little, if any, attention to the needs of young females. In every site studied, the young people themselves often expressed choices that differed across occasions, audiences, and such volatile issues as the relative power of male and female neighborhood gangs. Most policymakers, meanwhile, saw far more need for structured recreational and vigorous activities for boys than for girls; if idle, boys could be in the streets "causing trouble," while girls were more likely to be at home or in shopping malls.

Dichotomies persisted throughout our study between the reality that policymakers perceived and the reality of the everyday life of youngsters in inner cities. We try here to represent both worlds as they are constructed from the very different perspectives of the urban young themselves and those outside the lives of the young people. Most of the young considered in this volume are those whose families and communities suffer from all or some of the blows of late 20th-century urban life: decaying housing, drug and alcohol abuse, extreme swings of poverty, high rates of crime and violence, and educational neglect. Among the youth organizations we studied were local units of national organizations (e.g., Camp Fire, Girl Scouts and Boy Scouts, Boys and Girls Clubs), as well as community institutions (e.g., centers established by parks and recreation boards) and grass-roots organizations founded by community residents. All of these neighborhood-based organizations serve as places where young people can go when they are not in school, at home, at work, or on the streets. These organizations are frequently characterized, especially in impoverished communities, as alternatives to both home and street life.

Both public perceptions and policies for the lives of many young people in the United States—in schools as well as in youth organizations—often focus on concepts such as self-esteem, identity, peer relations, and acceptance of authority, especially as these relate to ethnicity and gender. These concepts often appear simultaneously with perceptions of community locale—especially for inner-city youth. Policymakers, educators, and youth workers often think first of strong ethnic identification as something that young people need and may even demand. Yet the young people's sense of salience of their own ethnic membership in their daily lives is likely to be either conditional or latent. The voices of urban youth in the three metropolitan regions of our study contend that their *embedded identities,* or multilayered self-conceptions, represent far more than simple labels of ethnic or racial membership.

Chapter 1, "Ethnicity and Gender in Theory and Practice," examines how the ideas of youth on gender and ethnicity contrast with those of adults from their own communities, with mainstream institutions, and with the media. We consider views of gender that lie behind numerous policy and program decisions for youth organizations. The chapters that follow demonstrate the power of specific cases, points in time, and rituals of events from humanistic and social science perspectives.[6] The cases illustrate the multiple views of ethnicity, gender, and identity that young people and their institutions hold and the force of historically established and organizationally reinforced perceptions of youth policymakers.

Chapters 2, 3, and 4 enable the reader to hear how youngsters work in youth organizations to shape themselves as something different from their portrayal in the media or by those who formulate youth policies. These fictitious portrayals sit in opposition to what the young people themselves hold as their self-image or presiding narrative. The youth we hear in these chapters know that they have self-selected away from the freedom and perils of other affiliations in the streets or in the projects. The identities the youngsters themselves carve out in the youth organizations that they judge to be effective are detailed from what may be viewed as a humanistic perspective. "Belonging," as a phenomenon of human consciousness, is seen to depend much more on how those in one's immediate environment ask questions, give directions, frame time and space, and reflect expectations than it does on verbal declarations of collectivity or acceptance or on common labels. Subtle differences in fine-grained matters of daily life constitute self-identities far more than do abstract, broad-sweeping assumptions of labels—ethnic or otherwise.

McLaughlin, in chapter 2, lays out the ways in which the identities of inner-city youth are embedded in the multiple and situationally diverse environments of community, neighborhood, family, peer groups, and local institutions, such as churches or youth groups. The neighborhood institutions that find acceptance in the eyes of local youngsters are those that enable them to find a sense of balance within harsh, inner-city conditions. These institutions are themselves embedded in the local context and are responsive to the particular realities and needs of neighborhood youth, be they gang boundaries, family circumstances, or pressures from school. These neighborhood-based organizations often have a strong sense of having to construct themselves and sometimes have a sense of doing so in spite of or against funders' requirements or national directives.

Ball and Heath, in Chapter 3, illustrate how dance groups—often portrayed by outsiders as simply "ethnic" and revolving around distantly related folk history or literature—work instead on close-up, "real" problems. These dance groups shape their environments as supportive families that center on showcase productions for which the youngsters themselves sometimes write scripts and coach younger dancers. Here the sense of self links up closely with the security that comes from accomplishment as a member of an active, supportive group. And the members of these groups often disdain the calls for loyalty to an ethnic or national group that they perceive as too distant from their immediate or hoped-for future life. Youth organizations offer "negotiable zones" in which youngsters experience guided participation in social units that mirror the kind of social commitment expected from mainstream institutions in the areas of employment, government bureaucracy, medical care, and education.

Chapter 4 looks inside the life of gangs of several ethnic groups in Los Angeles and reflects their view of "what's out there" for them. To outsiders, all gangs look alike, but Vigil shows how gangs of different ethnic groups vary considerably in their activities, their acceptance of females, and their sense of territory. Gangs in a single metropolitan region can develop specializations of tasks, as well as turfs, colors, and a preferred range of talents within the group. Yet the same factors of multiple marginalities and social control, as well as lack of economic opportunities, contribute to the origins of gangs of all ethnic groups and suggest promising policy responses.

Chapter 5, by Fine and Mechling, illustrates that "white ethnics" of middle-class families, like their inner-city counterparts, take up in their youth groups language and rituals—what adults often regard as their "play"—to mark them as belonging to small groups that have responsibilities, long-term goals, and allegiances. Within such groups (Boy Scout troops, for example), young people create rituals of separation into smaller groups. They come to view the collective as reinforcement of a sense of unity in membership that sets them apart from those outside, both at the current time and in the future. Moreover, in middle-class groups, such play features strong developmental imperatives, as youngsters see themselves primarily through what they do—through activity and accomplishment identifiable as successful and enjoyable in their terms. These are goals and expectations that they learn to carry into their own school and work lives.[7]

Chapter 6 considers similarities among youth organizations at the level of their linkages. Traditionally, agencies that serve youth have worked as individual units, often in competition with each other. By the late 20th century, foundations and politicians began to push and pull youth organizations to collaborate in their use of resources, types of programs, and scheduling of public events. However, as this chapter by Langman and McLaughlin shows, the benefits and objectives of collaboration looked very different from the outside than from the inside. Fundamental differences, ranging from conceptions of youth and the role of gender and ethnicity to the need to honor local street gangs' turf, stood in the way of collaboration.

James's chapter 7 offers the sweep of this century's view, from political figures and social leaders, of what youth organizations should do as "friendly intruders."[8] Politicians had long regarded ethnicity and gender in poor, urban youth in light of their potential to harm society. Children of color, especially boys, represented a threat; young women, both as future partners of these males and as mothers, were seen instead as possible reformers and positive influences on willful young men. Yet as the public perceived that more and more very young women were bearing children and that these young mothers were unprepared and unable to care for their children, resentment festered. It became easy to designate those with cultural habits unfamiliar to the middle-class mainstream as deviates. The dominant policy model and driving force behind program assumptions thus became one of reform of *deviation* and *delinquency*—both terms defined in contrast to a criterion of "normal" life within a mainstream nuclear family of stable income.

The relegation of young men and women to separate domains—sometimes for recreation and sometimes for reform—shifted when coeducation became the norm in public education. But among most ethnic groups, males and females who had not yet reached puberty separated themselves when choice was possible (on playgrounds and in leisure times outside of school). Hansot's chapter 8 illustrates how, in inner cities, the major supports for attaining maturity as a male or a female—or as a parent or a worker—easily fall away and the young can be left with short-term, unpredictable frameworks for their lives.

In the book's final chapter, McLaughlin and Heath set the conversations of those looking in from the outside at youth against the views of the youngsters themselves. This chapter proposes some transformations necessary for youth organizations that wish to be effective with urban youth and suggests policies that might support such organizations. This chapter urges a changed public view of inner-city youth that will enable policymakers to think about youth in ways that will support environments of affirmation and activity. These proposals represent considerable challenges for youth policymakers and for educators who have considered partnering with youth organizations in the future. The authors examine these opportunities and suggest certain organizational and philosophical adjustments necessary to engender and sustain youth groups that will work from the perspective of inner-city youth.

By the 1990s, neither the ethnic nor gender identities of past decades could translate into the practice and survival of daily life for inner-city youth. This book looks at the little universe of youth-based organizations that serve inner-city youngsters through rituals, processes, and structures that make room for building identities. Inner-city youngsters have no place, except the place they make for themselves, and certain youth organizations have allowed them to do just that. These groups have enabled the young to have a sense of a range of identities that transcends and transforms. Most important, these groups have enabled the young of inner cities to know both that there are choices and that they can help decide what it takes to make the choices necessary to create the terms of their own existence.

Notes

[1]This research project,"Language, Socialization, and Neighborhood-Based Organizations: Moving Youth Beyond Dependency on School and Family," was funded by the Spencer Foundation. Senior associates who worked with Heath and McLaughlin were Merita A. Irby, Harvard University, and Juliet Langman, University of Delaware, who collected data and worked closely with teams of 20 junior ethnographers in the youth organizations studied. Ali Calicotte and Steven Balt assisted in data collection and maintenance, and Jeffrey Lox managed the complex qualitative data sets and developed a computer program to analyze the language data.

[2]Funded by the Spencer Foundation, this conference included all of the authors included here (except Ball). Also attending the conference were individuals with long-term experience in a variety of types of youth groups, including Joanna Lennon of the East Bay Conservation Corps in Oakland, California; Michele Cahill, school and community services, Academy for Educational Development, New York City; and Felicia Bute, a community organizer with experience in several midwestern metropolitan regions.

[3]Roosens (1989) notes in his study of ethnicity in various parts of the world that after the 1960s, middle-class members of ethnic groups created situations for the use of ethnic labels in order to boost the political power and public visibility of such communities. Breton (1991) echoes this view in his study of the governance of ethnic communities.

[4]Motivational Educational Entertainment (1992) elaborates on the unpredictability of urban environments from youth's perspective in *Reaching the Hip-Hop Generation*.

[5]In 1990, the Boys Clubs of America became the Boys and Girls Clubs of America, and the Girls Clubs of America became Girls Incorporated. The latter organization argued that research indicated that organizations for girls consistently had fewer resources and less funding and that this disparity reached about two-to-one funding for boys' groups over girls' groups. Girls Incorporated adopted an affirmative action approach to providing positive environments for girls and young women in an attempt to counter what they regarded as patterns of societal discrimination against girls.

[6]Michael Novak (1980) outlined for the *Harvard Encyclopedia of American Ethnic Groups* the concept of "new ethnicity" and what its study might mean for researchers. He noted that ethnicity had been much more studied by social scientists than by humanists and that the failure to bring these perspectives together had resulted in a "lumping" process in which the *individual*—whether it be the human, the time, the place, or the event—was unexplored. This neglect led to minimal attention to values, memories, narratives, and systems of meaning that emerge, develop, shift, and reshape themselves in the individual.

[7]The importance to young people of *doing*—of being active and with peers—is clearly illustrated for middle-class urban youngsters. See, for example, Csikszentmihalyi and Larson (1984) and Heath (1991). Both studies illustrate the extent to which middle-class youngsters seek out active ways of being with peers.

[8]In her study of child care and parent participation in schools, Joffe (1977) used this phrase to characterize how government and state intrusion into child care in the

1970s threatened public understanding about family life. We adopt it here for its logical extension to similar threats seen by youth policymakers in the increasingly expansive roles taken on by youth organizations. To whom do children "belong?" To parents or to societies? And if the latter, then what should the distribution of responsibility be among the courts, social service agencies, youth organizations, families, and schools? Critical to any answers to this first question is the point at which children or the young enter the realm of public life and public responsibility.

References

Breton, R. (1991). *The governance of ethnic communities*. New York: Greenwood Press.

Carnegie Council on Adolescent Development (1992). *A matter of time: Risk and opportunity in the non-school hours*. New York: Carnegie Corporation of New York.

Csikszentmihalyi, M., & Larson, R. (1984). *Being adolescent: Conflict and growth in the teenage years*. New York: Basic Books.

Heath, S. B. (1991). "It's about winning!" The language of knowledge in baseball. In L. B. Resnick, J. M. Levin, & S. D. Teasley (Eds.), *Perspectives on socially shared cognition* (pp. 101–124). Washington, DC: American Psychological Association.

Joffe, C. E. (1977). *Friendly intruders: Childcare professionals and family life*. Berkeley: University of California Press.

Motivational Educational Entertainment. (1992). *Reaching the hip-hop generation*. Philadelphia: West Philadelphia Enterprise Center. [A study prepared for the Robert Wood Johnson Foundation.]

Novak, M. (1980). Pluralism: A humanistic perspective. In S. Thernstrom (Ed.), *Harvard encyclopedia of American ethnic groups* (pp. 772–781). Cambridge, MA: Harvard University Press.

Roosens, E. (1989). *Creating ethnicity*. Newbury Park, CA: Sage.

1

Ethnicity and Gender in Theory and Practice: The Youth Perspective

Shirley Brice Heath
Milbrey W. McLaughlin

This chapter lays out the numerous perceptions, policies, and practices that surround ethnicity and gender. Youth bear conflicting messages about the image and reality of these two concepts as applied to their own identities whenever political, economic, demographic, and educational conditions shift in their communities. Since the 1960s, organizations for youth have come and gone, along with emphases on ethnicity and gender shifting in response to rapidly changing community demographics and local needs. Failed schools, street violence, and helpless parents have made youth organizations the only safe place for many inner-city youth. In response to the corrosive consequences of "minority" labels, effective youth groups have promoted activities to build culturally grounded self-respect. At the same time, teen pregnancies, girl gangs, and violence directed toward females have led youth organizations to weigh seriously the political push for coeducational programs in light of their own concerns for the special needs of young women in the inner city. In the context of these challenges to the saliency of ethnicity and gender in the core identities of youth, this chapter examines the backgrounds of the presiding narratives that young people take for themselves to try to ensure their survival.

All of it is now . . . it is always now . . . there will never be a time when I am not
crouching and watching others who are crouching too . . . I am always crouching. . . .

Toni Morrison
Beloved

Ethnicity and gender—are they essential dimensions of identity for youth?
To be sure, young people must sort out these two features among the many
other influences on who they are and who they will be.[1] The multiple
dimensions of their decision making fail to be captured in the deceptively
straightforward titles of many youth organizations—Girl Scouts or Boys and
Girls Clubs—or in the ethnic emphasis adopted by groups dedicated to celebrating and enhancing ethnicity—like African American theater groups or
Ballet Folklórico.

Both in theory and in practice, conceptions of ethnicity and gender
enjoy neither simple nor agreed-on meanings. Disciplinary, political, social,
temporal, or cultural perspectives create competing and often dissonant theoretical notions of ethnicity and gender. In practice, the actions and beliefs
of individuals and organizations that apply conceptions of ethnicity and
gender, as well as the perspectives and realities of the individuals and organizations to whom they are applied, generate still more and different meanings. The conceptions of ethnicity or gender adopted by programs and
organizations devised for youth matter to young people only as they themselves assign relevance to these efforts and to the selves they celebrate in
those contexts. Understanding the organizations and activities that inner-
city youth judge to be effective requires appreciation of the evolution and
contextualized application of ethnicity and gender in theory and in practice.

Shifting Meanings of Ethnicity

Ethnicity takes on both *subjective and objective* meanings, both as an internal assignment for the self and, more often in the United States after the
1980s, as a label given by external sources. Ethnicity may be a subjective
belief that a group holds regarding its common membership because of
shared descent or historical background and similarities of customs, language, and sometimes of physical type. But the cultural and linguistic features that mark the boundaries among groups from the perspective of outsiders may not be acknowledged by those enclosed within them. Thus,
through power, force, and public labeling, certain groups can designate
others as "ethnic groups" and work to ensure that a division exists between

members of those groups and outsiders. It is also possible for those designated as being from one ethnic group to change their ethnic membership by adopting new customs, behaviors, and language habits, and it is not uncommon for such changes to be prompted by a desire for political or social gain.

Ethnicity is sometimes used synonymously with *culture*. Although all groups possess separate behavior, beliefs, and language that distinguish them culturally from surrounding groups, they may not equate these with ethnic membership. For example, cultural habits are, to some extent, chosen by members of groups, and both socioeconomic mobility and population movements alter and elaborate patterns of behavior as fundamental as religion, child rearing, and language. Humanists, who for decades used *culture* to mean *high culture*, began only in the 1960s to acknowledge the anthropological meaning of the term as referring to the ways of believing, behaving, and valuing of a self-defined group of people. Well into the final decades of the 20th century, humanists often equated culture with style and referred to nationality or period labels when talking about particular works or schools of art. Periods of history, bodies of literature and art, and museum collections bore labels that marked them as of Eastern or Western cultures, as Italian (or French, Estonian, or Russian) literature or art, or as of Romantic, Modern, or Postmodern periods. The widespread use of labels in museums, textbooks, and formal education institutions to indicate ethnicity emerged only in the late 1980s, when humanists began to attend to areas such as Chicano or African American art, history, and literature.

Ethnicity and *race,* often uttered in the same breath in the United States, are socially constructed labels. In the late 1800s, for example, physiologists, anthropologists, and politicians declared the people of Wales, Scotland, Ireland, and Cornwall to be "racially separate from the British," and those of Western Ireland and Wales were further labeled as "Africanoid." The declaration of racial or ethnic membership by political fiat is well attested in the history of Nazi Germany, South Africa, and the United States, where being "black," "Jewish," or "Indian" was decided by legal decree regarding parentage, customs, names, and even dress.[2] Less easily accounted for historically are the numerous occasions when small groups have chosen to escape the ethnic labels given to them by outsiders by simply moving to another region and adopting different customs of eating, dressing, worshipping, and speaking. In the United States, such shifts have historically been referred to—usually in a pejorative manner—as "passing," but in other nations of the world, such changes may receive no negative assessment. Instead, they may be recognized as worthy moves to improve one's station in life.[3]

Social Ethnicity

Ethnicity has always and everywhere been a series of creations brought about by the situations through which individuals or groups move. Perhaps nowhere is the "constructed" and contingent nature of *ethnic* identity more evident than in the inner cities of the United States at the end of the 20th century. Often without a solid grounding in the facts and passions that forged concepts of ethnic membership in American history, especially during the Civil Rights era, the young of high-rise multiethnic projects and linguistically diverse communities develop their own theories and practices about the role that ethnic membership can play in their contemporary lives.

These conceptions of ethnicity reflect their changed and changing neighborhoods and policy environments. Since the 1960s, the perpetually economically troubled inner cities have shifted drastically in response to community demographics, economics, religious emphases, and ethos. In the rebuilding of inner cities following the civil uprisings of the 1960s, local residents established small businesses, and urban housing projects were home to populations relatively homogeneous in culture, language, and ethos. Many institutions for youth turned to ethnically and culturally based names and activities. Cultural centers, dance troupes, and artists' groups took to storefronts, and T-shirts sported local business advertising on the back and cultural and ethnic pride slogans on the front. Throughout the early 1970s, "Black is beautiful" rang out as a frequent call to the memory of Stokely Carmichael's rallying cry and Martin Luther King, Jr.'s dream. The place of history, literature, and culture stood central in Malcolm X's calls to revitalize African American identity in churches, homes, community centers, and storefront galleries and bookstores. European American, Puerto Rican, and Mexican communities also began in new ways to appreciate and celebrate their ethnic heritage and particular roles in the course of American history.

But the kind of ethnically homogeneous links among local businesses, residents, and youth that led in the 1960s and 1970s to calls for ethnic unity and pride diminished by the late 1980s, as urban neighborhoods became increasingly diverse linguistically and culturally. Neighborhood businesses of the past decade all but disappeared. Waves of refugees and new immigrants, bringing a host of different economic, social, and personal goals, as well as multiple languages and cultures, moved into inner-city neighborhoods. Some of these brought with them habits and skills in small-business entrepreneurship that they put to work in inner-city communities. They moved in bringing fast-food and convenience stores, liquor stores, pawn shops, and check-cashing services—small enterprises of long hours, high risk, and steady market demand. It became harder and harder for the youth of groups long established in the United States, such as African Americans, second- and third-generation Mexican Americans, and Filipinos, to find adult models from their own groups in locally owned businesses or in the professions of their communities.

Simultaneously, a variety of drugs hit the streets, creating what many disgruntled, confused, and eager youth saw as their only viable business opportunity. Relentless marketing promotion of *the* shoes and garments for youth who wanted to fit in, along with a rapid increase in the number and visibility of African American-, Puerto Rican-, and Mexican-origin entertainers and athletes, fed aspirations of inner-city youth for quick money—and lots of it. Family values, community strengths, and pride in historical and personal achievement through education dropped away. Despairing and desperate parents, usually without the extended family support system that had sustained the generations before them, turned more and more to drugs, alcohol, and physical abuse of each other and of their young. Public outcries over the inadequacies of education and the spread of the crime and violence of youth gangs invariably pictured minority and inner-city youth as those leading the United States in its downward spiral.

Meanwhile, city museums and galleries, as well as Broadway shows, celebrated African American, Latino, and Asian American writers, artists, and actors and drew middle- and upper-class patrons from all ethnic groups while rarely touching the lives of inner-city youngsters. Cultural expressions of ethnicity for those who had both time and leisure multiplied, and cities that had never had an upper echelon of people of color in politics, society, and culture joined the ranks of cities such as Philadelphia and Chicago, which had long had a strong upper stratum of people of color.

In the 1980s, the children of these advantaged families found they had to give themselves labels driven by politics and institutional decisions. For example, on college campuses, many of the children of second- and third-generation immigrants from India joined Asian American theme houses and culture groups, because the ethos of campus life moved students toward self-labeling to be part of the newly prized cultural diversity on campus. The offspring of interracial marriages often felt compelled to call themselves *black* and join African American theme houses although they had grown up in communities where such labels were not applied to them. If professional socioeconomic standing had gained them acceptance in predominantly white institutions, they were often likely to have been effectively isolated from having to think of themselves as "minorities." It was not at all uncommon for students whose families of Latino origins had lived for several decades with a mainstream middle-class "American" identity in a midwestern town—speaking English, participating in local social and cultural organizations, and eating hamburgers and roast beef—to be pressured to self-identify as "culturally different" on college campuses or as "ethnic minorities" for other purposes. By the mid-1980s, ethnic labeling had become one channel toward upward mobility or, at the very least, social recognition as a member of a particular group for specific institutional purposes.[4]

Ethnic consciousness involved more than recognition of racial heritage or migration history. For some groups, especially "white ethnics," the key labels that outsiders attached to them were in the 1980s and 1990s those of nationality or religious membership (Polish, Italian, Jewish, Catholic, and so on). Assignments of region of origin become important also for immigrants from Central and South America, as well as for those from islands of the Caribbean. The same was true for individuals of Southeast Asian origin, who distinguished among themselves on the basis of class *before* immigration, as well as the time and place of refugee camp experiences before coming to the United States.

Political Ethnicity and Conflicting Signals

Against this backdrop of differences of class, race, and immigration history came the confusing and contradictory mesh of affirmative action and ethnic celebration on one hand and considerable public proclamation of equality and equity on the other. Although much rhetoric promoted cultural pluralism and diversity in education and the media, employers, educators, and health service workers simultaneously heard messages that told them not to see color or to attend to race, sex, creed, nationality, or handicap in hiring and evaluation. Moreover, by the late 1980s, for many young adults, a sense of privilege came in *not* identifying as ethnic. Marriages across different races, nationalities, and languages dramatically increased in number, and parents often did not want their children boxed under one ethnic label. Children with one African American parent and one Puerto Rican parent and several Portuguese or Dominican Republican friends saw only psychological hazard in proclaiming a single label for themselves. At the same time, affirmative action and integration policies, as well as college financial aid packages, called for self-identification into one or another ethnic group in order to receive certain types of consideration or attention.[5]

Meanwhile, city councils and local wards tried to carry out what they saw as a political mandate: celebration of ethnicity. Parks and recreation boards sponsored ethnic fairs or holidays, such as Cinco de Mayo for Mexican-origin families. Political leaders failed to understand the resistance such celebrations encountered in communities that now included Haitians, Puerto Ricans, and El Salvadoreans, as well as African Americans and Southeast Asians. Many middle-class leaders of the groups so celebrated charged that such events were often mindless and perpetuated stereotypes; moreover, they resented having outsiders come in to see their "exotic" dances, art, and food. Other nationalities in the same neighborhood resented the additional noise and intrusion of strangers (such as police to handle crowd control) that street fairs or cultural exhibits could bring. Some immigrant groups who wanted their celebrations kept exclusive to members of their own group resented pressures from city officials to open their affairs to the general public. In short, many political officials tried in their policies for inner-city neighborhoods to engender peaceful and educational displays of ethnic membership or group pride and to give a "caring and human face" to government through support for folk celebrations. Many inner-city residents saw these policies as exploitative of their cultures and as wasteful of scarce resources. What neighborhood spokespersons wanted instead were solutions to the difficult problems that endangered their lives and property: increased security, better public housing maintenance, and cleanup of abandoned sites that attracted derelicts and drug dealers. Frustration over these many needs sometimes led groups to lash out against others different from themselves in food preferences, child-rearing practices, and language. The magnitude of their problems and a sense of helplessness made any cosmetic or entertaining celebration of ethnic cultures seem trivial.

The meaning of *white* as a racial or ethnic label bore no fewer political problems than did labels for people of color in the 1990s, especially following the breakup of the former Soviet Union and the Eastern European bloc. Descendants in the United States of newly forming or aspiring republics rose to proclaim their long-submerged identities and to defend their compatriots' actions abroad, shown in nightly newscasts as whites killing whites in the name of ancient grudges. Whereas militant African Americans during the 1960s and early 1970s had sometimes termed "the white man" as the universal enemy of people of color and the wielder of economic and political power, by the 1990s, corporate powers and major employers in many parts of the United States were almost as likely to be from Asia, the Middle East, or Europe as from the familiar European American cities of one's own city or state.

In earlier years, required norms of dress, procedure, timeliness, and language usage had been tagged "the white man's way," but companies run by foreign or minority executives and managers insisted on similar habits. Fol-

lowing the 1960s, the cry had gone up that African American or Latino political leaders would make a difference in the quality of life for subordinated
populations. However, by the 1990s, it seemed that neither ethnic nor
national affiliation noticeably altered hiring practices, work incentives, or
production loads in the economic sector, or social policies for the poor in
the political sector. It became less and less clear what difference being non-
white made once individuals came to power economically and politically.
Thus, ethnicity and culture both advanced and receded as labels or sources
of identification after the 1960s, and the multiple meanings of ethnicity created an inconsistent mix of policies and programs for youth in American
society that adults felt ill-prepared to sort out for them.

Labels of Ethnicity

Social and political shifts in conceptions of ethnicity that began shortly after
the massive immigrations in the first half of the 20th century created a backdrop of inconsistencies and irritations. Intergenerational differences surfaced over views of the importance of ethnicity in the policies and programs
of youth organizations. Individuals who had achieved middle-class status
following childhoods of poverty sometimes returned to their old neighborhoods as youth leaders and adopted instrumental and symbolic views of
ethnicity for the youth organizations they directed. They wanted to reinvig-
orate youngsters with the sense of ethnic pride they had achieved in the
1960s and 1970s, and they tried to shape community organizations to celebrate ethnicity. They took pride in the fact that some national educational
groups and collaborative boards for local institutions (such as museums,
parks, and youth organizations) called for celebration of ethnic identities
and, in some cases, for both gender and ethnic segregation in schooling and
certain community activities. But by the 1990s, nothing about ethnicity and
gender in the identity of inner-city youth went down smoothly or in pre-
dictably stable ways.

Even names made a difference. Arguments over terms—*minorities, ethnic groups,* and *races*—dominated some youth organizations' board meetings. Staff members debated how effectively multicultural materials and celebrations would go over in institutions previously all black or all white.

Youth organizations had to respond to naming trends in the public
media. General consensus removed the hyphen from almost all published
ethnic labels; populations whose labels had been previously hyphenated
argued that the hyphen connoted hybridity or an absence of wholeness. In
addition, many argued that some groups should not be referred to solely by

racial terms (*black* or *white*) while others were tagged with the names of their families' homeland or general region (such as El Salvador or Southeast Asia). A particularly widespread controversy surrounded the use of *African American* as a replacement for *black* or *person of color.* Once presidential candidate Jessie Jackson used the term *African American* in 1988, many saw a way out of the negative connotations that had come to surround *black, colored,* and even *Negro.*[6]

Just some of the ambiguities surrounding ethnicity became evident in the very labels that Americans used to mark ethnic membership. Those who migrated from Mexico, Central and South America and the Caribbean, as well as those with years of residence in the United States, debated the use of terms such as *Hispanic, Latino,* and *Chicano.* Others who might be so generically labeled preferred specific terms to identify their homes as Puerto Rico, Mexico, or a specific Caribbean island. Controversy over terminology among these groups left the general public confused about the appropriate choice of labels. Especially for those who sought parallelism in reference, *African American* and *European American* became the preferred terms to replace *black* and *white* or *Negro* and *Caucasian.* Academic quarreling about such parallelism called for continental or geographic source of origin to be applied uniformly across all groups. But it was not easy to reconcile the fact that some labels took no notice of national origins, religious preference, or racial membership and that preference for labels could shift often—even in the usage of a single individual.

In 1980, at the time of the publication of the *Harvard Encyclopedia of American Ethnic Groups,* the rise of ethnicity and assertions of language choice in various parts of the world outside the United States attracted considerable attention.[7] However, in the United States, social scientists persisted in their view of the "new ethnicity" as "posttribal," arguing that every group seemed destined to need to become aware of and accept the culture of others. The United States in the late 20th century had a love-hate relationship with cultural diversity and strong push-pull tendencies toward multiculturalism and pluralism in institutions from schools to public arts. As a consequence, the public seemed to want on one hand to discern and label any possible source of ethnicity or cultural diversity while on the other hand to claim to promote integration and cultural homogenization to deny differences. A large urban school district, for example, in the last decade passed a regulation that students could change their designated ethnicity only once every three years.

American struggles for integration and equal opportunities available without regard to "race, creed, color, or national origin" were followed rapidly in the 1990s by insistence on equivalent assurances regardless of sexual preference or age. These struggles were celebrated by the media in situation comedies and advertisements that featured ethnic diversity and various positive portrayals of "rainbow relationships."

"Political correctness," a slogan and signpost of the time, signaled awareness, sensitivity, and a feel for "otherness" that bore some similarities to the new cultural and political self-consciousness that marked nations newly emerged from former Soviet and Eastern bloc unions. Meanwhile, simultaneous with the sensitivity of the newly politically correct public, the United States' legal and educational systems were often locked in a persistent bureaucratic stance of acknowledging no differences among groups of people.

Within the United States, federal mandates of the 1960s and strong state and local regulations forbade discrimination, while social pressures promoted respect and sensitivity for differences. But increasingly in the 1990s, as more and more African American, Latino, and Southeast Asian individuals achieved positions of economic and political prominence, the general public found it relatively easy to accept that such individuals had escaped the "burdens" of their race and ethnicity to "make it." They had the option to leave the labels behind.

Within the inner cities, public housing projects, and urban schools, a tendency toward ethnic labeling by outsiders became more and more paradoxical. Political figures and the public media dropped older names, such as "Little Italy," for particular regions of cities and referred instead to the names of housing projects or specific street names. Schools and employment offices asked gingerly about "ethnic membership" in their requests for residents to fill out paperwork for public benefits. Yet state and federal mandates still required instruction in the mother tongue of students with a large representation in certain schools. Community residents often objected to such categorical "takeover" by the schools of their language, which families often felt should be reserved for home use or considered a habit that must be dropped by the next generation to get ahead.

Youth Organizations

Life is like quicksand.
(You sink in everyday life)
Growing up is like T.V.
(It's boring)
Boys are like pimps.
(We too cool)
Girls are like pick pockets.

(They slip in your pockets when you
sleep and take all your money)
Making new friends is like a test.
(It's hard to do)
                                    Fredrick McNeary

Those attracted to youth organizations in the three inner cities of our research were young people who had felt these tensions and more. Many faced crises daily and knew they had to find ways to escape gangs, drugs, and the tortures of their disrupted community and home lives. Many needed and wanted ways to ground themselves. By the early 1990s, it was common for young people of inner cities to be unable to name even half a dozen African American or Latino figures—either distant or close up—who had made a difference in the course of their histories or aspirations. Far more often, they could name current athletic or entertainment stars. More often than not, schools proclaimed multicultural education but reserved study of the history of "other" Americans for special days or weeks (such as Black History week or Cinco de Mayo). Many classes on such topics as multicultural literature limited enrollment to academically successful students, and general or remedial classes rarely included more than the names and dates of non-European political leaders, scientists, or artists. The ethnically centered youth organizations of the 1960s and early 1970s had all but disappeared. It was as though the poor of the inner city could no longer wrap their identity primarily in their ethnicity; they needed first a core of personal efficacy achieved as a member of a close and personally connected group.

The youth organizations that remained were primarily local branches of national organizations, such as the Boy Scouts, YMCAs, and Girls Clubs, and community resource centers that offered services ranging from day care to senior citizen programs, along with opportunities for athletics, arts, and drama for neighborhood youth. With nothing constructive to do in their out-of-school time and afraid of life on the streets, young people with the motivation to find something for themselves sought out youth organizations that they judged to be effective: safe places to be with their peers to engage in enjoyable activities through team building with predictable adult support. When the majority of those attracted to such organizations coincidentally might have the same ethnic background, youth did not consider common ethnic membership as a necessary part of belonging. Because of friendship patterns among youngsters and the neighborhood-based quality of such organizations, many groups served constituencies of one predominant ethnicity only until community demographics shifted enough to alter social alignments among the young. Even in large public housing project areas, where many ethnic groups shared apartment living, young people often chose most of their friends from their own ethnic or linguistic group. Yet, in contrast to assumptions about the importance of ethnic identity as held by some adults, the young did not see ethnicity as the centrally important attribute of their own identity. Local youth organizations, holding similar views, resisted the formation of teams or troops of youngsters that were all Puerto Rican, all African American, or all European American. The organizations arranged jamborees and regional get-togethers to bring different troops and leagues together in a search for common themes and interests that transcended ethnicity or gender.

Youth organizations provided opportunities for youngsters to build a sense of self-efficacy and a series of prevailing narratives of success in different events and kinds of activities. These programs took in youth of all ethnic groups and promoted strong pride in the unique and specific accomplishments of their organization and its membership. They tailored program content and institutional processes to the interests of the young and incorporated young people into participatory roles of all sorts.[8] Diversity of talents, styles, and ideas among the young added to the repertoire of resources available to youth organizations, which often had to struggle with limited funds and a shortage of adult staff members. Arts and athletics topped the list of activities youth organizations offered, for these provided involvement in planning, preparing, practicing, and performing— with final judgment coming from outsiders (audiences, other teams in the league, and the public media). A sense of worth came from being a member of a group or team noted for accomplishment; a sense of belonging came from being needed within the organization—to teach younger members, help take care of the facility, plan and govern activities, and promote the group to outsiders.

Youth leaders provided a familylike frame for the work of their organizations. They advised and guided youngsters, letting them know they cared, and often reminding them in word and action "we're here for you." Many times these leaders and the volunteers they recruited did not share ethnic membership with the youngsters; acceptance came through respect for the young people and knowledge about their communities. Adults reflected their respect by holding youth responsible for worthwhile tasks and achievements and by bearing a consistent attitude toward discipline and infractions of rules. Often, a policy so simple as requiring youngsters to show up at the youth organization twice a week, or to call in to say why they could not be there, amounted to what the youth called "being family." Accountability applied to everyone in youth organizations—places of safety where no one could bring weapons, drugs, or gang insignia—and everyone knew they could belong.

Gender and Its Roles

My sisters, you must never let a man
tell you he's the boss
or he wears the pants
Never let a man hit you or even
take that chance.

Tisha Zinn

While ethnicity had come to be more and more a fluid academic concept after the 1960s, gender in both theory and practice escalated as a public issue and sociopolitical concern. Access to employment and job mobility, medical research and services, and control over women's bodies in abortion, pornography, and advertising hit the headlines on a regular basis by the 1990s. On the streets and in radio and video, violence directed toward women that was set off by competing claims of "possession" by a member of the opposite sex increased. Lived experiences every day told the young that their gender mattered as much as if not more than their ethnicity to their patterns of survival and their identity.

Gender figures centrally in the images or narratives of the self that all individuals hold and is perhaps the strongest affective "hook" by which youngsters come to know themselves and become attached to certain behaviors, norms, and evaluative frames. When the context for the development of gender is relatively free of dramatic and dangerous influences and circumstances, gender roles are complicated enough. But within inner cities, decisions related to how one plays out gender roles can make the difference between life and death. Shooting up with someone to appear macho or having sex to try to ensure sustained financial support can result in AIDS or any one of a number of venereal diseases. Every inner-city youngster knows these facts, but making wise decisions about how to be a man or a woman is much tougher than facts can suggest.

Gender refers in its everyday sense to societal distinctions between masculine and feminine, and in such usage, it is distinguished from the term *sex,* which relates to the biological and largely binary distinction between male and female. By the 1980s, it became commonplace to talk of gender as "constructed," because *masculine* and *feminine* are learned behaviors and are continuously variable. Across societies, these and related terms (such as *manly, womanly,* and *macho)* carry different degrees of emphasis on what is regarded as *sexual* as distinct from generalized personality traits or mannerisms (such as *brusque* and *assertive* or *gentle* and *caring).* In general, across contemporary societies, masculine is more prized than feminine, but matters of situation, age, occupation, education, and culture determine judgments of both what will be judged as either masculine or feminine and when traits of either are appropriate. All societies are "gendered" in that their constructions of gender represent a critical division that carries economic, political, religious, and social consequences.

Labels that refer to sex and gender came more and more to provoke considerable discussion in the 1980s. Many social scientists urged the use of the term *sex* or *sexes* to refer only to biological attributes and use of the term *gender* to refer to socially constructed assignments and socialized features of behavior. Previously, these debates, along with quarrels over the meaning of *feminism,* had remained within academic institutions. But when television situation comedies, cartoons, and popular music began to refer to such issues as feminism, they entered the street—if only in retorts from young women that they did not want to be called "ho' bitch," but "Miss Ho' Bitch."

Early socialization experiences and especially relations with male and female family members provide the base on which children, sometimes as early as age eight or nine, enter into peer relations that begin to temper family norms of masculine or feminine. In the subsequent years into adulthood, the young try to construct their sense of gender identity in a tug-of-war between peer and adult norms—with strong influence from public media, music, and film representations as well. Hormonal changes and spurts of growth and body changes accentuate the need for young people between the ages of 9 and 11 to reconcile their emerging sense of themselves as sexual beings with their social relationships and patterns of friendship.[9]

Messages from some adults about the relationship among sex, sexual activity, and responsible behavior often conflict with both the media's representations and the close-up experiences of young people. Young people often have to develop their own metaphors and rules for how sex relates to "manhood" and "womanhood."[10] And in the inner city, girls can easily see rejecting the status of daughter, gaining the attention of older males, and having a baby as marks necessary for their transition to womanhood. For boys, *male* and *sex* are synonymous, pregnancies are a demonstration of virility and power, and denial of parenting responsibilities is a claim to independence and freedom. Forced to be grown-up in the face of neglect by either absent or substance-abusing parents, boys and girls assume many "adult" responsibilities early in life, often with little or no recognition or support. Once they can get away from the house, it is tempting to "hang on the corner" for attention and adventure. Males who deal in drugs and have ready cash can buy sexual favors with clothes, gold, and trips to the hairdresser. Girls, once marked by such status, face double jeopardy when they are dropped from a male's favor: loss of material goods and loss of attention. The next step seems easy: "The only way I'm gonna hold onto him is have his baby." Young women who discover that this next step does not bring sustained attention come to feel like "dogs and whores—nothing but a piece of meat." Coming up from such a low opinion of self and a seemingly confirmed identity can take twice as much support as staying out of the path to despair.

Culture and Gender

Imagine the world
filled with perfect families,
Children, husband, wife
And there would be no death.
We would have everlasting life.
Imagine there were no gangs.
Aya McNeary

The confounding of gender identity with what it means to be "an adult" is an area in which scholars in gender studies have found it difficult to untangle definitional issues of gender from those of ethnic membership. With the heightened awareness of feminist concerns and increased sensitivity to multicultural issues in the 1980s and 1990s have come key questions: To what extent is it appropriate to talk about ways that different cultures define gender roles? Is subordination or exclusion by the larger society more the result of ethnic or gender identity? How do answers to these questions intersect with matters of age and class? Although society can think of members of an ethnic group as a community, members of the same sex do not necessarily have a sense of communal membership—even when they are of the same ethnic group. They are in fact often in brutal competition with each other. Individuals of the same sex take on very different gender roles depending on class, education, occupation, and perhaps most important, culture and individual determination.

However, in general, gender hierarchies show up in all the domains of social behavior that make cultural and class differences evident: dress, demeanor, preferences for types of work and leisure, ways of relating with others, and primary roles valued both in the ideal and in actual behavior. Divisions of labor with regard to the rearing of children and to waged or salaried labor have been central in defining gender roles throughout history. For much of that history in most parts of the world, no overarching political or social theory had the strength to dislodge the rigidity of these roles.

Females were for the most part primarily responsible for bearing and rearing children, preparing food for family members, and maintaining the household, while males held responsibility over domains farther from the household or communal center.

Within these very general outlines of duties across history, various patterns of status for males and females have given differential access to religious, economic, and social powers; acknowledging this fact, scholars have tried to determine the mechanisms that have constrained women in social systems where women's possibilities for advancement have clearly been limited or dictated by males. The inner city is one such site. There, boys and girls have relatively few opportunities for close association with role models that can tell them how to move beyond the constraints evident in their communities. In some urban housing projects, as many as 8 of 10 households have no stable adult male member.[11] Hence, both boys and girls see early on the lack of balance in the division of labor between men and women of the neighborhood. Women are much more visible to the children of such housing projects—in the halls, laundry centers, and nearby markets. Women have more occasions than they would like, to talk of the need to keep the young away from where the men are: on street corners, in parking lots, in jail, or dead. Even in communities of single-family homes with two-parent households, men are much less visible than women, for men often have work that is migratory or work two jobs and are rarely evident on the sidewalks of the neighborhoods.

Moreover, relations between the sexes often appear violent in public as well as close up, and the uneasy balance of dependence and independence—love and hate—between males and females leaves the young of both genders insecure. To find security, the young seek arbitrary and risky courses of action and relationships. For example, female gangs as independent units of violence rather than as appendages to male gangs emerged in some cities in the late 1980s and quickly became known for the hardness of their leaders, the ruthlessness of their violence against other females, and their ability to terrorize entire areas of a city. Male gangs had long provided bonding opportunities for young boys, as well as occasional economic support. Now, females wanted their own secure group and more of the financial take for themselves.

As domestic violence increased dramatically, young boys watched older versions of themselves inflict harm and pain on the mothers and sisters who had nurtured them. *Masculine* or *male* often became synonymous with bruising, dominant, unpredictable, and boastful, while *feminine* or *female* were expressed as separate yet connected, passive and aggressive, grasping and retreating, or strong and unapproachable. In the most hostile of household circumstances, little room existed for the daily rites and rituals of manners, dress, speech, and attitudes that in more stable households reminded and reinforced young children's sense of the multitude of subtle, gentle, small ways to express maleness and femaleness. The habits that textbooks describe as reinforcing "gender constancy"—the understanding that a girl is a girl and a boy is a boy, as well as acceptance of "gender stability" (a girl will grow up to be a woman, and a boy will grow up to be a man)—for children as early as age three had little chance in homes of unreliable and unstable adults in short-term and often exploitative relationships.[12]

For families and relations within inner-city environments of the late 20th century, several key factors determined the relative positions of males and females and the ways in which the immediate and the public environment constructed their roles. Job opportunities for males and females with low levels of skills in urban zones were drastically cut from those of earlier eras of factory work, unskilled manual labor, and domestic labor. Without access to jobs or land ownership, the growing youth population saw no way to reveal their gendered selves in work. Distant models were athletes and entertainers whose life-styles and material wealth offered many attractions but only one chance in a million of similar achievement. Lacking the future work orientation or home ownership orientation so powerful in the public image of what makes a man or a woman in suburban American life, the young emulated models of achievement obvious in their communities— which often involved destructive and dangerous sexual or criminal pursuits.

The long-term consequences of becoming a parent and providing for one's children were overshadowed by hopes for immediate acceptance and clear identity marking. As urban housing projects became more and more mixed ethnically and culturally in the 1980s, the generalized norms of early sexual experience as a way of gaining gender identity spread across cultures and often put the young and their peers in conflict with the values of their parents and grandparents, who held the ideal of school, job, and then family for the future of their children.[13]

What amounted to a dual society emerged in many urban areas. Young adult males and females adapted the norms of gender roles into which they were socialized as a way to adjust to the predominant situation in which females had greater access to welfare and work than males. Meanwhile, the sets of choices by which males without education could either prove themselves or find approval decreased while peer norm increased the stigma attached to studying for school success or trying t get ahead. When to these peer pressures was added the lure of community gangs (often directed by organized crime leaders in state penal institutions), young males had little leeway in which to negotiate options. Females, on the other hand, often looked to pregnancy and motherhood as a way out of difficult, lonely, or abusive home situations. Finding favor with males and becoming pregnant could, in many inner-city communities, bring approval to females from their peers, as well as provide favored negotiating positions with schools, welfare agencies, and bureaucratic institutions. As individuals responsible for nurturing an infant, young women could extract greater sympathy from societal institutions than could males, who often found themselves distrusted and feared.

As most young mothers found that their new status brought little relief, they also confronted new problems or obstacles. Males, generally relegated by welfare regulations to absence or to work at two jobs, often drew more from continued male peer associations than from life as a father and a breadwinner. Roles for young women and young men contracted and concretized as many of the institutions that had lent social control for sustained family life in past generations, such as churches and gender-segregated religious clubs, no longer endured in inner cities.

Gender in Youth Organizations

I need
Someone to love
When I'm feeling lonely
I need
Someone to hold me
When I look around
I feel lonely with sorrow
But I'll just sit here
And wait for a better tomorrow.
                Amora Lewis

Into this void of communication, modeling, and sustained presence, effective youth organizations came to meet some of the needs of inner-city youth. Gender roles figure prominently here. By the late 1980s, clubs that included girls as young as 10 and 11 years of age often began classes on birth control, prenatal health, and child care. Such clubs also offered time for games, sports, and outdoor explorations for girls. Clubs that allowed only males rarely offered classes or courses that projected the boys into adult roles of cooking, cleaning, or caring for children. Instead, they provided sports activities such as boxing, swimming, and basketball to boys collected into similar-age groups.

Gender-segregated youth organizations thus differed in the extent to which they provided role-playing of future tasks, specific skills, and responsibilities for young women and men. Boys' organizations explained their programs of high physical activity as necessary to "burn off energy" or let the boys "play out their frustrations" in safe, rule-governed activities that taught important norms of sportsmanship and team play. Leaders saw the boys as building skills, as well as a sense of physical prowess and strength—both critical for survival on the streets. For girls, youth leaders saw it as necessary to help them to role-play what they would become as adults, as well as provide them with opportunities to develop physical prowess, sportsmanship, and a sense of being on a team.

Gender-segregated organizations, as well as coeducational groups, provided youngsters with opportunities to participate in group decision-making, to take part in maintenance chores of youth centers, and to plan public performances or displays. Almost all ensured much time "just for talk." Some groups had "clubs" with compulsory attendance twice a week; others held "family meetings" that gave adults and youth opportunities to say what was on their mind in an accepting and caring atmosphere. In such talk, only harsh or "hurtful" language was ruled out. Many organizations included both boys and girls on boards that met on a regular basis and heard matters pertaining to funding, insurance regulations, and programmatic decisions. Leaders emphasized the importance of such occasions for young males and females to make decisions together as members of a board or council; they saw these situations as modeling power sharing between males and females—occasions that were infrequent in the households of many youngsters in inner cities. The most common metaphor for these youth organizations was "family."

Situated Constructions

Appearing at your deepest rest,
Controlling your mind at its best,
Sometimes there's good things happening to you,
Hoping your dreams will someday come true
Making you think you're really there
But then you wake up
To hideous glare.

Steven Hill

Ethnicity and gender, both social constructions, will always reflect many features of an individual's up-close and broader environment. The social mores, disciplinary lenses, ideologies, commercial marketing, and political economy of the time lend definition to conceptions that drive public ideas and policies. Ideas about ethnicity and gender also depend on where a young woman or man sits. Generational differences in the nature and significance of ethnicity and ways to play out gender roles find their ways into policies and programs for youth. "Ethnic pride" or being a "lady" or "gentleman," sometimes prized and pursued by adults but seen as outdated or irrelevant by youth, can also represent a threat for youth—one more boundary that could, if flaunted, add to gang, turf, or girl-boy struggles ever ready to erupt into violence. Organizations that youth judge to be effective include adult leaders who can be trusted to know that survival in the inner city represents something distant from a mere celebration of ethnicity or gender. Far more complex and embedded in achievement, responsibility, and an immediate support network are the conditions of identity necessary to resist violence and drugs. For this reason, it is possible to see African American, mixed race, and recent immigrant boys and girls join in club or family meetings to acknowledge that "village collaboration" and a strong sense that "we're in this together and it won't be easy" can keep them together to resist the temptations of the street created by those who have no such pride and supportive network. Many youth leaders allege that such unexpected ways of calling youth to "be strong" and "show color" illustrate that it is far more than symbols and labels that bind youth to promising self-images.

Youth organizations see inner-city youth's socialization to healthy gender roles as especially necessary to protect them from commercial and physical exploitation and isolation. Within youth organizations, young men and women write raps to denounce violence against women and the equation of gender with sex. They script and produce dramas that expose the senseless futility of gang turf battles; they coordinate musical programs to celebrate themes of hope. They come together often to remind each other they can have futures in spite of what they see going on around them with their parents and their friends. They want to see themselves as able to move from their "crouched" positions of either subversion or submission. They want resources that will help them to lift themselves in theory and practice above their overwhelming sense that "all of it is now"—has to be now—and that there will be no tomorrow.

Notes

[1]Data for this chapter were drawn from fieldwork and interviews done in youth organizations of the three major metropolitan areas studied under a research project, "Language, Socialization, and Neighborhood-Based Organizations," funded by the Spencer Foundation. For further discussion of the three urban regions studied, see the Introduction. The poems and brief prose pieces that appear throughout this

chapter were written by members of the youth organizations included in this study.

[2]For discussions of the Irish case, see Curtis (1971), Harris (1964), and Gossett (1965). Whitten and Szwed (1970) provide a very useful overview of the various uses of the term *race* in the second half of the 20th century.

[3]Among African tribes, for example, individuals may choose to shift their identity as a member of a particular tribe based on altered regional economics or politics or based on marriage or other rites of adoption. (See case studies of such shifts in *Ethnicity,* Vol. 1, No. 1.)

[4]In the late 1980s and the 1990s, some African American scholars (Steele, 1991) pointed out that affirmative action programs and college financial aid programs invited individuals to self-label for certain benefits. Those who had previously not chosen particular ethnic self-ascriptions did so under institutional pressures.

[5]Numerous social scientists and journalists took up the tough question of whether "minorities" and "underrepresented groups" should assert more strongly their similarities or their differences with respect to the "majority." See, for example, Steele (1991) and Williams (1991).

[6]Scholars have examined the various meanings and interpretations of labels for those who are American slave descendants (Baugh, 1991; Smitherman, 1991). The latter reports a survey that showed that "at least one-third of African Americans are in favor of the name change and that such support is seemingly strongest among African American youth, particularly those in college" (p. 128). African American women are least in favor of the change, often arguing that far more important matters deserve the attention of the American public and "black people." In this book, we use *African American* with the view that currently this term most closely aligns with the general practice of referring to other groups: Asian American, Italian American, and so on. The term *black* is retained in all quotations that originally included this label. For the same reasons, we refer to white Americans as *European American,* except when another term for this group appears in directly quoted material. At the time the fieldwork of this study was carried out, *Latino* held a slight edge over *Hispanic* among individuals who led youth agencies in neighborhoods populated by Puerto Ricans, Mexicans, and refugees from Central America, as well as immigrants from Latin America. But preference for labels changed often and according to age, time of migration, amount of education, and audience, and no steady majority voice emerged on the choice between these two terms and specific national identifiers (such as El Salvadorean). The politically neutral decision was in most cases to be as specific as possible when referring to known individuals or groups and to choose the country of origin as the label.

[7]For the most part, the names that particular groups called themselves came to assume prominent attention only in the next decade. Autonomy in language, representation in the United Nations, and control over schooling became familiar pleas from small groups in Europe, as well as Native Americans in Canada. These requests for recognition, as well as careful attention to names, broke into widespread demands after the breakup of the Soviet Union in 1990. Ethnic warfare and harsh divisions dominated the world's news.

[8]The duality of domains of competence and positive judgments by those regarded as important helps explain why contexts that are holistic and include indi-

viduals of different ages and ability levels tend more toward the creation of strong self-images than environments without these features (Harter, 1990). See also Spencer and Dornbusch (1990) on the role of units beyond the family in creating global self-esteem in nonmainstream or "minority" communities.

[9]In general, girls begin their pubertal growth spurt at a mean age of 9.6 years, and the first menstruation appears within 10.5 to 15.5 years of age for girls in the United States. For boys, although testicular growth begins around age 11, the onset of the release of sperm usually occurs between the ages of 12 and 14.

[10]These changes co-occur with growth spurts that often allow girls to grow taller than boys at the early stages of adolescence. Girls' added height and emerging breasts and hips often make them more attractive to older boys than to their own-age peers and may lead them into relationships that result in sexual intercourse earlier than their male counterparts. For discussion of pubertal process, see Brooks-Gunn and Petersen (1983), Brooks-Gunn and Reiter (1990), and Kreipe and Sahler (1991); on gender-related role expectations during early adolescence, see Anderson (1990, Chapter 4).

[11]The study of "gender" roles as such centered after the late 1980s on women; see, for example, Morgen (1989). The usual justification for this tendency was that all studies before the late 20th-century feminist movement generalized from a focus on males, with little consideration for the roles of women or their relations to economic, political, and religious segments of a society's culture; see, for example, the essays of Morgen (1989). Since the 1970s, the position of African American males has been an exception to the general omission of males from gender studies; see Anderson (1990, Chapter 4), Gibbs et al. (1988), Hannerz (1970), and Stack (1974) for examples.

[12]These habits range from choice of toys and dress to reminders about "how little boys (or girls) behave" and also promote sex-role attitudes that have strong impact on developing gender relationships (Maccoby 1988, 1990; Stangor & Ruble, 1987).

[13]Anderson (1990) details the complex interrelations of changing public norms and changing ethnic compositions of neighborhoods with shifting sexual practices and images of self and children for young African American males and females. Heath (1991) describes how high-rise public housing projects of the 1980s undermined earlier community socialization practices that sent clear signals to young children about gender-appropriate behaviors and attitudes.

References

Anderson, E. (1990). *Streetwise: Race, class, and change in an urban community.* Chicago: University of Chicago Press.

Baugh, J. (1991). The politicization of changing terms of self-reference among American slave descendants. *American Speech, 66,* 133–146.

Brooks-Gunn, J., & Petersen, A. C. (Eds.). (1983). *Girls at puberty: Biological and psychosocial perspectives.* New York: Plenum.

Curtis, L. P., Jr. (1971). *Apes and angels: The Irishman in Victorian caricature.* Washington, DC: Smithsonian Institution Press.

Gibbs, J. T., Brunswick, A. F., Connor, M. E., Dembo, R., Larson, T. E., Reed, R. J., & Solomon, B. (Eds.) (1988). *Young, black and male in America: An endangered species.* New York: Auburn House.

Gossett, T. F. (1965). *Race: The history of an idea in America.* New York: Schocken.

Hannerz, U. (1970). What ghetto males are like: Another look. In Norman E. Whitten, Jr., & John F. Szued (Eds.). *Afro-American anthropology: Contemporary perspectives* (pp. 313–328). New York: Free Press.

Harris, M. (1964). *Patterns of race in the Americas.* New York: Walker.

Harter, S. (1990). Self and identity development. In S. S. Feldman & G. R. Elliott (Eds.), *At the threshold: The developing adolescent* (pp. 352–387). Cambridge, MA: Harvard University Press.

Heath, S. B. (1991). The children of Trackton's children. In J. W. Stigler, R. A. Shweder, & G. Herdt (Eds.), *Cultural psychology: Essays on comparative human development* (pp. 496–519). Cambridge, MA: Cambridge University Press.

Maccoby, E. (1988). Gender as social category. *Developmental Psychology, 24,* 755–765.

Maccoby, E. (1990). Gender and relationships: A developmental account. *American Psychologist, 45,* 513–520.

Morgen, S. (1989). *Gender and anthropology: Critical reviews for research and teaching.* Washington, DC: American Anthropological Association.

Sander, J. (1991). *Before their time: Four generations of teenage mothers.* New York: Harcourt Brace Jovanovich.

Smitherman, G. (1991). "What is Africa to me?": Language, ideology, and African American. *American Speech, 66,* 115–132.

Stack, C. (1974). *All our kin: Strategies for survival in a black community.* New York: Harper Torchbooks.

Stangor, C., & Ruble, D. N. (1987). Development of gender role knowledge and gender constancy. In L. S. Liben & M. L. Signorella (Eds.), Children's gender schemata. *New Directions for Child Development, 38,* 5–22. San Francisco: Jossey-Bass .

Spencer, M. B., & Dornbusch, S. M. (1990). Challenges in studying minority youth. In S. S. Feldman & G. R. Elliott (Eds.), *At the threshold: The developing adolescent* (pp. 123–146). Cambridge, MA: Harvard University Press.

Steele, S. (1991). *The content of our culture.* New York: Beacon Press.

Whitten, N. E., Jr., & Szwed, J. F. (Eds.). (1970). *Afro-American anthropology: Contemporary perspectives.* New York: Free Press.

Williams, P. J. (1991). *The alchemy of race and rights: Diary of a law professor.* Cambridge, MA: Harvard University Press.

2

Embedded Identities: Enabling Balance in Urban Contexts

Milbrey W. McLaughlin

The civic, community, and neighborhood settings in which urban youth grow up furnish different signals and supports for their social identity, worth, and possible futures. Young people construct their identities within these embedded, diverse, and complex environments, a reflection of such elements as local political economy, peer relations, family circumstances, civic supports, churches, schools, and neighborhood-based organizations. This chapter explores the significance of these embedded contexts for youth and the character of the neighborhood institutions that enable youth to find balance in the harsh actuality of their urban environments. The institutions from which inner-city youth derive support and hope are institutions that are enmeshed in the lived realities—not imagined conditions or construed circumstances—of urban youth. Neighborhood-based organizations that enable youth to construct a positive sense of self and to envisage a hopeful future have roots deep in the local setting and have caring adults who provide bridges to mainstream society.

When something violent hits you, you can't help but lose your balance and fall. And after you pick yourself up, you realize you can't trust anybody to save you. . . .

Amy Tan
Kitchen God's Wife

Balance and trust embody key elements of survival for inner-city youth. Their sense of self is framed in the several identities they must assume in multiple arenas—family, neighborhood, and schools as well as community organizations, the streets, local economic realities, churches, and youth groups—that compose their environment. These elements combine to shape the ways in which young people perceive themselves and their sense of competence, future, and social membership. "Something violent" hits almost every young person living in America's inner cities. The flagrant violence of street crime, the concealed violence within families, and the silent violence of emotional neglect and absence of nurture are commonplace in urban neighborhoods.

For too many young people, the violence that is part of their lives disables or deflects any positive sense of future or even a secure conviction that they have a future. Learning to trust no one but yourself and to limit hopes and expectations underlies young persons' strategies of survival in urban contexts. Beyond the close-up, harsh realities they experience are public media portrayals of them and the places they live blaring out on the evening news. Vanishing communities, depressed economies, and disappearing families provide few direct supports to contradict these depictions and few models of successful escape from these depictions. "Ain't no makin' it" in legitimate or mainstream society becomes the perceived reality of most inner-city youngsters (MacLeod, 1987; Williams & Kornblum, 1985).

Commentaries and analyses of the urban environments in which youth move and mature typically take an undifferentiated cast. The institutions of the urban context—most especially schools but also churches, families, and community organizations—come off as meaning the same thing. From the perspective of policymakers, government officials, and analysts, urban communities bear a structural and institutional sameness. All urban centers have schools, parks, police, social services, community organizations, and other publicly supported institutions to serve youth and their community. All urban centers have private resources in service to the community: churches, neighborhood organizations, and philanthropic initiatives. Aside from funding levels, membership statistics, or demographic features, little distinguishes one community from the other in the view of those at the top of the policy system.

However, the view from inside—the youth's perspective—reveals quite a different landscape. The experiences of youth growing up in one urban area can and do differ in many important ways from those of youngsters growing up in another urban environment that may be only two blocks away. Most important in these differences are not the status and character of individual institutions but the collective determination of the environment in which local youth develop and mold a sense of identity.

For many inner-city youngsters, the institutions and opportunities in their communities and neighborhoods and personal lives do not add up to much. An African American woman, active in her community's youth organization, comments: "There are so many broken lives—broken spirits, broken hopes. How else can you understand the drugs, and the violence, and the kids having kids? The inner-city environments break kids." A youth worker describes his objectives for inner-city youth in stark terms of survival:

I want these kids to have a positive life. That's where I put my energy. If they can be a doctor, great, but I just want them to live. If they can "duck the bullet"—not just the bullets that come from the gun, but from the verbiage of peers, a girl pregnant by 16, a man incarcerated by 18. That's the bullet.

A social commentator, summing up the life prospects for inner-city youngsters, says: "These kids don't have a chance."

How do youth growing up in America's inner cities duck the bullet? How do they construct and pursue alternatives that enrich rather than endanger their lives and provide them with images of productive futures? How do young people navigate the tough territories of inner cities to construct a positive identity and a perception of themselves as members of society? For most youth, balance is hard to achieve and even harder to sustain in the teenage years. The youth organizations effective by virtue of youth's engagement with them described their success primarily in terms of helping youth to achieve "balance"—sure footing and sense of purpose—in their communities as well as an ability to negotiate different roles in different places—to draw on an array of features to give them several identities, all of which are anchored in a secure sense of self.

This chapter draws on our three study sites—River City, Lakeside, and Big Valley—to show first how the embedded contexts of inner-city communities challenge young people as they negotiate the various boundaries that confront them and how even within the same community, differences in neighborhood history, families, and structural and spatial arrangements of parks, schools, and public transit create substantively distinct conditions for the evolving self.[1] Remarkably similar across these different contexts, however, are the attributes of youth organizations that have enabled youth to find balance within these inner cities.

The City Level

At the city level, communities as enacted by local government, social structures and traditions, civic leadership, and political economies are quite different places to grow up in. Local factors combine to create qualitatively and quantitatively different environments in terms of opportunities available to youth, values and expectations that shape their development, and supports or obstacles associated with paths to maturity and productivity (Schwartz, 1987). Beyond institutions and the dollars that sustain them, communities constitute diverse cultures in which youngsters come to know themselves and to form a sense of their personhood and future—as a male or female, a member of an ethnic group, a member of a social class, and a future worker and parent.

Local Economy

An obvious and critical aspect of context in terms of youth's developing sense of personhood and place in broader society is the health and character of the local employment market. Local opportunities to have a job, to see parents and friends at work, and to have the self-respect that goes along with involvement in productive enterprise are critical to any youngster's sense of personhood. Through much of the 19th and early 20th centuries, jobs have provided inner-city youth with a way to supplement meager family incomes, as well as with adult roles and associations. Adolescents unsuccessful in school could find jobs and respectability in work within their communities. Others could plan on jobs with local industries after high school graduation, following in the footsteps of their fathers and neighbors.

But by the end of the 20th century in most urban communities, youth had little hope of deriving their worth from the local labor market. Some argue that the ghetto's worst feature from young people's perspective is that it closes them off from images of success (Wilson, 1987). Jobs dried up as industry left urban centers, as technology replaced unskilled and even skilled labor, and as competition from abroad eroded entire industries (such as steel and automobile manufacturing). Although there were differences among our three urban sites, the general job situation for urban youth was grim throughout.

In River City, the late 1970s saw the closure of the heavy industries that had provided employment for generations of River City families. Suddenly, adults were unemployed, and young people, who used to count on a mill job even without a high school diploma, faced a severely depressed local economy and bleak job prospects. Women, who until then had played the traditional role of housewife, had to find work outside the home in order to make ends meet.

In Lakeside, the final two decades of the 20th century offered few legitimate jobs in the inner city, especially for males. The city lost more than 300,000 manufacturing jobs during the 1980s alone. A young African American gang member snapped angrily that "the only work around is nigger work." A Hispanic gang leader talked quietly about the low-level jobs the few employed adults have in his neighborhood—employment he sees as numbing, dead-end work: "A job like that is giving up. Just isn't worth it."

In Big Valley, the swift collapse of the oil-based economy and the decline in ranching, on top of the closure of food processing plants and the mechanization of agribusiness, brought depression to the city's economy and eliminated the bulk of the unskilled jobs.

Youngsters see critical differences in their life chances in an economically sound industrial community versus the besieged economy of most urban centers. Teenagers in depressed communities grow to see themselves as superfluous in terms of mainstream society; drugs and crime offer an attractive alternative to no productive employment. "The streets are an equal opportunity employer," quipped one cynical young man. Youngsters say involvement in such illegitimate activities is one of the few ways they can demonstrate their competence in an environment that seems to offer them no future or legitimate means of support: "Why do we steal and deal drugs? Because there is no work for us. If we could find work, we wouldn't be doing this stuff."

The absence of employment for youth and adults in inner cities not only makes the young deeply pessimistic about their futures and the value of school but also means the young have no opportunity to learn how to work, or to learn the skills and habits of the workplace either through their own involvement or through the models provided by adults in their lives. Inner-city youth often stop trying to meet the terms of the mainstream because they do not see the payoff: They see nothing in their community or their families to support a positive future perspective, and this lack of positive role models and hope for a positive future may be their key risk factor (Auletta, 1982; Dryfoos, 1990; Schorr, 1988; Wilson, 1987).

Conceptions of Youth and Ethnicity

A less obvious impact on youth's developing sense of personhood is the conception of youth held by members of the local community. Communities view childhood and youth differently. Some see young people as a resource to be developed; others, as a problem to be managed; and others, as adults-in-waiting. Ethnicity and race further complicate these local conceptions of youth.

In the old European traditions that dominate River City, adults try to hold their children to traditions of respect for elders and to the rule of "don't speak until spoken to." As a result, community responses to youth offer few forums for the voice of youth to be heard, and heavy-handed, authoritarian European traditions characterize youth organizations. Youngsters have little legitimate presence at the community level, and city government, by the report of insiders, has not been very effective in working with or for youth.

Furthermore, the city has supported the image of River City as a city of neighborhoods and has left it to local civic groups to develop an interest in youth and to support programs for them. These neighborhood-based civic activities often came about in response to "problems" with youth, and the level of interest and support provided for youth has varied significantly by locale. This situation has been, according to a local youth activist, "both good and bad—good because people in the neighborhoods work together, bad because neighborhoods won't work together." As a consequence, there has been no coherent policy for youth in River City, and the level and nature of neighborhood support for youth has varied dramatically.

River City's strong, European American, ethnic enclaves have also included a latent racism that creates an unreceptive and often hostile environment for African Americans and newly arrived Asian immigrants. For example, a settlement house founded in the late 19th century to work with immigrants closed approximately 80 years after its inception primarily because a majority of the board did not want to admit African Americans, who were becoming a larger part of the neighborhoods they served. Until the late 1950s, African Americans were not permitted even to enter the settlement house. The executive director of the city's Boys and Girls Clubs was outraged by the racist attitudes of club officials in a European American ethnic neighborhood: "They told me that they didn't want those kids, meaning African American kids from the housing projects, walking through their neighborhood."

Despite efforts of some city officials, educators, or philanthropists to blur these boundaries between European American ethnic groups and "others," those boundaries remain significant in determining a perception of place in the broader community.[2] Although River City has managed to preserve some of the positive aspects of its ethnic heritage, the barriers and boundaries that accompany it work against community-level solutions or collaborative arrangements.

Lakeside, like River City, is a city of immigrants and a labor town. However, Lakeside's context for youth draws primarily from yet another frame: machine politics and organized crime. European American ethnics long controlled the city's government apparatus and the favors it could bestow. Patronage and "old boy networks" held in firm grasp the various "goods" for distribution. In this context, African Americans especially were clear outsiders, included primarily for token representation and displays of "fairness." In fact, the housing, city services, and benefits available to Lakeside's African American and Latino citizens have been traditionally far inferior to those available to European American groups living within the city. For example, park facilities in African American neighborhoods have often been little more than scruffy lots, in conspicuous contrast to the "country club" facilities available in more affluent neighborhoods. The consequence for African American and Latino youth and their families living in Lakeside has been a sense of personhood that is structurally and politically subordinated.

A local news commentator summed up what it is like to grow up in Lakeside for all but the advantaged few:

> Lakeside is one of the most structurally segregated cities in the country—segregated by housing. There are the black neighborhoods and the Hispanic neighborhoods. This distorts a child's life. But even more distorting are the gangs and drugs and crime that are part of a child's environment. It is like a minefield; more succumb than will make it through. Everyone is trying to get rich on drugs. Adult black males tell me that the biggest problem they have is with 10-year-olds dealing. Teenagers are now engaged in murders. There are now kids on bicycles shooting at cops. It is getting more and more fantastic . . . almost murder as an art form. It distorts a child's life. They are overwhelmed.

Gangs in Lakeside are big business, linked to organized crime and controlled by adults from the chief executive officer's "office" in an upstate prison. Asked what might be a headline for a story on local youth, this commentator paused and replied: "'If you're lucky. . . .' That's the headline."

A community worker who had worked in low-income neighborhoods in both Lakeside and River City saw important differences for youth growing up in the two cities:

> In River City, kids don't hurt as much. There are different problems for youth and youth policies. Both communities have been co-opted by the adult agenda and senior issues, but in Lakeside a particularly debilitating conception of youth exists. Youth are seen as expendable—life is expendable, especially if you are black.

In Big Valley, violence of the type that occurred daily in the lives of Lakeside youngsters was rare, but a similar "them/us" climate divided the community and generated rules of action that were well understood by all actors. Leaders in Big Valley, long controlled by an elite European American establishment, began to wrestle with these discriminatory conceptions of community in the 1990s. However, for the lower-class, Latino and African American youth growing up in Big Valley, trappings of second-class citizenship were everywhere—from the public schools they attended to the community services available to them, their families, and their neighborhoods. In large measure, the conditions and experiences of Big Valley's ethnic minorities were invisible to the city's social and political elite: "It's not our problem."

A European American social leader and political lobbyist expressed concern about both the perception and reality of indifference to the community's young people:

> We don't support [all of] our children . . . we are perceived as being very wealthy individuals who don't care, which is really bad news. We don't do enough for our kids. [But] I see us working harder at providing for our youth . . . the [proposed] youth curfew and its implications have really caught the attention to the community. And I think they're going to work harder at programs for our youth, all ages.

A local philanthropist commented that things could change but that it had been difficult for traditional Big Valley civic leaders to see problems such as gangs, homelessness, crime, and school performance as community-level problems that might affect them, too.

These community-level attitudes toward ethnicity and race get expressed in various ways: by the allocation of community resources, the presence or absence of voice in the community's power structure, and access to the local social structure. The priority or lack of priority afforded youth gives off powerful signals to youth about their value, social legitimacy, and future. Within the communities studied—especially Lakeside—African American and Latino youth responded to these community-level attitudes by retreating to the confines of their cultural group and by distrusting the possibility or desirability of ever becoming part of broader society.

Communities also shape young people's conceptions of self-esteem and presence. The messages about self and identity that urban youth get about themselves and their place are disheartening: "Society gives you the feeling that you aren't worth anything." "Negative is everywhere." And in all three communities, community leaders acknowledged that youth "just are not a priority." Moreover, the often fragmented voice of minorities at the community level fails to mobilize political support for change. Low-income minority youngsters and their families are typically isolated in their neighborhoods, effectively cut off from sources of power or secure support from the broader community.

Neighborhoods

The city sets the broad context for youth. But within urban communities, neighborhoods are "home" and are the most immediate and salient environments for young people. Neighborhood is where young people hang out, where they have their closest connections, and where their personhood is formed by the daily responses of the individuals and institutions they encounter. Although the character and contribution of neighborhoods are shaped by features of the larger community, neighborhoods further shape these broader influences and contribute their own influence to young people's sense of identity.

The maps that teens draw of their "community" frequently encompass no more than 5 to 10 square blocks and are marked with significant places in terms of "what you can do there" and "where you hang out." Many maps drawn by youth place their youth organization in the middle of their neighborhood map and show that the streets all lead to "their group" (see Figures 2.1 and 2.2).

The notion of neighborhood as a nurturing setting where older members watch out for and over neighborhood youth and where networks of "local knowledge" and intergenerational intimacy weave sturdy systems of support for young people and their developing identities is far from the reality that contemporary inner-city youth experience. (See Sorin [1990] and Anderson [1990] for analyses of traditional neighborhoods, their values and strengths, and the different realities of today's urban settings.) Such notions of nurturing neighborhoods embody, at best, times gone by. Instead of strong intergenerational families to provide love, education, socialization, and economic support, families in today's urban neighborhood are likely to be headed by a single female parent or to consist of two working parents. Connections to the neighborhood are difficult to maintain as transience for economic or other reasons reshuffles neighborhood composition on a regular basis.[3] The very physical structure of many inner-city neighborhoods influences young people's sense of who they are.

Vertical Neighborhoods: The Projects

Public housing projects in all our sites constitute pernicious environments for youth and their families. In Lakeside, African American youth are segre-

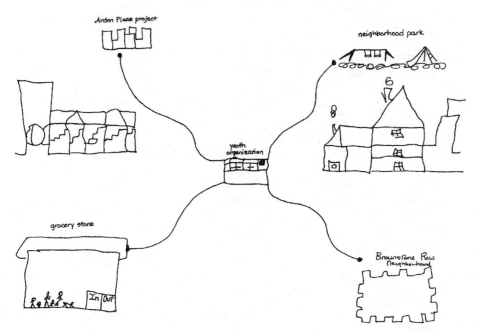

Figure 2.1

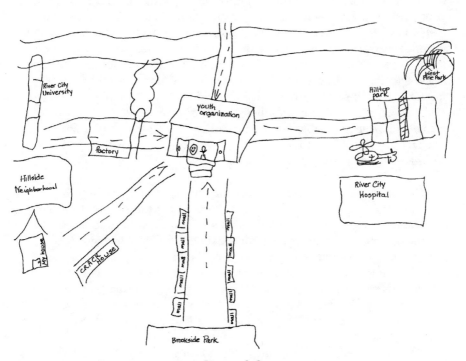

Figure 2.2

gated from the rest of the city in high-density housing projects in which adult males, positive economic role models, and personal security are in short supply. For example, Lakeside's Arden Place project, known as one of the nation's most desperate urban settings, counts fewer than 30 fathers among its 13,000 residents. Its empty parks reflect youngsters' justified fear of harm from gang violence; less than 5% of Arden Place residents hold a regular job. Housing authority guidelines disqualify most wage earners, thereby ensuring a context of welfare dependence. (See Kotlowitz [1991] for a description of such neighborhoods and their painful impact on youngsters who lack a positive sense of self and society.)

Physical safety is at issue every moment. Young people describe their neighborhood, where gangs are organized by high rise, as "a war zone. You never know where they're comin' from, or who they're shootin' at." Adults and youngsters talk about the importance of just getting on the bus: "If you can just get a kid on the bus, he will be safe," says a Lakeside youth worker. "The kids stand in the doorway and wait until the bus comes and they make a run for it . . . like once you got on the bus, you were safe."

The constant violence fosters perpetual fear and caution, as well as cynicism and numbness about the value of life or plans for the future. One youth wrote in his youth organization program: "Why have I forgotten to feel? I have forgotten to feel when I see Brothers dying every night." The violence also robs youngsters of the little recreational space available to them in their dense neighborhoods crammed with people and concrete towers. Parks are dangerous places because of drug deals and gang fighting. The park closest to Arden Place has been deserted for years by project youth after high-rise snipers killed two European American policemen. Gangs are an unavoidable fact of life in Lakeside's projects; the rare child remains uninvolved. A long-time street worker remarked that youngsters were joining up at an earlier and earlier age:

> Gang members used to be about thirteen. You started in the gang
> when you were about thirteen. Now you go over to Arden Place and
> you talk to seven-year-old kids. You see, you don't have to talk to
> them. You just come by and you see them throwing the signs and
> crossing their hands. . . . you've gotta belong to a gang if you live in
> a building, if you live in Arden Place. . . . it's very difficult unless
> your mother screams at them, "this is my son, and I don't want you
> messin' with him," makes sure you don't stay out, but you know
> you've gotta belong to a gang if you live in the projects.

River City youth who live in public housing projects have fewer concerns about daily shootings and violence, but in other respects their environment is similar to that of youngsters in Lakeside's projects in terms of absent fathers, unemployment, drugs, and teen pregnancy. In one such project, for example, where youth workers have been largely unsuccessful in establishing and sustaining programs, approximately 1,500 youngsters live in 415 apartments, 98% of which are headed by a single female parent. The majority of the residents in the project are under the age of seven. A community worker characterized River City's projects generally as "clusters of teens and children." Furthermore, River City's projects are out of the sight of the city, located high on the bluffs at the edge of town. And because only one bus a day comes in and out of the projects, the youngsters who live there rarely take the 30-minute ride "downtown," a strange and foreign place to them.

In both Lakeside and River City, youth talk about the stigma attached to "being from the project." "People just don't expect much of you," said a Lakeside teen. A coach of an Arden Place basketball team noted that people around Lakeside "were surprised that we're nice [when we visited in tournaments]. At first they don't expect [the players] to be nice because they are from Arden Place." A Girl Scout leader in River City, intent on bringing Girl Scouts into the public housing community, remarked that "there are stigmas attached to those who live in public housing; they are not invited to join in activities." Even within the Girl Scout program, however, a taint of neighborhood identification follows the girls to regional camps and jamborees. "It is race as well as class. Girls from the suburbs equate River City with 'bad.' And the worst offenders are their leaders." In this climate and for all of these reasons, she had difficulty in sustaining troops for public housing girls. These problems further diminish the neighborhood-based opportunities available for these young women.

Inner-City Enclaves

In Big Valley, there are few high-rise projects, but low-income minority youngsters are "ghettoized" by ethnicity. Overbrook, the traditionally African American neighborhood, had only one access street until the late 1970s. The community was sequestered on all other sides by fences and railroad tracks. Few public resources have been provided to Overbrook; the community has no library and enjoys meager recreational facilities. Latino youth live in another part of town, similarly isolated and enclosed by known neighborhood boundaries.

In the later 1980s, gangs began to form in Big Valley's inner-city neighborhoods, and outsiders see them as ethnic aggregates. One Latino youth worker downplayed the gangs, saying, they really are little more than groups of boys who get together and give themselves names. I don't call them gangs because they don't get together for violence . . . not that they don't do violence, but the primary thing is not violence. It is a social outlet.

However, the Latino director of a Big Valley Boys and Girls Club sees the situation as much more serious for youth and for the community:

Those gangs in the east and in Los Angeles—the Crips and the Bloods—are far more serious; they are corporate drug gangs. But Big Valley suddenly has the second highest level of gang activity in the state. They haven't taken over the schools yet [as they have in Lakeside], but they will if the community doesn't do something. In the Latino part of town, kids are afraid to come to the club because they are crossing gang turf. The park across from the building is one of the biggest battlefields. In the African American neighborhoods, though, gangs are really tough drug gangs.

Big Valley's traditional Latino neighborhoods are relatively stable and, in the view of residents, "haven't changed much. Everybody here knows everybody and if you have a problem you can usually find somebody to help you. A lot of people who moved away, moved back." Although unemployment is high and the emergence of gangs worries adults, Latino neighborhoods have relatively strong family networks, and even Latinos who moved away as they became economically successful remain deeply committed to the "old neighborhood." These neighborhoods worried about their youth being influenced by public portrayals of Latino gangs in Los Angeles and now call for improved, healthy opportunities for recreation in their communities:

We need to give kids something to do rather than tell them what not to do. There is nothing in our neighborhood for them. We have 14,000 people, a third of which are kids, and only one recreational center. It closes at 8 P.M. and on Saturday and Sunday. There is pee-wee [baseball], but you need money to join. One little park with three or four swings is all there is. We don't even have a water fountain. Across town they have nice parks and equipment. We have a recreation center in the middle of our neighborhood, it has a beautiful field. But the people across town are the ones who use it because you have to pay a fee. And I'm saying that's a total joke. If we want to keep our kids busy, we have to give them something to do. We have to give them something to create.

In River City, there remain a few urban neighborhoods reminiscent of those of old that support young people. For generations, many of the European American ethnic neighborhoods were bastions of ethnic tradition and social history. Houses in some neighborhoods were passed from parents to children; ethnic religious and social organizations drew neighborhood residents of all ages to festivals, religious observances, and cultural performances.

Today, in neighborhoods where ethnic members have spread out to more middle-class suburbs, the cultural center or club in the "old" neighborhood has in some cases become the center of the ethnic community, as reconstituted. In others, economic hardship has effectively isolated the remaining members from wealthier group members. Ethnic support groups as well as the social clubs have moved to the suburbs. Still, a number of ethnic groups have retained a commitment to heritage coupled with a contemporary dedication to "keep the kids off the streets." The festivals and cultural commemorations that define these organizations represent more than cosmetic decorations of ethnic life. "Rites of intensification," which provide youth with a strong sense of continuity and identification that is as immediate as geographical neighborhood, are augmented with a strong performance aspect that allows youth to showcase their uniqueness and talent in a community climate that still values and esteems European ethnicity. These youth find such centers to be powerful emotional and social neighborhoods of sorts.

Although these organizations honor ethnicity, consign a positive sense of belonging and history, and inscribe ethnic origin as a central aspect of a young person's identity, for young people, it is the performance aspect of the clubs that keep them viable (see chapter 3). Not only the people but also the organizations to which they belong do not cross rivers in River City. As people achieved a measure of economic prosperity and moved out into the hill areas—from the river banks to the suburbs—movement followed the rivers. "Neighborhood" for some groups of European American ethnic youth in River City exists on an expanded geographical base but retains much of the coherence and power of the old.

African American youngsters growing up in River City generally have no such sustaining, stable neighborhood environments. As in other sites, the emergence of single female–headed families and transience spurred by local economic downturns have eliminated the neighborhood networks and "old heads" who used to provide advice and a watchful eye. "It used to be," commented an African American woman involved in a church literacy effort, "that if a kid got in trouble or did something wrong, his mother would know it by the time he got home. No more. There is no one looking out for the kids. There isn't that kind of community anymore."

As in other urban areas, successful African Americans have moved out of inner-city neighborhoods to the surrounding hills and suburbs. Once away, a few bring their children back for church services as a way to maintain cultural traditions and religious identification. But these African American churches do not serve the same community-building function as did the European American ethnic centers of River City. According to African American civic leaders, their African American church is generally not meeting the needs of the neighborhood in which it is located:

> The black churches in the inner-city areas now have commuter congregations of wealthier middle-class blacks who drive in for Sunday Services in order to expose their children to "ethnic culture." They close their eyes to avoid the sights on the streets outside the doors of the church. In the black community in River City, only the Salvation Army is open all day.

An African American director of a Riverside Christian group commented that the African American churches are "too interested in gospel and [in] inculcating young people, and not enough interested in service to their community." Another African American youth worker involved in church programs characterized his church as largely disconnected from inner-city realities:

> Our churches are still strong, but the problem is that they are not strongly connected to the people who surround them. We are kind of out of step. We middle-class blacks have brought our kids back; now we need to act locally. But there is resistance among staid members of the church . . . they don't want to have street urchins in church.

The consequence for most African American youth in River City is the absence of a neighborhood cultural and spiritual center to socialize and support them.

And in one traditional African American neighborhood, civic action splintered the weak essence of neighborhood that had existed. Construction of the showcase River City sports arenas cut the Basin neighborhood in half and dispersed residents to a nearby ethnic European American neighborhood, causing massive interracial tensions and creating a hostile neighborhood environment for African American youngsters. In River City's other traditional African American neighborhood, youth lost their sense of place and space with the growing "yuppification" of the housing stock and complaints from new residents about noise and street activity. Youngsters now avoid this neighborhood, largely because of its location at the center of a newly gentrified area and their association of it with gay males.

Caring and Involved Adults

Inner-city youth in these communities and neighborhoods also had substantially fewer resources than are typically available to middle class youth in terms of caring and involved adults. Like working parents everywhere, inner-city parents are squeezed to find time to involve themselves in their children's school or extracurricular affairs. Single-parent families pressured by unmet child care needs, long hours searching for work, and multiple jobs often find the time and energy needed to involve themselves hard to come by. Positive mentors for youth are one of the most cherished assets that a community can have.

These pressures are seen to greater or lesser degrees in most American neighborhoods, but Latino and African American youth experience them differently. In all of our research sites, Latino youth had a far greater measure of adult involvement, advocacy, and commitment than did their African American peers. Latino adults are generally ready to volunteer in church, school, and neighborhood organizations; African American parents are generally not ready to do so. Latino parents and community members have developed vital neighborhood organizations to support their children's performances, such as Ballet Folklórico, and have begun to acquire an active and effective voice at the community level through their own persistence.

Parents are little involved with their children's activities in River City's African American neighborhoods. (See Anderson [1990] for an elaboration on the role of volunteerism and civic involvement in urban neighborhoods and on their decline in African American inner-city neighborhoods.) The Little League coach for the Parker league expressed sadness over this lack of parental participation but added, "at least I don't have any trouble with the parents of my players telling me what to do and interfering with practice." The regular spectators at ball games, he continued, are not parents but local "park dwellers," men whose ready advice and criticism are animated by a good amount of alcohol.

In Lakeside, differences between Latino neighborhoods and African American neighborhoods are apparent on most all fronts that require participation: voting, school reform councils, and political action groups. African American leaders attribute the low level of involvement in the African American community to "the decline of the black churches" and higher level of involvement in the Latino community to the existence of effective political action organizations in the Latino community: "They can really get their people out and their voice heard downtown." As frustrating as low levels of involvement in community affairs are to African American civic leaders, the lack of parental involvement in the lives of their children is even more frustrating to youth workers. One young African American social studies teacher who also coaches a successful basketball team with a strong tutoring component for young African American teens from Arden Place became angry about the apparent indifference of the community:

> Parents asked me to see what I can do with them [their kids]. Parents are hoping that by being with us [they'll do something positive]. But parent support is minimal. For example, in 1988, no parents came— *not one*—to the awards banquet. They came this year only because I visited each of the parents so every kid was represented by someone.

In Big Valley, Latino parents tend to be more involved in political activities and in their children's development. A youth director at a community Catholic Church, a young Latino male studying for his master's degree in social work, underscores the importance of community in Latino culture: "With Hispanics, community is part of the family. Community augments the family."

A Camp Fire staffer in Big Valley also commented on problems with getting volunteers to work with their programs and on differences between African American communities and Latino communities in this regard:

> We have horrific problems with volunteers, especially in the black community. Volunteering is a modeled thing. There are few models for volunteers in the black community. Many of the black mothers have jobs and are just not around. Hispanic women, in contrast, tend to be home.

The lack of parent or adult volunteers has direct consequences for the character and number of programs available to young people in the neighborhood. As the River City Girl Scout leader commented, the problem posed a fundamental dilemma. She felt she needed to have someone from the public housing project lead the troop to provide direct links to the local community and to bring relevant local knowledge to the activity, but these parents and adults were those least able to volunteer their time. This meant either that girls in the project then either had no Girl Scouting available to them or that their troop was led by someone from outside their neighborhood. The troop leader saw the root problem for her organization in terms of insufficient understanding of the realities of young people and their parents living in public housing:

> We've gotta do something with the parents. We can't negate that they exist. Without the adults, you can't have the girl. The problem within

our own organizations is a lack of understanding about the problems that minority women, especially those who live in public housing, face. How do you offer hope to kids whose parents have given up?

Instructors in Lakeside's very successful Liberty Street Theatre group defend community parents: "With the exception of one or two parents, they aren't involved at all. But it's hard. It all goes back to babies having babies. Most of the parents of these kids are probably just in their 20s themselves."

Low levels of adult involvement in neighborhood youth activities mean fewer or no scout troops, athletic teams, staffed recreation centers, and tutoring activities. Low levels of involvement by caring adults mean fewer active champions for the needs and efforts of youth. Low levels of parental and adult involvement in young people's lives exacerbate the "invisibility" that inner-city youth say they feel.

A theme in our interviews with young people was their sense of being isolated and unseen in their neighborhoods, their schools, and even their families. A Latino gang leader told us:

Except for the holidays, you'll never see a whole family sittin' together eating dinner, you know, like a regular family dinner. It's just like, you know, you're there, but you're not really there. Everybody ignores you.

A Boys and Girls Club director in Big Valley asserted that by ignoring its young, society was creating a

living time bomb. Kids aren't dumb. They know people have abandoned them. Upper-income parents provide too much money and too little time to their kids. But lower-income kids are just struggling to survive. Their parents cannot and do not pay much attention to them.

Ironically, anonymity was greatest for youth in the high-density neighborhood of the public housing projects. Youth often said that they felt part of a faceless mass, unknown as individuals outside their families or peer groups.

Youngsters growing up in America's inner cities have simply less of everything than their suburban counterparts. Their neighborhoods have fewer corner groceries, libraries, and attractive parks. A Lakeside Latino community activist noted sourly that the only publicly supported institution in their neighborhood was the county jail. Neighborhood schools generally are the worst in the city. In addition to scarce human resources, the economic privations of inner-city neighborhoods shape the character and quality of activities available to youth in multiple ways. Cookie sales bring in very little cash, money is not available for uniforms, youth productions have few of the high-tech or glitzy supports available to youth in affluent suburbs, and parents cannot or do not volunteer. On almost every front, inner-city youngsters have less, and what they do have is of lesser quality.

The real and perceived boundaries that circumscribe a youth's environment generate young people's perceptions of themselves as human beings and as social participants and also establish perimeters for their understanding of possibilities and futures. For inner-city youth, their neighborhood and the context it provides are all they know. A youth worker in Big Valley pointed to the stunted exposure evident in a youth's comment on arriving at a crosstown destination: "Are we still in the state?" A River City youth advocate said:

> These kids growing up [in the inner city] have grown up with violence, incest, abuse, horrible stuff. They really don't know about the outside world. They think their neighborhood is their entire world. It cripples them. And it defines their sense of self.

Cumulative Contexts

What does it all add up to for young people? On one hand, these nested contexts add up to substantively different places to grow up in terms of the broader community and in terms of neighborhood culture. The local contexts for youth in these three sites are as striking in their differences as in their similarities. Even larger structural changes—economic shifts most especially—affect youth differently depending on the neighborhood in which they live and their particular family circumstances. On the other hand, it's all the same. These embedded contexts do not add up to much for inner-city youth. Few resources are available to them, and even fewer are dedicated to them. There are few employment options or opportunities to understand what it is like to have a job. These social situations establish youth's perceptions of paths to maturity and the future.

Inner-city youth feel lonely, isolated, and disconnected from larger society and its institutions: schools, churches, and workplace. In this context—in the fierce communion of the streets and the barren economic life of inner-city neighborhoods—the deep pessimism, low self-esteem, and destructive behavior that corresponds to this sense of personhood are not surprising, nor is the hope of the youth advocate that they "just live, just duck the bullet." The street becomes the refuge for youth who can no longer bear a sense of failure and invisibility in their family, school, economic life, or community. Passivity and fatalism become directives for self.

It is not surprising that a theme in our interviews with youth was the inevitability of jail or death as futures for young men and the inevitability of early, single parenthood for young women.

Enabling Balance: Neighborhood-Based Organizations

What kinds of organizations and activities enable youth from inner-city neighborhoods to find balance and to construct a positive sense of self in terms of productive futures and larger society? In River City, Lakeside, and Big Valley, some programs and institutions played an effective and positive role in the lives of urban youths in that they attracted their participation and commitment. Furthermore, the young people involved with these institutions were more successful than their neighborhood peers in navigating the damaging aspects of their environments to construct positive, productive identities. Many finished school and found steady employment. Some went on to college. They made commitments to family and the neighborhood. They ducked the bullet.

These neighborhood-based institutions took diverse forms: Theater groups, tumbling teams, basketball teams, and Boys and Girls Clubs are but a few examples. They had diverse institutional histories and identities: Some were sponsored by churches, some were local organizations affiliated with a national organization, and some were the product of a passionate individual committed to the neighborhood and its youth. All of the enabling institutions, however, shared common attributes in terms of institutional design, philosophy, qualities of leadership, and attitudes essential to their effectiveness in the inner-city context.

Inclusive and Proactive

The needs of inner-city youth do not come in neat bundles or tidy problem definitions. Just as the identities of youth are embedded in the character and resources of their communities, neighborhoods, and families, so are their needs enmeshed and interrelated. Inner-city organizations that connect youth with larger society, promote a positive sense of purpose and personhood, and provide the resources that youngsters need to reach adulthood are not single-issue, single-purpose institutions. Even activities with an apparent narrow purpose—tumbling, basketball, or theater—address multiple needs for youth. They serve as tutoring centers and counselors; they broker linkages and opportunities to the world of work; and they provide assistance in the form of loans, emergency food supplies, or family assistance. These organizations, in short, serve as "family" for youth, meeting their needs and promoting their growth much in the inclusive way a family would.

Furthermore, like the idealized family, these organizations take a proactive role in shaping the young person's evolving sense of identity, goals, and connections to larger society. Unlike youth organizations that bring resources to the table and wait for youth to partake, these organizations are aggressive both in recruiting youth and in shaping their identity. "We don't sit back and wait for kids to come running up to us asking, 'what's the meaning of life?'" said the director of a high school inner-city outreach program.

Nor do adults involved with urban youth assume that young people have much idea about alternative futures that may be available to them. The coach of a winning basketball team from Arden Place put it this way:

> These kids can only imagine what they have some familiarity with; my mission has to be enlarging their vision, their perspective, and sense of the possible. These are kids who can't imagine anything but life in the projects.

In all of our sites, adults who worked with youth took an active—if not aggressive—role in assisting youngsters' construction of a positive self-concept and expanded view of alternatives they could hope for. "It's not enough," snapped one program director,

> to admonish kids to stay in school. What do they see around them that suggests that it makes any difference? You have to take them to show them what alternatives are, what exists outside their neighborhoods. Talk and high-sounding rhetoric don't mean a damn.

Inner-city youth need not only an enlarged vision of choices, alternatives, and self. They also need the direct involvement of adults in developing an understanding of what realistic goals might be and an identification of strategies to achieve them.

Shields Against Neighborhood Life

Organizations that enable inner-city youth to find balance and footholds do so by shielding them from the streets and the destructive aspects of neighborhood life. Some of these shields are physical, such as strong, fortress-like buildings where youngsters are safe behind sturdy doors, or vans that transport youngsters through hostile gang territory. Others of the shields take the form of rules of membership that preclude gang membership, involvement with drugs, "or anything negative." Still another shield comes in the outward signs of membership that protect youth from gang involvement. A street worker said:

> As long as you are involved in something, school, sports, the gangs will leave you alone. It is the unaffiliated youth they're after. If a kid can show them "I'm not a gang member, I don't want to be a gang member," you can stay out of gangs.

These youth organizations provide that kind of inclusive identity.

Clear rules of membership support protection within the organizations. Each of the effective youth organizations in the three sites described here established a few clear, firm, and consistent requirements of membership; enforcement was swift and certain. In the brutal context of gangs and tumult of the street, youth organizations that enable youth to find and maintain balance establish what one leader called "neutro-turf." But life on that turf takes place with firm rules and active involvement in programs and projects led by adults who have high expectations of youth.

Local Construction of Identity

"There is no fixed formula for working with kids in the inner city—you have to start where they are, and you have to work with local resources to find the right way to work with kids." Each of the organizations effective in working with inner-city youth is palpably local. Each draws on local resources, sinks ties into the local community, and responds to the issues and needs particular to the neighborhood. Each sees youth in the context of their families, neighborhoods, schools, and peer associations. Each values local knowledge and understands interconnectedness. In places like Lakeside, that knowledge is essential to program design and operations. A gang leader advises:

> Better neighborhood programs better look not only at city boundaries, but there may be a thousand more boundaries out there of gangs, you know. So I feel like that whatever they put on one side of the park, they should put on the other side of the park . . . if it's not what you be, it's where you live, it's how you look. Like if you dress with Jordan clothes on, they gonna mess with you because they say, "Hey, this motherfucker's in a gang." Don't matter if you are or not.

As this youth points out, local knowledge can be essential to safety.

Localness assumes strong ties to the community so that programs can shape and be shaped by their context. These strong ties are both informational and instrumental. They provide the networks of personal knowledge that support personalization and individual responsiveness. Local knowledge permits staff to intervene on behalf of youngsters with family or other institutions. For example, traditionally low levels of African American parent involvement in an after-school sports and scholarship program was changed only after a community member on staff personally called each mother to chide her about her absence and insist that she "get on in here."

People who are foreign to young people and their culture and who lack an understanding of the challenges involved in growing up in their neighborhood are hindered from the outset in making productive connections with youth. Young people need to be understood in the context of their gangs, their schools, their families, and their neighborhoods. Ethnicity and race vary considerably in the extent to which they figure as a core feature of young people's sense of themselves and others. For example, a European American activist working in Big Valley's Overbrook neighborhood to organize adults and rally the neighborhood association to press for more and better community services for the neighborhood's children reflected: " . . . many people don't like me working in the community because I'm white, not black."

The importance of local ties, character, and credibility for effective youth organizations poses a dilemma for program operation and governance. An executive director of a Lakeside affiliate of a national organization complained about being stuck between needs for community involvement and fund-raising:

> We believe in community control, but community people cannot generate or control the resources. So we have a bunch of oinkers on the board who are far away from the community [and who are] making decisions about their programs. My personal challenge is to get my board members to see the oppression these kids live under.

The director of a community-based organization faced similar issues because of the board of directors that governed his organization as a result of funding realities:

> [The composition of the board of directors] is a dilemma that faces all social service institutions if they purport to develop alternative institutions and serve poor neighborhoods. Our board is overly populated with bankers and lawyers; a majority of our 29-member board are not members of this community. There is only one black, although this neighborhood is 45% black; there are a few Latinos on the board, but

most don't live in this neighborhood. There are no Polish-Americans on the board, and this neighborhood has been traditionally Polish. I think the board essentially is unresponsive and unaware of the problems they could be addressing. Board members simply can't see the needs of the population.

Conceptions of Youth

A striking difference between effective and not so effective organizations that serve youth has to do with their conceptions of youth. The majority of youth-serving programs view youth as a problem and try to fix, remedy, control, or prevent some sort of behavior. From youngsters' perspectives, this single-focused, problem-based program strategy fails on two counts. First, it is too simple. The needs or problems of inner-city youth can rarely, if ever, be circumscribed by a single-issue effort. Teen pregnancy, drug use, involvement in crime, and school failure have multiple roots and require inclusive responses. Second, such "lack of" programs too often only reinforce youth's view that something is wrong with them, that they are somehow deficient, and that they are a problem. It is not surprising that youth do not elect to participate in such organizations or activities to a significant extent. The youth organizations that attracted and sustained young people's involvement gave visible and ongoing voice to a conception of youth as a resource to be developed and as persons of value to themselves and to society.

Many aspects of program design signaled the positive value of youth and positive expectations for their future. Youth activities geared toward tangible products or performances provided a sense of accomplishment and success. These activities gave youth concrete evidence that something could be gained by sticking with an effort and provided what one youth worker called "visible victories" for youngsters who have had few such positive experiences in school, in their family, or in the community.

These performances and productions also offered a socially integrating sense of purpose that served as a hook for other things, most especially tutoring activities. Such programs also bear witness to youth that choices matter, that effort can pay off, and that at least some adults believe what they do with their lives is important. The future perspective embedded in the productions and activities is generally outside the neighborhood and family experiences.

The norms of discourse and interpersonal interaction within these institutions were rooted firmly in the positive. Put-downs by either staff or youth were firmly and absolutely disallowed. To a person, leaders in effective youth organizations stressed the critical importance of respect for the youngsters: "We treat them like kings and queens, and we value honesty."

Adults who work with inner-city youngsters agree that nothing is more important than establishing a sense of youngsters' self-worth and of the value to society's institutions of the contributions they can make. Program staff contrasted these norms of behavior and interaction with the messages that youth received in school:

> We spend at least an hour every afternoon making up for all of the negative stuff kids hear about themselves in school. All they hear all day is that they can't do it. We have to reassure them every day that they can. Teachers want things orderly and controlled; they want to be in charge of the kid; they use punishment to keep things in line. All that negativism accomplishes is to further belittle the kid.

Many adults in these settings stressed the importance of alliance with some well-grounded cultural history as a component of general self-esteem and social competence. Youth workers underscored the importance of cultural awareness and pride and of youth's development of a positive sense of this aspect of their identity. Within the broader community context, there is often little with which to ascribe value or pride to African American or Latino youth.[4]

Youth workers see development of self-respect as an African American or as a Latino as an important element in enabling youth to make positive connections to the broader, culturally diverse society. African American adults are passionate as they point to the community contexts and institutionalized racism that "have forced African Americans to turn inward and to lose all self-respect." "It's gotten to where young black men don't expect anything of themselves or of their peers." The self-hatred of young African American males appeared as a consistent concern among inner-city youth leaders.

Ethnic or racial awareness, in the view of youth workers, can impart a richness lacking in the emotional lives of young people, as well as a sense of personal history: links across time, generations, and place generally unavailable to youth raised in anonymous, turbulent inner-city environments. Youth leaders who make ethnic or racial awareness a central part of their program philosophy and orientation said that this emphasis represents not "ethnic chauvinism" but rather an effort to reconcile individual identity and larger social diversity. These leaders stress the fact that for all their ethnically diverse youth groups, discussions of their different cultural histories offer an expanded vision for each and for the organization as a whole. These youth workers describe what theorists put forth as enabling features of the new ethnicity: "Under the conditions of the new ethnicity, a capacity to enter into multiple perspectives, and to see the same matter from more than one point of view seems to represent a clear gain for the human spirit" (Novak, 1980, p. 45).

Other adults involved with programs for inner-city youngsters minimize issues of ethnicity to stress general cultural values. For example, the African American leader of a world-traveled tumbling team from Lakeside advised his young people to focus on what is common to people rather than what is different:

One thing I teach these young people is that it had nothing to do with how they come into this world, just like the white kid had nothing to do with how he came into this world. And so, realizing those things to be true, you shouldn't spend one second of your time [emphasizing] different ethnic backgrounds. The bottom line is that I teach my young people citizenship, brotherhood, fairness, and sportsmanship. When they go out, they look at people how I look at people, and that is that color is nothing.

Youth leaders of both philosophies offered inner-city youth a firm bridge to the mainstream.

Stable, Consistent, and Caring

Unreliability and inconsistency build a way of life in inner cities; effective youth organizations make explicit efforts to follow through with commitments, to provide stable relations with adults, and to be consistent, predictable resources for youth. Youth workers say: "When folks pop in and out of kids' lives, it leads to a feeling of insecurity; we are trying to give predictability." "If you want to be a change agent with these kids, you've got to interact with them three or four times a week, you've got to work on the whole person."

Stability and consistency are essential to establishing a climate of trust and to making credible claims of caring and support. Young people are in desperate need of the things that adults can provide, but they learn from the street and family to trust no one but themselves. The most essential contribution that youth organizations can make to the lives of young people is that of a caring adult who recognizes a young person as an individual and who serves as a mentor, coach, gentle but firm critic, and advocate.

What these kids really need most is not more money or expanded programs. They need someone who cares for them. Our goal is to get kids to realize that regardless of what's going on at home, you've still got people here who love you.

These caring relationships not only provide an intimate adult for youth, but they also furnish a value system—religious or secular—that allows youth to see alternatives. More important, they furnish a system of beliefs and a structure for action where none existed before.

The need for stability and consistency makes tough demands on youth organizations and their staff. Many who choose to work in youth organizations do so with a sense of mission and of contribution to the community or cultural group. Economic rewards are few, and demands on personal resources are often overwhelming. Only the most passionate few can involve themselves for an extended time in organizations dedicated to inner-city youth. An executive with the Lakeside Girl Scouts commented on her departure: "I'm a manager, not a missionary. I'm burned out. I need to see results."

Finding individuals willing to make that commitment is no easy task. But most of the leaders of the effective organizations insist on staff stability and somehow manage to secure it. "I always ask applicants how long they plan to be with us," said the director of an Arden Place youth program. "If they say for the rest of their lives, I don't believe them. But I insist on a commitment of 4 to 5 years."

Bureaucratic requirements of "professional qualification" further exacerbate the difficulty of stable, consistent staff. Often, so-called qualified staff—individuals qualified by virtue of education or advanced training—are neither able to make the connections necessary to provide consistent, caring relationships with young people nor willing to make long-term commitments to program or place. Instead, their commitment may be to their career—for example, social worker or recreation specialist—or to the organization—for example, the Boy Scouts, YMCA, or Boys and Girls Clubs—where advancement often means leaving a specific place or neighborhood.

Flexible and Responsive

Leaders of effective youth organizations also agree on the importance of flexibility and the ability to develop programs and processes that respond to the situations that youth and their families bring with them. Flexibility is fundamental to building trust and to demonstrating genuine care. One director commented that too many programs "service" rather than serve youth.

Effective programs often provide activities in nontraditional settings, at nontraditional hours, and with nontraditional personnel, and pay little heed to orthodox boundaries of the service sector, bureaucratic compartments, or professional parameters. The programs and the terms on which they are offered take their shape from the needs and contexts of those with whom they work rather than from bureaucratic guidelines, accountability precepts, or objectives formulated at geographic and cultural remove from the local contexts (Schorr, 1988).

This need for local flexibility generated bureaucratic tangles for many of the nationally based organizations we observed when leaders attempted to adapt "national's rules" to local realities. A few individuals associated with national organizations bent or flatly ignored regulations. For example, a YMCA director, forbidden by national regulations to permit gang members into the building, closed at the usual time and then opened 15 minutes later as a community building available only to gang members. Such youth leaders simply did what they felt was necessary for the young people in the neighborhood they served.

Other limits to flexibility are found in funders' requirements. Leaders of neighborhood-based organizations complain that philanthropic organizations "jerk us around" with their apparently constantly shifting priorities and short time horizons. Government programs are restrictive in terms of eligibility requirements, allowable expenditures, and collaborative relationships. Both public and private funders alike demand "accountability" and outcome-based evaluations that require a focus on things that can be counted and controlled. Youth directors counter with their need for flexibility and the changing face of the communities in which they work. Examinations of public health and social service programs agree with youth organization leaders:

> Pressures to quantify have crippling effects on the development of the kinds of programs most likely to help high-risk families. Current methods of demonstrating effectiveness do not capture the essential extra dimension that characterizes successful programs. Organizations are pressed to shape their objectives and methods for intervening with an eye to easy measurement, and cannot be blamed for choosing to narrow rather than broaden their efforts. Many of the most effective interventions with high-risk families are inherently unstandardized and idiosyncratic. (Schorr, 1988, p. 268)

A Latino woman active in Big Valley neighborhood associations pointed to the limits on flexibility and on local decision making inherent in many funders' administrative structures—in this instance, those of the United Way:

> I have seen that the United Way has not been as effective as it should have been in delivery of services to minority neighborhoods. The United Way needs to decentralize their operations. The real need is for programs that will steady the community and be adaptable and flexible to meet the changing community . . . they try and "trickle down" but ineffectively.

Local needs for flexibility, for day-to-day autonomy, for adaptations that bend if not ignore standard operating procedures were key to effective youth organizations but contrary to policy and bureaucratic demands for standardization, accountability, and bureaucratic control.

Leaders with "Fire in the Belly"

The individuals who provided leadership to the effective youth organizations described here were as diverse as the organizations themselves: a former Marine, a minister, a teacher, a long-time community "mom," a state representative, and a retired professional athlete. They all had "fire in the belly." To a person, they were passionate about the young people with whom they worked, about the neighborhoods they served, and about the failures of conventional public and private efforts to meet the needs of inner-city youth. All described their involvement in terms of a lifetime mission. All had or developed deep roots in the community. They did whatever necessary to respond to needs as evident—not imagined—and to create the confidence and context of positive futures for these youngsters and families. They subscribed to a view that although they may not be able to change the community, they could change people and touch youngsters' lives. The director of a neighborhood center for Latino youth said this touching of lives is what made her work rewarding:

> It is all worthwhile when the kids give you this [showing us a picture drawn especially for her by one of the center's kids]. It was just being able to make a difference. I have kids from my organization who say, oh, gosh, thank you for helping me, you know if it weren't for you, I wouldn't have gone to school. There's not hundreds of those, but there is a good handful and I still keep in touch.

An African American youth leader committed to his sports group said much the same thing:

> I get satisfaction out of the fact that I've made a difference in the lives of a lot of young people. I just believe that serving as a good role model, serving as surrogate parent, will help society. Who knows, some of these young people may become tax beaters. But they also may become a taxpayer and a giver. They may become someone very important to society [or to the young people in their community].

Leaders see personal contact as key to effective relations with youth. The director of a buzzing, active inner-city Boys and Girls Club contends that personalization works both ways: "I have to get out and touch the kids. I have to put a human face on the administration, to have the kids know who I am." That knowledge provided important role models for inner-city youth. The leader of Lakeside's very successful tumbling team put it this way:

> When you look at the number of youngsters I have on my team and you consider that about 68 [out of 75] of them are black and that there are only two fathers in 68 households, we have a big problem and that makes my job more important. I became a surrogate father to these young people. And in some instances, I am the only real male they've had an opportunity to affiliate with who didn't drink, didn't swear, didn't smoke, wasn't unfair, wasn't unkind to them, was yours truly. And so, I rule by example. And I just think that a lot of what I am trying to teach will be a part of their lives forever—hopefully.

Passion, commitment, and personal contact ground the effectiveness of these leaders, as do personal knowledge and credibility. With few exceptions, all of these youth leaders have "been there." They come from the neighborhood or neighborhoods like them. Many have been gang members, and many have survived the projects. Having a preponderance of staff with backgrounds similar to those of local youngsters and their families makes a big difference in organizational credibility. Having been there matters for a number of reasons. Obviously, the understanding imparted by similar experience allows youth workers to see youth in context and to empathize with their self-perception. Having been there enables policies and programs that connect with the living reality of youth, not imagined conditions or supposed circumstances. Youth affiliated with gangs, especially, need to feel that the adults they are involved with are at least as tough, streetwise, and scarred as they are. A former gang leader, now a street worker for a YMCA program, holds street credibility as key to work with gangs:

> Get the gangbangers [to work with youth] because, you know, they're the ones that know the streets, that know what's goin' on. You know, they are the guys who would be able to communicate with the other guys. Otherwise, these guys, if somebody else came up to them, like I said, if you were to come up to them out of the blue and say "Hey, we got a program goin' on over here," they're gonna look at you like you're crazy, you know. But I come to them. They know me, and I know them. They're gonna have confidence in me, they're gonna trust me.

Effective leaders use such local knowledge and credibility to craft programs and resources that provide the connective tissue between estranged, cynical inner-city youth and the broader social institutions essential to their productive futures and positive conceptions of self. This connective tissue is spun from personal knowledge of youngsters and their setting and from knowledge of social, political, and economic resources in the larger community. These effective leaders all act as brokers, catalysts, and coaches, making the contacts and linkages necessary to enlarge the opportunities available to youth and providing the introductions and confidence necessary to access.

The disconnections between the professionalization of leadership in youth organizations and the kinds of skills and expertise necessary to be effective with urban youth are enormous. There is no training for the manner of leadership essential to youth organizations, and leaders committed to local youth and to neighborhood have no "career ladder." If they want to stay in their neighborhood organization, they are caught in a flat salary structure and career path. The rise of professionally trained administrators as mandated by many public and private agencies renders leadership an anonymous function defined by the responsibilities of bureaucratic controls. The typical youth professional is notable not for fire in the belly but for advanced degrees and certified competencies. These competencies may advance balanced budgets, but they have little to do with establishing the climate of trust and of connection and the individual courage necessary for effective youth organizations in the inner city. Instead, passion and commitment matter. The founder of the Lakeside tumbling team, who claims 7 days of vacation in 18 years, constructed his epitaph:

> When I die, I don't want anyone to say "He took my money," that he did it because of money. I'm motivated by love of kids. I have a commitment, I have a mission. On my tombstone, I just want someone to write, "He cared." He cared, but not for the money.

Enabling inner-city youth to find balance in their lives comes down to enabling trust in and positive involvement with adults. Leaders with fire in the belly are an ingredient essential to constructing the environments in which such trust can be nurtured and sustained. These leaders understand the importance of organizational attributes of persistence, safety, and flexibility and organizational messages of succor, security, and personal dignity, because these leaders understand youth and the challenges of embedded identity and balance in context.

Acknowledgments

Juliet Langman and Arnetha Ball gave this chapter a careful reading; their comments were extremely important in bringing clarity to complex points and smoothing rough edges. This chapter draws extensively on fieldwork carried out by research associates Merita Irby and Juliet Langman and research assistants Ali Calicotte and Steven Balt. The work reported here was supported by a grant from the Spencer Foundation to Shirley Brice Heath and Milbrey W. McLaughlin for a 5-year research project entitled "Language, Socialization, and Neighborhood-Based Organizations."

Notes

[1]River City, Lakeside, and Big Valley are pseudonyms, as are all names of the organizations and neighborhoods mentioned in this chapter. Except where otherwise noted, all quoted comments were made by respondents in the course of our fieldwork. To preserve the confidentiality of sites and individuals, we identify respondents only in terms of their community role.

[2]European American ethnics, too, tend to be exclusionary. A director of the Irish Center commented that their center "got bogged down by the people governing it. You were not welcome if you were not a member, and you couldn't join if you weren't Irish. The problem is that people built fences around themselves."

[3]For example, the registrar of a secondary school in a neighborhood we studied reported that she logged as many youngsters in the school as out of the school in a given week and that the school has an overall turnover rate of almost 70% in a given year. Likewise, the principal of an elementary school in an African American neighborhood reported that fully 50% of the students were not completing the year at her school.

[4]In fact, this stress on ethnic pride and on marks of uniqueness finds its way into organizations that draw European American inner-city adolescents—frequently the minority in their schools. Similar to their ethnic peers, these youth do not identify with mainstream culture; they turn frequently to heavy metal or the occult in search of an identity that distinguishes them from the mainstream.

References

Anderson, E. (1990). *Streetwise: Race, class, and change in an urban community*. Chicago: University of Chicago Press.

Auletta, K. (1982). *The underclass*. New York: Random House.

Dryfoos, J. (1990). *Adolescents at risk*. New York: Oxford University Press.

Kotlowitz, A. (1991). *There are no children here*. New York: Doubleday.

MacLeod, J. (1987). *Ain't no makin' it*. Boulder, CO: Westview Press.

Novak, M. (1980). Pluralism in humanistic perspective. In W. Peterson, M. Novak, &

P. Gleason (Eds.), *Concepts of ethnicity* (pp. 27–56). Cambridge, MA: Belknap Press of Harvard University Press.

Peterson, W., Novak, M., & Gleason, P. (Eds.). (1980). *Concepts of ethnicity.* Cambridge, MA: Belknap Press of Harvard University Press.

Schorr, L. (1988). *Within our reach.* New York: Doubleday.

Schwartz, G. (1987). *Beyond conformity or rebellion.* Chicago: University of Chicago Press.

Sorin, G. (1990). *The nurturing neighborhood.* New York: New York University Press.

Williams, T., & Kornblum, W. (1985). *Growing up poor.* Lexington, MA: D.C. Heath.

Wilson, W. J. (1987). *The truly disadvantaged: The inner city, the underclass, and public policy.* Chicago: University of Chicago Press.

3

Dances of Identity: Finding an Ethnic Self in the Arts

Arnetha Ball
Shirley Brice Heath

Why did some youth organizations of the 1980s and 1990s look to the per-forming arts as activities to attract youngsters? Youth leaders in dance, music, and theater recognized that the ethnic revitalization goals of the 1960s and 1970s had to be greatly supplemented for both the second- and third-generation children of European American ethnics and African American youth from inner cities. Performances had to bear up to high standards, engage a sense of both the past and the present, and center on group cohesion. Three programs described here indicate the importance of creating a sense of connectedness for youngsters through strong discipline, group achievement, and mutual expectations of high quality. The lan-guage of leaders goes a long way toward creating these contexts; frequent positive reinforcement and opportunities to help create and reflect on both practice routines and the arrangement of performances are essential. Both words and actions build a sense of work and play that offer strong attrac-tion to youngsters in dance.

My people had used music to soothe slavery's torment or to propitiate God, or to describe the sweetness of love and the distress of lovelessness, but I knew no race could sing and dance its way to freedom.

Maya Angelou
The Heart of a Woman

Urban youth organizations in the 1980s looked increasingly to the arts to find ways to attract what they regarded as "at-risk" youth away from drugs, dangerous diversions of their communities, and apathy with regard to academic achievement. These organizations included not only "Old World" ethnic groups, but also African American and Central American or Mexican American youth. Artistic activities, such as drama, mural production, and dance and musical performance, came to compete with athletics as key participation opportunities for young people in these organizations. These artistic endeavors sometimes rivaled athletic pursuits as attractions for young people and as events that adult leaders believed could build discipline, commitment, and a sense of group solidarity. This chapter describes several of these endeavors—one targeting European American youth from working-class neighborhoods around their city and two focusing on inner-city youth of African American and Latino backgrounds.

European American dance groups developed in the late 19th century as occasions to bring young and old together in regional folk festivals. However, in the 1960s and 1970s, these experienced a rebirth when they helped move the internal activities of individual sociocultural groups into the larger public arena. National legislation that favored "ethnic heritage," folk festivals, and a general valorization of ethnicity made possible public occasions for several groups to come together. Hungarian dancers now joined Croatians, Irish, and those of other national backgrounds in competition and performance at regional festivals attended by audiences that embraced the new ethnicity that called on those "in the know" to celebrate many different ethnicities, not just their own.

Since the 1920s among African American communities, jazz, gospel, ragtime, blues, and other art forms have both brought community members together and served as a way out of the ghetto for star individual performers. Many Americans remember with pride the contributions of artists of the Harlem Renaissance; many can name individual key artists in song, dance, and literature who worked their way out of discouraging and destructive backgrounds to achieve fame and financial success. But until the 1980s, youth organizations, especially those in inner-city areas with residents in poverty, did not look to the arts as the primary framework or basis for activities to attract youth. The problems of young people had been too persistently cast as needing direct and practical solutions rather than what many regarded as the frivolity of the arts.

Why then did some youth leaders of the 1980s look to dance or any of the performing arts as activities to attract youngsters? Who were the leaders who did so, and what was the nature of the youth populations they targeted? Before the 1980s, youth policy leaders generally viewed the performing arts as either irrelevant or extravagant in troubled urban areas and as unnecessary in communities of European American ethnics. But broadened understanding of the potential role of the arts in creating for young people a sense of story, intense holistic involvement across a range of activities, and a connecting quasi-spiritual bridge to both a past and a future led some youth leaders and philanthropic foundations to try immersion in the arts for youngsters.

In the 1980s, second- and third-generation European American immigrants left their old neighborhoods and scattered across diverse residential areas throughout their cities, where they joined working-class or middle-class communities whose families had no strong links to the dance and folk music of their forefathers. For certain ethnic groups, grandmothers and grandfathers, as well as mothers and fathers, determined to find ways to bring young people of the same ethnic heritage together—to retain pride in their past, to be sure, but also to help fill the time of young people in disciplined, adult-supervised activities. Drugs, alcohol, and activities their elders labeled "promiscuous" knew no spatial or class barriers, and suburban and working-class youngsters were more frequently than ever before seen as under threat from societal forces.

In general, youth leaders and community representatives who argued the value of the arts were performers from the neighborhoods or ethnic groups whose youngsters they wanted to involve in the arts. Many of these performers—particularly African Americans—had their beginnings in the 1960s and 1970s, in the height of ethnic pride movements centered in storefront theaters, galleries, bookstores, and social halls of local churches. There, they had formed their texts to critique the status quo and national and local political leaders, as well as to call people back to search for their roots. The history of dance as an expression of ethnic heritage, culturally valued narratives and forms of movement, and social protest underscored these leaders' special commitment to this art.[1]

But the turn to dance in the 1980s for youth differed in substance and rationale from earlier decades' endorsement of dance as primarily for ethnic identity or societal critique. Now, youth were drawn to dance, drama, and other forms of art as a means to form strong, safe group affiliations. In addition, some youngsters in the 1980s needed art to express current dimensions of their lives: their battles with drugs and gangs and their efforts to cope with ways to announce some achievement and identity for themselves.

Performers from inner cities who had gained prominence outside their communities after the 1960s had returned two decades later to find their old communities places that differed greatly from their earlier memories and their most recent performance demands. They had achieved success in national and regional cultural centers frequented by middle-class patrons for whom entertainment—not reclamation or revitalization of a lost ethnic identity, as had been been the case in earlier years—was a primary goal.[2]

Now, community or group identity, especially in the old African American neighborhoods, seemed highly elusive, and entertainment certainly did not appear to be a warranted goal of youth programs. Residents of high-rise project housing were now ethnically and linguistically diverse, whereas before they had been relatively homogeneous. Drugs, prostitution, and gangs were never far from the daily life of any urban child; it was rare to find a youngster who had not seen death come suddenly, seemingly out of nowhere, for friends, acquaintances, and sometimes family. Unlike in earlier decades, strong families, active community leaders, and political protest rallies that drew state and national attention rarely appeared in inner-city neighborhoods; instead, many of the old communities were now portrayed on the late night news as places of brutality, where residents took their violence out on their neighbors. These returned youth leaders in the arts learned quickly in the 1980s that youngsters of their old neighborhoods needed focused projects and group affiliation through which they could express their sense of what was happening in their communities and their places and possibilities there.

The youth leaders and performers who wanted to bring dance back to neighborhoods thus targeted two primary groups. The first of these—and by far the largest group—were populations of inner-city neighborhoods, especially residential projects, that housed primarily African Americans and recent immigrants from Southeast Asia, Central America, and the Caribbean. The second of these consisted of the geographically scattered youth of second- and third-generation Old World immigrant families. Older members of groups such as Hungarians and Croatians felt a strong need to recreate a sense of connection to the past for their young—no longer growing up in linguistically and culturally homogeneous neighborhoods but now spread throughout urban middle- and lower-middle-class neighborhoods in several regions of the nation. Moreover, events in the early 1990s in Europe gave impetus to a prideful sense of connection to old homelands and their traditions. The performing arts of these groups came to be central to the entertainment of the folk festivals that had begun to flourish in the early 1970s. These festivals celebrated immigrant ethnic groups, often in regional or state festivals in which ethnic performing groups competed against each other before panels of international judges. Maintenance of ethnic folk traditions in dance and music through competition in folk festivals came to be one way of reintegrating—at least for this event—the young into some of the old ways. (See, for example, McCullough [1980] on the use of dance and music to revive European immigrant cultures and to alleviate social fragmentation of such groups.)

We look here at three different performing arts groups, all centered on dance and established for the benefit of local urban youth. The leaders of all of these groups heard the insistent public message of the 1980s: "Do something to get kids off the streets." But these youth leaders chose to do more; they set out to use dance and music, sometimes combined with drama, to create a sense of connectedness for youth. Led by performers who had already achieved a reputation on the stage or travel circuit, these youth organizations looked to artistic endeavors for young people that would bind them together in a group focused on work culminating in a showcase performance. The central focus of our close look at these groups is the language they used to build strong discipline, group achievement, and a communal sense of mutual expectations of high-quality performance.

The customary American focus on artistic achievement as an *individual* rather than a group attainment was firmly set aside by these organizations in their commitment to build a sense of membership and group achievement. These groups turned to music and dance as group activities parallel in their goals and functions to athletic teams. Practices, planning, and performance drew individuals together in joint enterprises in which the diverse talents and interests of the members could meld for group acclaim.

The leaders of all the groups considered here saw their work as filling a void not only in the arts but also in community building. These leaders felt that the public media, schools, and government had dropped their interest in ethnic pride of the 1960s and 1970s and that now community groups had to step in to give young people a sense of belonging, achieving, and connecting publicly to something positive. Some youth organization leaders lamented that their institutions offered the only "family" atmosphere youth had or the only chance youth saw to participate in something that would tell them about themselves and build a sense of pride and spiritual connection to a positive heritage.

An Island in the Center

In Lakeside, small storefront enterprises line the busy four-lane thoroughfare that cuts through one series of massive 1950s housing projects now reputed to be one of the nation's most dangerous urban areas.[3] Squeezed between a small insurance office and an abandoned small grocery is the Liberty Theatre. No sign marks its location; its front windows are covered by heavy drapes, and the windows of the double front doors are barred. At all times, the doors remain locked, and there is no back way into the building. Anyone who enters must knock and be let in by the dancers and performers within; the entrance opens into an anteroom filled with big sofas and several youngsters working on their homework while waiting for practice or rehearsal to begin.

Directed by Henri, an African American in his early 40s, the Liberty Theatre is the center for several arts programs and workshops that meet not only in this location but at a local youth center and a nearby church. Begun in the late 1960s under a European American director who held workshops for dancers and performers to create their own materials, Liberty switched in the mid-1980s to a focus on workshops in African folk dance, oral history, and innovative African American drama for the adults and youths of the neighboring housing projects. All of the dozen or so actors and directors at Liberty perform elsewhere, some have their own production company or band, and some teach at studios on the other side of town. Funded primarily through foundation support and private donations, Liberty has five paid instructors; other instructors volunteer.

After achieving success with his own production company elsewhere in Lakeside, Henri returned to his old neighborhood to work with Liberty. Henri wanted to work with youth in the performing arts and also to serve as an African American role model: "I have a responsibility to these kids, especially as a black male. In this community, women have a high visibility; black men don't." He cited Liberty's goal as doing "more social work than we do theater." With Liberty for nearly 20 years, Henri explained the focus of the 1990s: "We try to teach them [local young people], nurture them along. A lot of these kids aren't getting a lot of attention. . . . We're not here to make performers out of them. We're here to make them better people." Henri saw Liberty as not only offering a positive alternative to the ways that families and schools treated youngsters but also offering the public media opportunities to cover events that cast African American youngsters in a positive light. He described most media representations of ghetto youngsters as "brutal," giving the public the impression they are incapable, threatening, and unworthy. "We have to do things . . . challenge the kids' thinking . . . challenge how they feel about themselves."

Liberty Theatre offered such challenge through an integration of dance, instrumental music, voice, theater and improvisation, and speech and writing classes that emphasized differences between African American English vernacular and mainstream American standard English.[4] The youths who came to the theater ranged from age 4 to 18, with older youths bringing younger brothers and sisters along rather than babysit them in the projects. Unlike most children's theaters that work to perfect short-term productions that parents and friends will attend, Liberty focused on producing a video-tape as their final performance; instead of building sets, they filmed on loca-tion—in the projects, in local churches, or on the streets. The premiere showing of the finished video project took place at Liberty, with friends invited to attend for a big party, but life in the projects did not afford the luxury of going out at night safely. Thus, a primary goal of making the videotapes was for the youngsters to be able to take the tapes with them to play wherever and with whomever they wished.

Melanie, a full-time African American teacher and dancer at Liberty, compared the lives of the children in the nearby projects with her own when she grew up in the projects of New York. She remembered opportu-nities to skate and to get together for "good fun" with her friends, but the projects offered no safe recreational areas for youths and instead presented them daily with pain, violence, unpredictability, and death. However, dur-ing the 3 hours or so a week that students practiced at Liberty (although many hung out there even when they were not due for practice), she saw "their creative juices flowing" in writing, speaking, dancing, and singing activities. The youths "create their own performances . . . working out what they want to have as the basis of a script, dance, or song," and the themes they selected were those of their everyday lives.

Melanie offered the case of the group's most recent production—written and performed by the troupe. The script began with the random shooting in the projects of an 11-year-old boy, moved through news reports of the event, and ended with the boy's funeral. The youngsters wrote the script, adapted a poem written by one of the youngsters to be the words of the theme song of the drama, and helped in the actual videotaping and editing of the final video production. Throughout this production, youngsters heard Liberty's staff explain that the news commentator at the scene of the shoot-ing and on the evening news hour could not use African American English vernacular but only mainstream American standard English. For those who played the roles of reporters and broadcasters to achieve appropriate dic-tion, word choice, and eye gaze required considerable attention and prac-tice. Youngsters wrote their scripts for the evening news broadcast, imitat-ing broadcasts of national networks by both reading from prepared scripts by the anchor and improvising humorous personal asides in the transfer from anchor to sports or weather reporter. Henri also explained that young-sters who played local residents interviewed in the projects at the scene of the shooting should speak rapidly, in the local dialect, and without a pre-pared script.

The funeral, complete with 11-year-old Fowler as preacher and with an actor playing corpse in an open casket borne by pallbearers, brought much talk about the pattern of chorus and response to the minister's sermon and the movement of the audience to the singing of the choir. Consultants on all these matters included the youngsters, for whom funerals were frequent events, and they offered advice on the dresses and veils of the mourning mother and older sister, as well as on the pace of movement of the pall-bearers down the central aisle.

Negotiation within situations and across settings and roles is the common theme that Liberty's staff members emphasize again and again. Their materials are not tributes to fallen African American heroes or ancient African history and culture, but the everyday life of the projects and what it takes to survive the struggles there. These materials come from the young-sters, as well as the adult volunteers and instructors, who bring direct experiences, real scenes, and familiar plots into their preparation and interpretation of scripts.

As the instructors work with the youth, they do so in language that structures and soothes at the same time that it makes unflinching demands for excellence and commitment. At the beginning of each new production, when new members may be joining the group, the youth make up the rules by which they agree to work. Tracy, a dance teacher, reminds class members: "Everybody, even old people [returning participants who may have been involved in prior performances], take a look at these rules that you all made up and adhere to them or you will be told to leave." Calls to think, remember, listen, make sure, and look at themselves (in the mirror that covers one wall of the studio) pepper the instructors' directions to the young-sters. Questions ask the dancers and singers to think about "what if?" and to draw on their experience:

> When you're doin' a dance and it causes you to stand up like this,
> what happens when I start doin' this? My arms are gettin' tired, right?
> That's why you gotta do exercises, to sustain 'em so they'll be used to
> stayin' up. OK? Ready. Hand out. OK? Palms are facing straight up.

Explanations of "what," "why," and "how" slide in between brief tele-graphic directives of "left, right, shoulder up, and up, down, up down, up, let's go."

Instructors always move with the youths, never asking them to do any-thing they do not do themselves. Shouts of encouragement, such as "There you go," "That's all right. Keep on. That was good," come fast and furious during the dance instruction, along with demonstrations and simple instruc-tions such as "Lift left, lift back, lift right." Talk is both professional (using technical dance, music theory, and theater terms) as well as connected to the youngsters' everyday vocabulary. Instruction is often tied to brief exchanges in which the teachers provide opportunities to laugh at themselves:

> In a plié, we gotta keep the back straight, OK? So it's not this. This is *not* a plié, guys. See what I'm doin'? That's a no-no. OK? It's sittin' down so you have to pick up your chest. And it's sittin', just like you were gonna sit. When you sit down, you sit, like this. You don't sit like this [laughter from dancers]. Same way when you dance. You have to sit in your plié. OK?. . . . Keep those butts tucked in. OK? Don't stick 'em out.

Negative directives within instruction are balanced by positive directives: "Don't turn 'em in. Make sure your knees go over your feet."

The philosophy of building a sense of success in a group, negotiating all sorts of situations, and working to perfect an end product find expression in the language of the leaders and the youth as they talk within and about their activities. During times assigned for work, practice, and preparation, instructors do not allow any straying from the task. Youngsters who do not abide by the rules the group sets at the beginning of every cycle cannot return to Liberty during that particular cycle. Predictability in terms of activity, personnel, events, and evaluation standards is ensured. As final production nears, instructors intensify their directions to the cast; shouts, strong calls to responsibility, and fast-moving action whip final rehearsals into a feverish pitch of emotion and activity. The youngsters describe their own fears during these days: fears of losing their concentration, making wrong moves, or disappointing their instructors.

The leaders take pride in seeing their young actors and dancers grow into commitment to their own excellence. The instructors see relatively little that is similar between their own childhoods and those of the youngsters of the 1980s and 1990s:

> The dangers out there are greater, and many come from their immediate neighbors and not just from the media, the police, and the schools. Drugs, AIDS, violence, and sickness are as common to these kids as baseball, Martin Luther King, and school buses were to me as a kid.

Tracy talks of her desire for some of the youngsters to survive and still be willing to commit to staying in the community. Born in the projects, she left for a short while for the Marine Corps and jobs ranging from security guard to bank teller, but she returned and chose to raise her son and daughter in the projects. A tough woman of intense energy, she has since taken in two other young boys who are friends of her children and have no stable household of their own; her home and Liberty have become the major support group for these youngsters.

Henri explains the philosophy as well as practices of Liberty as searching for ways "to make these kids proud of themselves as capable of doin' something *good,* really good. They need that, and they'll never come to do it unless we let them know they can." Although most of the instructors wear African or African American hairstyles and dress and their T-shirts usually sport slogans of African or African American pride, they explain their activities as building pride through doing and being *right now.* They must deal with the present, and to the extent that they can make history relate directly to ways of coping now, they do so. Together, the staff and youth study African and African American folktales and adapt these to performances that pick up themes of concern about life on the streets today. The trickster, wily one, and gullible fool live as much today as in the bygone days of folklore.

Liberty Theatre's adults want their activities to bring the youth success within a relatively short time in a structured and predictable environment. They see their role as enabling youth to use their minds and bodies creatively to re-create, assess, and interpret their daily lives and to reconsider their heritage. Sadly but "realistically," the leaders report that they regard this integrative goal as having to replace the relative luxury of expecting youth to grab onto the abstractions of African or African American heritage or simply the brotherhood of ethnic membership. The actualities of daily perils in their lives mean that Liberty has to be a place not only to explore the past but also to cope with the present and learn to hope for some future. Fowler, the young minister in the production that Liberty referred to as "The Funeral," summed up his sense of Liberty: "They help you here to know that you gotta learn to walk around what's out there. Keep your head up and keep on goin'."

A Little Bit of Old Europe—for Now

It is the end of February in River City, and the late afternoon sun is hidden by a mask of gray, with the promise of snow hanging heavy in the air. Thirteen-year-old Tommy and his 8-year-old sister Elena wait in the parking lot of the Brotherhood Hall for the Juniors' rehearsal to begin. Within minutes, 40 other youngsters between the ages of 5 and 18 join them, and they move into the hall, along with several adults carrying bags filled with colorful costumes for this dress rehearsal. Several of the young people carry instruments: horns, violins, flutes, and tamburitza. They file in through an anteroom with walls lined by glass cases filled with trophies, playbills in many languages, and posters of similar dance groups in other parts of the country. Once in the room, they put on their dance shoes, set up their instruments, and warm up—either on their own or with a bit of coaxing from parents or other adults standing by.

A loud shout from Laurie, the director, scatters the group—younger dancers into a small side room with two other adult leaders, and the remaining boys and girls in their places in the large central hall. Tommy's mother stands to the side of the room, ready to begin the tapes for each number as the group moves into rehearsal. Laurie stands in the center of the room, a clump of 12- and 13-year-old girls around her waiting to try out various capes, scarves, and headbands that Laurie pulls from a nearby bag. Suddenly, "Guys, shut UP!" rings through the air, and simultaneously, the room becomes an ordered array of colorful pegs standing at attention and waiting for direction as Laurie moves to the side of the room and faces the whole group.

> OK, I don' wanna scream 'cause I'm not feelin' good, and I'm on a
> real short fuse 'cause I don't. . . . I want to get everything done, you
> guys wanna learn your words, the new Croatian tune, and it's gonna
> be a real grueling session. Ready? [She nods to Tommy's mother.] Start
> Macedonian.

This practice, the last before the two dress rehearsals next week that will precede their annual benefit concert, continues in a feverish pitch. Laurie checks in with each youth, asking about instruments, whether they have memorized the words of the song they will sing in Russian, approving the color of a scarf, and conferring with adults about arrangements for next week's rehearsal.

Only one of over twenty such organizations in the greater River City area, Laurie's group is one of the best. The youngsters have won acclaim in the past several folk festivals. All who are in her group of Juniors began dancing by the time they were eight years of age. They must both dance and play a musical instrument as well as sing. To continue in the group requires many hours of practice across the years; the youngsters must memorize their music, the words of their songs, and their dance steps, and they must practice, practice, practice. Youngsters who emerge from Laurie's group are accomplished musicians, and many win scholarships for their talents and skills. Thus, parents are willing to drive miles to make sure they attend practice with Laurie. Supported by a local Catholic church, with some help from the Brotherhood, the Juniors began in 1972. Their executive director, Rich, a short, stocky man of Croatian descent, is a well-known tamburitza player who teaches music to the young people, and his wife

Laurie is both choreographer and dance director of the group. He talks with pride of the role of the tamburitza band, folk plays, and dancing in the history of Croatians and of the irony that by the 1980s there were more tamburitza players in the United States than in Yugoslavia, where the young people do not want to play the instrument. All of the leaders of the Juniors were members of some earlier versions of the Juniors in decades past, as were the parents of today's youngsters. Thus, the social life of parents parallels in a central way a key aspect of their own children's time spent in Juniors' practice.

Local brotherhoods provide scholarships for some of their young people who go on to college. Today, the dance groups consist of young people of many different immigrant backgrounds from Europe, whereas the groups formerly attracted only Croatians or Serbs. Recruiting young people is a constant need, for as older dancers leave, the troupes must have younger ones to take their place to keep standards high.

The constant social nature of the Juniors attracts the young, for they not only give more than 40 performances a year, but they also attend a small number of festivals, meeting with other ensembles, traveling, and getting reinforcement through parental support and pride as well as awards. Practices take place once a week year-round, with only an occasional week off in the summer. The summer, moreover, is reserved for intensive week-long workshops and journeys farther afield to festivals in other regions. The annual spring concert is the culmination of the year's work on new routines. New materials are introduced in a 1-week workshop in mid-August, and at this point, the young people begin their focus on perfecting their routines for the spring performance.

Adults who grew up in several close-knit neighborhoods of River City, where they could still occasionally hear their mother tongue and know that all their neighbors attended the same church and came from the same background, have now scattered across the region, particularly to the more comfortable outlying suburbs. Some old neighborhoods, bound together by a keen sense of their experience and identity as immigrants, as well as by a strong devotion to the church as the community social center, remain relatively intact, with grandchildren buying their grandparents' old homes. Other old neighborhoods of immigrants from Europe had by the 1990s become home to African Americans or had simply become blocks of boarded-up and abandoned houses. Parents who support their youngsters in the Juniors see the dance troupe as one way both to keep their kids busy with friends "of their own kind" and to ensure that their children continue to see themselves as members of their own Old European immigrant group. In the 1980s, the dance groups began to include children of several such groups and expanded their repertoire of music, language, and dance beyond Croatian to Serbian, Macedonian, Russian, and so on.

Rich explains that the parents expect the dancing to teach the youth "sociability, discipline, cooperation, concentration. We don't intend to train them as dancers—most of the kids do not go on to do something specifically related to the music and dance training they get with us." But with the dance troupe and in their mingling with other ensembles, they learn songs in several languages and acquire a feel for their roots. The Juniors, in spite of the competition among local organizations, see themselves as a large extended family. Any community who wants to form a new group must pay a fee to the regional brotherhood and thus gain the benefit of being within the network that the "family" can offer. In addition, a national brotherhood sponsors summer festivals, the proceeds of which go to provide scholarships for youngsters from the dance groups.

The language of practice, as well as the before-and-after of each such occasion, rings with a sense of family. Laurie knows the youngsters by name and calls after them to pick up their coats, to remember to check on a friend who was not present for tonight's practice, and to practice by themselves or with a partner to memorize the words to a song.

> Guys, is everybody's partner here tonight? You know you guys aren't holding belts [a prop in one of the dances]. Huh, what are you holding? You two are partners? You two are partners? OK. Ready? You guys remember this?

Throughout practices, Laurie asks questions of the dancers and asks them to pretend they are in different scenes, in different places in the dance, or in the actual performance. She shouts brief directions to groups about to move onto the practice floor for a particular number, as she orchestrates the 10 or so different dance numbers—many with the addition of instruments and singing—during rehearsals. Her negatives—"don't," "won't," and so on—either accompany reminders or appear in her questions to the youngsters: "Don't forget to call Roger to get him here next week"; "You won't fail to be here, right?"; "Don't you, aren't you in any small orchestras?"; "Don't you stand next to her?" She expects the older dancers to see that the younger ones know their parts, can carry their instruments, and have the words to songs memorized. While she directs one group, she turns to older students and sets them to work with younger dancers.

Many of the young dancers admit that their commitment to the Juniors keeps them out of after-school activities and other extracurricular events in which their school friends participate. The travel and the competition in a well-known and regionally respected group, as well as whether their friends are in the dance troupe, determine their commitment and how long they stay with the troupe. Most look forward with certainty to being the first in their families to go on to college, and the possible scholarship to a local university offers some incentive, as well as the assurance that once at that university, they will have a ready-made social group in the well-known Juniors' group there. For most of the youth, as well as for many of the adults who label themselves "realistic," their Old World ethnicity is really "food, fun, and festivals" and a commitment to what they see as working-class values and morals—hard work and honesty.

Commercial entertainment, middle-class mainstream values in leisure and recreation, and new friendships in culturally diverse neighborhoods have as much attraction for the youngsters' parents as for their children. The work ethic, along with regular gatherings in regional Catholic churches also populated by descendants of Old World European groups, push the young people along in their goals to achieve and not to stray too far from parentally sanctioned activities before they reach their mid-teens. For most of the young people in the Juniors, the idea that they are "ethnic" holds little salience; the salience rests with the view that "I'm special, because I'm on stage. I have worked hard and now I'm showcased."

A Web to Reach Out

The school yard is silent except for the occasional sound of the tetherball chains hitting against their poles in the late afternoon wind. The after-school playground would be completely deserted were it not for a small group of preschoolers and their day-care supervisor hurrying for their bus and three young girls intently practicing dance steps outside a portable bungalow. Almost an hour has passed since school was dismissed. The dance teacher arrives and unlocks the door, and the waiting students, now 13 or 14 in number, enter an oversized bungalow adapted for use as a dance studio. Hardwood floors have been installed and mirrors hung the length of one entire wall. During the school day, the room doubles as headquarters for the instrumental music program. Chairs and music stands are moved to the side as students begin to shed their outer clothing to reveal cut-off jeans or biker shorts that serve in the place of leotards and tights. Students find a space on the hardwood floor as the dance instructor plugs in the portable "boom box" music system and calls for their attention.

Philip, the director of the program and the Almaz Dance Studio in a nearby town, is from the Middle East, where he danced with a national company before coming to the United States 10 years ago. His wife, Candy, a Pacific Islander, is also a dancer, and together they have launched a dance training and performance program to reach out to inner-city youth, primarily African Americans, in their belief that dance will help the youngsters academically and personally. The program began in the mid-1980s as a 15-week pilot program at an inner-city middle school and expanded by the end of the 1980s to include 300 students between the ages of 7 and 14. "I know that dance changed my life," Philip says, "and if I can give that to just one kid, then I've accomplished something." He had once studied at the Alvin Ailey School in New York and felt that many youngsters in inner cities could use dance to make their way up and out of the grim circumstances of their childhood. All they needed was a chance: "One of the reasons I teach these classes is to let black kids see they can do anything white kids can do. Not just basketball and track, but being doctors." Structured to develop academic, personal, and physical skills, the program prided itself on an ability to develop concentration, discipline, memory, mathematical concepts, perception, and problem-solving skills of the youngsters.

Twice a week, Almaz instructors went to the schools to teach the students on site, usually in a gymnasium or in a classroom equipped with special flooring. Following warm-ups, the groups moved into specialized routines for practice and repetition. The language of leaders of these sessions generally followed the format of a brief introduction of the immediate activity (warm-up, routine, and so on), instructions and counts during dance, and summation—often of preparations for a coming show or for pulling together routines for a particular dance. Particular language features included the following:

- Spontaneous start-up with brief verbal introduction ("OK, let's do it from the beginning").
- Polite forms of request for starting or stopping ("Could you start from here?").
- Frequent questions directed to the group in a heart-to-heart manner, asking about specific group problems, such as why more students were not attending or why attitudes were not better ("Just tell me what you think, what is the problem why it's not going. . . . What's the problem?").
- Abbreviated directions, usually with counts and specific brief verbal reminders of the next routine ("Okay, let's do one more time. Let's go. . . . And five, six, seven, eight. One and two, three, four, five and six, seven, eight. One, two, three, four, five, six—stop. From here after we go—[demonstration follows]").
- Specific responses to questions or comments called out from the floor by students (Student: "No! We're supposed to go from four!" Instructor: "Yes, four, five, six, seven, eight.").
- Calls to refocus the group's attention on dancing ("Now, listen, but

some of you, like—Gorgeous, I'm talkin' to you—").
- Use of generalized terms for collective names or personal engagement ("[Name of student], where you goin', honey?" "OK, guys").
- Talk to individual students during generalized talk and demonstration to the entire group ("One—[aside to individual student: I talked to your mother] three and four [aside: let's set a time] eight").

Each class ended with an introduction of some new material for a dance being planned for either a school event or for the end-of-season production to be held at the dance studio. At the beginning of the year, these sessions often had 30 or more students, but as the term wore on, students decreased their voluntary participation and came with less frequency. It was not unusual for a new student to enter or an old student to return midway through the term. Sometimes, classes that began with 30 students ended the term with only 8 dancers. A concerned Philip lamented: "Some of them we'll reach—I don't care if they're going to be professional dancers or not. That's not the point. The point is that they're working close with a teacher, and that's going to reflect for all their lives." He admitted that he was "firm" with the students, wanting them to develop "the discipline needed to see any commitment through." He noted: "I work with them tight and I get to know them. On one side they like it. On the other side, they don't like it. You see . . . they have to be accountable."

Philip, Candy, and the other instructors occasionally asked students to compose their own steps and to attend master classes taught by professional dancers and instructors. Although much of the music and many of the routines learned in the classes were neutral with respect to ethnic identification, the director made efforts to learn more about the language and music of the students' backgrounds. He reported that he often listened to African American radio stations and collected jazz recordings in an effort to do a better job of choreographing pieces for his students.

School administrators and teachers saw Almaz as a type of incentive program to motivate students and to influence, albeit indirectly, their academic achievement and social development. But the youngsters' dance participation was highly marginal to school administrators' and teachers' many other concerns about the youngsters' education. For many of the young people and their parents, the goals of the dance program seemed distant, and the bits and pieces of dance performance they saw appeared to have little to do with students' academic life. Both parents and school district personnel occasionally queried the kind of dancing and the purpose of the instruction Almaz instructors offered. At one point during the term, several members of the school board expressed their desire for less focus on dance that might be seen as "African" and more on dance "like ballet."

These comments came along with complaints from parents and students that Philip did not understand their children's cultures and was too strict. When Candy and Philip performed a Latin American dance together in the youngsters' school program, some parents and teachers were outraged at what they regarded as their inappropriate costumes and sexually explicit movements. Conflicting cries that they were culturally insensitive came, on one hand, from community leaders who saw them as perpetuating stereotypes by having the youngsters perform only dances that were "too African" and, on the other hand, from teachers and parents who disapproved of dances from other cultures they regarded as too sensuous and loose. Philip, frustrated by these misinterpretations and by some students' unreliable attendance and commitment, explained that his goal was "to educate the real soul of the child. This, I think, is the most important thing."

But the schools had less regard for his view of the child's "soul" and more for their schedule and expectations. The administration imposed certain constraints that determined participation in Philip's dance program. In spite of the goal of the Almaz Studio to help youngsters who were under-achievers academically, the schools ruled that only those who maintained a C average could participate. In addition, Philip had to fit instruction into a regular school period (40 minutes), which meant that instructors and students always felt rushed. Routines and workouts had to be reduced to approximately half the time they usually took in the studio. Parents saw the dance program as "a nice outlet, you know, instead of runnin' the streets and, you know, gettin' into things that are not good." Many, however, insistently worried that the instructors were not culturally connected to the youths and that both their choices of dances and music and their ways of relating to the students sometimes did not fit what they saw as the youngsters' needs.

Dance as Expression and Involvement

What do these cases mean? How might youth policymakers interpret these close looks at several performing dance groups? The anonymous nature of folk art and dance has stood for centuries, cutting out a central focus on the individual or the professional. The adaptation of such arts to particular situations and cultural circumstances has depended heavily on the "reading" of the current scene by the performers and on their adherence to a sense of the value of their performance for the group at large. Moreover, art as communication with its own symbol systems and nonverbal channels has been judged by many societies as more effective for social control than direct explication. Yet dance carries its own narrative—its own stories of past events, dreams, or foreshadowings of events to come. These narratives, as well as their strong support of movement both violent and subtle, allow much to be communicated that might not be verbalized directly. Spiritual beliefs, mysterious forces, and states of involvement outside the clearly representational or "rational" infuse dance and music and bring to performers and audiences alike a sense of togetherness and critical energy that transcends that of a collection of individual units.[5] In youth organizations, the praise and appreciation, the unifying dictum of being "in step," "on cue," and "on the same beat," as well as the opportunity to be heard and seen in legitimate publicly sanctioned settings, bring the collectivity together. No single individual could gain such an audience, and the power of the group transmitting as a single body remains in the forefront of consciousness in dance troupes of youth organizations.

The performing arts, like all symbols of culture, change with social and economic processes. In each of the cases presented here, leaders felt that their focus on collective communication through dance with youngsters had to struggle constantly against the attractions of commercial entertainment, highly individual-centered performance, and expensive costuming and instrumentation. The key symbolism of much commercial entertainment that attracts young audiences derives from references to sexuality, individual achievements, and often violent competition. The organization, philosophy, and language of the urban youth organizations described here recognize the attraction of such themes to contemporary youth but strive instead to bring the young people together to find a sense of identity in supportive groups. As one parent from Henri's Liberty Theatre put it, "For our kids, by the time they are 11, the sad reality is that there are only two places they can go: to jail or to be dead." These youth organizations seek to help students to envision other alternatives. They value highly the potential their groups offer for communication through dance, music, and drama, as well as the safety of the practice halls, travel, and performance sessions.

However, financial realities close in on all urban youth organizations committed to the performing arts. One director explained:

> These kids see fancy stuff on TV, musical videos, and stuff, and they
> think we can do that too; they don't want anything homemade lookin',
> scruffy, or amateur. That means they also expect us to be high tech,
> and we just don't have the money for that, and foundations don't want
> to pay for that kind of equipment for the ghetto.

To film the funeral, Henri had to arrange for a full film crew to cover the several sites of the show. Likewise, Philip and Candy of the Almaz studio had to struggle continually to have a sound system "the kids will approve of." The Juniors depended heavily on Brotherhood and church funds, as well as on high entry fees for each chapter, to support their costumes, instrument upkeep, travel, and competition fees for folk festivals.

Comments from program directors and staff, as well as Philip and Candy's experience with the Almaz outreach program, suggest that two primary performance or presentation criteria enable artistic groups to beat out their competitors for the commitment and attention of young people. Groups that can meet these two criteria manage to attract youngsters over a sustained period of time. The first of these is demonstration that the organization can mount a major performance accompanied by technical support in the form of video recordings, the latest in recording devices, and public presentation beyond the community. Under these circumstances, as with Liberty Theatre, young people play central roles in the use of the equipment, as well as in the performance. They commit their time consistently so as to produce what they regard as a professional production. The second performance criterion that attracts young people is competition that takes place within the context of a fun-for-all context. Travel, costumes, performances, food, and festivals—repeated year after year and attended by individual families over a long period of time—can compel young people to want to belong. As with the Juniors, they acquire a sense of family obligation and enjoy the peer support. Primarily because of constraints raised by the schools, the Almaz Dance Studio could neither engage the youngsters in high-tech productions nor in competitions; thus, very few youngsters got hooked on the hard work, practice, and focused attention that Philip wanted desperately from them.

However, even when youth organizations meet these two criteria, the demand that young people make for "lookin' pro" can conflict with their sense of the need "to dig in and practice." One adult leader explained:

> These kids think from TV and advertising that everything that looks glitzy and smooth comes easy. When they have to get down and work, they either decide to hang in there or to "bag it." And it's discouraging to us a lot of times, because the difference between "hangin' in" and "givin' it up" can be something that happened on the street or at home, and it's totally out of our hands most of the time whether or not a kid sticks with us.

Other leaders, especially those from the same cultural and class backgrounds as the youth with whom they work, disagree or at least hang on to the belief that what their organizations do can make a difference between succeeding or failing to keep a youngster's interest.

Words such as "credibility," "connection," and "communication" appear most often in their explanations of what counts in their effectiveness with youths. The young people themselves put these ideas in other words: "They want us to do our best," "They let me know I *can* do something," and "This is my family—the only family I've got—they're here for me, and I know it—I come here, I feel safe, I'm a different person." The language of instructors at Liberty Theatre and with the Juniors demands and supports, affirms and commands, involves and directs.

The language of these youth leaders differs in several ways from that used by Almaz instructors in the classes in public schools. First are the range and frequency of verbal supports. The youngsters who danced with the Juniors and the Liberty Theatre heard quick prompts, such as "keep it up," "that's the way," and "nice job" throughout their long practices. Philip and his instructors, greatly pressured by time, peppered their talk with an occasional quick "good" or "let's go" but offered no other positive verbal prompts.[6]

A second language feature that distinguished Almaz practices from those of Liberty or the Juniors was the amount of talk to individual students that took place in front of the large group. Called by the students "clowning," Philip's practice of talking to a particular student about his or her needs, misdeeds, or the meaning of a particular phrase used by the youngsters came in for derision. Parents identified this practice as a case of the instructors not being from the same cultural backgrounds as the students and not understanding "just how kids are." This clowning feature included direct public threats to exclude individual youths from the forthcoming performance if they did not listen, remember routines, follow routines, and attend practices regularly, as well as direct responses to students' questions or comments during practice.

A third difference was evident in the extent to which Henri and Laurie—in contrast to Philip and his instructors—asked the dancers questions of "what if?" to engage them in thinking about the hypothetical possibilities of certain nuances in their performances. Henri and Laurie also repeatedly used words such as "will," "would," "gonna," and "can" with the youngsters, as well as directives that engaged them in self-monitoring and staying on task ("look," "think," and "listen"). Philip and Candy, in their short infrequent practices, had far less opportunity than Henri and Laurie to build the full engagement of the young people as responsible agents and monitors of their performances.

Verbal communication in all three dance groups played no more important a role than other forms of expression and displays of knowing. Both adults and young people spoke of the attractions of dance *per se* in the same ways: "release," "letting go," "being able to move," "expressin' my feelings without talkin'," and "bein' strong."[7] In addition, of the cases cited here, both the Juniors and Liberty Theatre valued the sense of bonding that came from the amount of local knowledge that old and young shared. Ways to talk, places to go, neighborhood characters and events, and occasional opportunities when the youngsters saw their dance instructors in their own communities went a long way toward binding these groups to the young. The Almaz Studio differed from these in its cultural discontinuity with the children it served, its strong links to the school district, and its central focus on improved academic achievement as a side benefit of dance participation. Laurie, Henri, and Rich, as well as other adults connected to their groups, stressed the importance of dance, performance, practice, regimen, and excellence in all of these. Although among themselves and occasionally in one-on-one talks with the youngsters they talked about other goals they had for the young dancers, they kept their talk to the performers focused on what students could and would do and not on what they were not doing and could not achieve.

Generally speaking, connections between community- or ethnic-based artistic activities and nonethnic institutions, such as school, appear to dilute the vigor and core philosophy of the performing arts of youth organizations. The schools with which Philip's program was linked were committed neither to dance nor to the enhancement of ethnic values.[8] There are some indications that activities in the performing arts contribute to the self-esteem and discipline that underlie academic success. However, it has never been possible to determine whether youngsters who succeed in dance and go on to academic achievement received their impetus from dance or any other art per se, from the focused attention and disciplined commitment that life in the performing arts demands, or from their own internal motivation to achieve regardless of activity. (See Hanna [1987, 1992] on the complexities of establishing causal connections between academic performance and artistic pursuits.) In other words, since accomplishment in the performing arts draws on not only numerous musical, kinesthetic, and rhythmic talents but also on a sense of narrative and history, these same skills—cognitive, expressive, and integrative—can with proper motivation and self-drive carry strong transfer value to academic pursuits. But motivation and desire from the individual must be present for sufficient practice and performance to take place and for these other benefits to take effect.

Moreover, groups such as Liberty Theatre and the Juniors involve the youngsters in creating and reading written language. All sorts of literacy events—occasions when youngsters' actions and talk spring from or occur with written materials—slip into practices and performances repeatedly. Laurie reminds her dancers to read and memorize the words to their songs. Henri and the Liberty Theatre young people carry scripts around; papers, pencils, and discarded wall charts made of butcher paper often clutter the studio and offices. Posters, T-shirts, playbills, trophies, certificates, captioned photographs, and news clippings announce past performances and competitions at the Brotherhood Hall, Almaz Studio, and Liberty Theatre. When Melanie, Tracy, Henri, and other instructors work on diction and articulation or music theory, they often write the word or words of focus on chalk boards and ask the youngsters to spell aloud as they look at the written words.

Some have argued that art is a way of imposing order on a fundamentally disordered society.[9] For individuals and cultures that do not easily give themselves up to verbalizing the complexities about them, dance offers a conceptual and adaptive frame of expression across symbol systems. All of the dance groups described here place little or no importance on youngsters' "talking out" their problems with family, school, or street life. The focus instead on music, dance, performance, and talk is valued primarily to the extent that it supports these efforts. Communication is embodied in dance—engaging the kinesthetic, visual, musical, and spatial, as well as the narrative. The power of dance to give itself over to improvisation, shifts in numbers involved, and movement from one performance arena to another permit creativity from youngsters in environments of support and encouragement. Some instructors see dance for its value in enabling youth to express deep, often unspoken feelings of religious, political, and social experience by engaging the entire body.

For urban youth organizations that want to attract youth away from the seductive life of the streets or the violence and sexual exploitation promoted in much commercial entertainment, the organization of instruction and of performance stands at the center of the effectiveness of dance. Contexts for learning and doing must be communally connected, highly credible and predictable, clearly and consistently structured, and strongly supportive of diverse talents. Young people must find in these organizations opportunities to bond with each other in a group task and a commitment to excellence. They must feel secure, knowing they will not be singled out randomly for censure before the group. Through the sense of belonging that comes from inclusion in such an organization, young people achieve layers of conviction in their ability to be worthy.

Central in dance is the extraordinary and diverse work that mounting a successful performance season after season or year after year takes. Youngsters have to stay in shape, perfect techniques, learn routines, and help maintain equipment, costumes, and music. The young people say of their practice halls or studios: "There's always something to do, no way to come here, hang out, and do nothin'." Youth leaders agree that "lettin' kids do nothin' gives the message they can't do anything. We don't let anyone around here just sit like a bump on a log. We expect 'em to be movin' and doin' all the time." Although the demand by youth that the performance look professional and be well traveled to reach a lot of people keeps leaders in a constant struggle for funding, space, and modes of travel, most agree these criteria can make the difference in attracting youngsters and maintaining their interest. Moreover, youth expect their instructors to be "the best," to know what they are doing, and to have proved themselves in the "real" world.

The enduring aspect of the artistry of dance—its extension beyond itself and its power to adjust and adapt, as well as communicate—must, then, go along with a stable organizational and supportive environment. This duality enables urban youth to move beyond an identification with dance as an ethnic expression or a political commentary to an immersion in the contraries that it and its organizations offer: structure and release, creative outlet and consistency of routine, and hard work along with expressive play.

Acknowledgments

The work reported here was supported by a grant from the Spencer Foundation to Shirley Brice Heath and Milbrey Wallin McLaughlin for a research project entitled "Language, Socialization, and Neighborhood-Based Organizations."

Notes

[1]The most comprehensive treatment of such roles for dance is Hanna (1987), which notes that during periods of national crisis, dance has brought to the public messages of accusation, pleas for social reform, and expressions of alienation. The antiwar ballet "The green table" (1932) warned of diplomatic deception as a path to war. The Alvin Ailey dance troupe, as well as numerous South African groups that toured the United States in the 1980s and 1990s, narrated both individual and group experiences with repression and violence.

[2]Sociologists have given considerable attention to the preferred leisure-recreation habits of specific ethnic populations, but especially urban African Americans. By the final decades of the 20th century, this research showed clearly that both socioeconomic standing and age exerted a strong influence on such choices. With the achievement of middle-class status, urban African Americans' preferences for leisure recreation generally matched those of other groups of their class: domestic informal leisure patterns (e.g., watching television or visiting with friends) and public activities such as visiting museums. Young middle-class couples of two-wage-earning families chose night life activities, often in discos and often with members of other racial and ethnic groups. See Woodard (1988) and Hutchison (1988) for summaries of this literature and critiques of use of the theoretical constructs of "race" and "ethnicity" in such research on leisure.

[3]Lakeside and River City are pseudonyms, as are the names of the organizations and neighborhoods mentioned in this chapter. Except where otherwise noted, all quoted comments were made by respondents in the course of our fieldwork and data collection. To preserve the confidentiality of sites and individuals, we identify speakers only in terms of their community role.

[4]Often referred to as black dialect or Black English vernacular, the informal or everyday language of African American English speakers received extensive attention from scholars and from the public media after the 1960s. Linguists established Black English or African American English as linguistic terms to refer to the highly consistent grammar, pronunciation, and vocabulary that many African Americans throughout the United States learned as their first dialect. By the 1990s, many educational programs and performing arts projects acknowledged its authenticity in informal occasions of African American life and worked hard to legitimate its broad acceptance on a parallel with the many varieties of nonformal English used by speakers from all regions and classes in the United States. The use of this vernacular by playwrights such as August Wilson and film producers such as Spike Lee came as part of the general new ethnic rebellion against mindless acceptance of modern, formal, standard language as superior to old, homey, and everyday or customary. In addition, both artists and audiences saw the revelation on stage and screen of the fact that middle-class educated speakers used vernacular or informal language as reflective of a new and deepened democratic force in the arts.

[5]Similar arguments have been made for decades about play as a safe arena in which to explore beyond that which can be verbalized. The sheer physicality of dance and its potential for creation ensure its inclusion in the broadest definition of play. Several studies suggest that in some cultures, the effects of movement on releasing pent-up emotions and on structuring responses and reactions over the long term differ by gender; see, for example, Pellegrini (1988, in press) on the differential social adjustments of young boys who engaged in rough-and-tumble play on the playground with those who did not. Several scholars contend that play is, in essence, "crisis oriented" and that it continually tests boundaries; play done in performance adds another dimension in that the response of the audience adds an immediate "critical" element that can further intensify the emotions and kinetic energy of the performers; see Schechner (1973, 1988) and discussions of individual cases in Hanna (1987, Chapter 6).

[6]Extensive language analysis is possible for the Almaz program as well as for the Juniors and Liberty Theatre youngsters. A computerized data bank of transcribed talk by leaders and performers during practices totals more than a million words. Ethnographic field notes and interviews over the course of several years with youngsters, leaders, and neighborhood members supplement these data. Discourse analysis aided by statistical analysis indicates the extent to which certain types of language made the Juniors' and Liberty Theatre's staff emphasis on excellence and sense of youth involvement evident to the performers.

[7]The therapeutic value of dance has had numerous proponents who maintain that it reveals information that often cannot be expressed verbally or in direct person-to-person interactions. What it reveals about the use of space, time, and body by an individual must, however, be interpreted with sensitivity to varying cultural

and class norms. Therapists who use dance must know how movements are culturally conceived and must not apply middle-class European American verbocentric ideals in their diagnostic evaluations (Hanna, 1987; North, 1972).

[8]Across the nation in the 1980s, school districts established individual schools committed especially to the performing arts. Many of these had after-school programs that also gave private lessons to individuals and offered semiprofessional opportunities for performance. Among the most well known of these were New York City Public School's Harlem School of the Arts. Many private schools, established by parent groups and educators to ensure students' strong identification with a particular ethnic heritage, initiated performing groups that sometimes became part of the school's repertoire of entertainment groups. Other dance programs for public schools, such as the National Dance Institute founded by Jacques D'Amboise in the 1980s, brought numerous schools dance opportunities for their entire school population and recruited youngsters as performers and teachers for the Institute.

[9]Anthropologists have debated this point, especially since the 1970s. However, in the 1920s, Malinowski characterized culture as consisting of contradictory principles that could sometimes be given coherence through art. For this debate, see Fernandez (1973) and Mills (1973).

References

Fernandez, J. W. (1973). The exposition and imposition of order: Artistic expression in Fang culture. In W. L. d'Azevedo (Ed.), *The traditional artist in African societies* (pp. 194–220). Bloomington, IN: Indiana University Press.

Hanna, J. L. (1987). *To dance is human: A theory of nonverbal communication.* Chicago: University of Chicago Press.

Hanna, J. L. (1992). Connections: Arts, academics, and productive citizens. *Phi Delta Kappan, 73,* 601–608.

Hutchison, R. (1988). A critique of race, ethnicity, and social class in recent leisure-recreation research. *Journal of Leisure Research, 20,* 10–30.

McCullough, L. (1980). The role of language, music, and dance in the revival of Irish culture in Chicago, Illinois. *Ethnicity, 7,* 436–444.

Mills, G. (1973). Art and the anthropological lens. In W. L. d'Azevedo (Ed.), *The traditional artist in African societies* (pp. 379–416). Bloomington, IN: Indiana University Press.

North, M. (1972). *Personality assessment through movement.* London: Macdonald & Evans.

Pellegrini, A. D. (1988). Elementary-school children's rough-and-tumble play and social competence. *Developmental Psychology, 24,* 802–806.

Pellegrini, A. D. (in press). Boys' rough-and-tumble play, group composition, and social competence. *British Developmental Psychology.*

Schechner, R. (1973). *Environmental theatre.* New York: Hawthorn.

Schechner, R. (1988). *Performance theory.* London: Routledge.

Woodard, M. D. (1988). Class, regionality, and leisure among urban Black Americans: The post–Civil Rights era. *Journal of Leisure Research, 20,* 87–105.

Gangs, Social Control, and Ethnicity: Ways to Redirect

James Diego Vigil

This chapter describes the emergence, development, and current state of ethnic gangs present in most urban communities in the 1990s. Social, political, and economic conditions of migration and adaptation in the United States set the stage for gangs to develop and to take over socialization roles traditionally held by families and schools. Long-term studies of Mexican American, African American, and Vietnamese American gangs in Los Angeles form the basis of the descriptions given here of gang life and analysis of their origins and maintenance. Proposed are practical ways to build from the context and rationale of gang life and to create innovative effective youth programs. Solutions to gang problems require acknowledging that gangs fill socialization voids and offer attachments, commitments, involvements, and beliefs for young people in need of affiliation and achievement. Social change programs can include gang members held to responsibility and commitment in new roles, but such programs require sustained support through jobs, community-based support groups, and radical approaches to schooling.

I live smack in the fissure between two worlds, in the infected wound: half a block from the end of Western Civilization and four miles from the start of the Mexican-American border, the northern most point of Latin America.

Guillerma Gómez-Peña
Documented/Undocumented

Why do young people join gangs?[1] What roles do ethnicity and gender and the desire for affiliation and achievement play in the formation and maintenance of gang subculture and gang membership? The ethnic traditions of the streets can provide answers to these questions. Although gangs have been an urban problem in the United States since the 19th century, gangs added new dimensions that placed them in a different light in the late 20th century. Drug use and trafficking, gangbanging, and wanton drive-by shootings raised public alarm to a new level. Specially trained law enforcement "gang" units, probation programs, and court sentencing "crackdowns" took aim at the "gang problem," but to little or no avail. Thus, by the late 1980s, more and more public servants and observers began to rethink how the problem of gangs might be approached and rectified (Huff, 1990; Sahagun, 1990, 1991). Some made a complete turnabout in shifting from law enforcement to socially based solutions to the problem, creating renewed interest in unraveling the causes of gang formation and behavior and the dissolution and redirection of gangs.

Many poor ethnic families, primarily from southeastern Europe, immigrated to the United States in the late 19th century looking for improved working and living conditions. Although adaptation was difficult for all family members, it was the immigrant children who underwent especially intense culture change pressures. When the parents left their traditional culture and rural, peasant ways of life, they had no idea that they would be "doubly" stressing their children by subjecting them to urban slums with deteriorated and substandard housing and to a modern urban culture that placed unfamiliar demands on them. Nor were parents aware that traditional means of social control, anchored in the small community and in close, extended families of the peasant village, would be totally transformed in these new American cities, where public servants, such as schoolteachers and police, would come to dominate their lives.

Instead, what occurred for generation after generation of different ethnic immigrant groups was that the street life of the cities began to affect detrimentally the character of many of the immigrant children, especially by loosening established means of social control and unevenly introducing new ones. Young males lost connections to established social institutions, such as family and schools, and made their own street adaptation. Early on, large portions of these youth formed street gangs from groups that social reformers then referred to as "pavement" children. Through the turn of the century and until the 1940s and 1950s, these European American ethnic gangs caught the eye of both the public media and researchers.

Many social programs then took the form of settlement houses, recreation and social opportunities, and even make-work projects as the public became more open to the social experiments of the Progressive Era and the budding welfare state (see chapter 7). Researchers of that era also noted how social and environmental problems caused the gang problem. By mid-century, it was clear there were different types of ghettos, or urban slums, that produced different kinds of street groups. The ebb and flow of the economy played a role in the development of street gangs. When the economy was relatively strong, increased opportunities for employment helped stabilize the lives of the majority of the European American ethnic children, who could at least expect and get jobs and hope to start a family. Conversely, when the economy faltered, the chances for avenues of employment and a conventional life diminished. With some variations created by the history of immigration, location, and strength and sources of outside influences, the economic downturn of the late 20th century helped create the diversity of gangs across Mexican American, African American, and Southeast Asian youth in Los Angeles.[2]

Mexican American Gangs

The role of immigrant labor for Los Angeles and the southwest United States in general has always been filled largely by Mexicans. However, it was after large-scale immigration to urban areas during the 1920s and subsequent decades that a street gang tradition emerged. At first, these groups were referred to as "boy" gangs of a mildly disruptive nature (Bogardus, 1926), but in less than two decades, they were simply noted as "gangs" (Bogardus, 1943). By the end of the 20th century, researchers and youth policymakers acknowledged a gang subculture with powers of its own. What had happened through the decades was that externally imposed barriers and obstacles—namely, working and living conditions—had taken their toll to affect large numbers of second-generation Mexican American youth.

Ethnicity and gender were crucial factors in this transformation. Coming from a different socialization experience, set in a mostly rural background and with a contrasting cultural orientation, Mexican-origin youngsters, especially males, found adjustment to the United States difficult. Processes of maturation and participation in the economic and social life of one's community changed when racist attitudes and barriers prevented full integration into the American mainstream. This in turn undermined responsibility and discipline for work and family duties among such youth. This discrimination was particularly evident during the transition from childhood to adulthood, when many of these males were traditionally expected to contribute to the household. In an industrial economy, they found the paths for achievement blocked or dramatically altered.

Marginalization of the population in various sectors of life resulted in a loosening of social control networks and the development of new forms of street socialization. This process (labeled *choloization* and taken from the term *cholo,* used in Latin America to describe Indians who are only marginally acculturated to the Hispanic urban culture) was linked to street socialization, which became a Chicano gang subculture. By the 1940s, a subculture of *pachuco* style syncretically combined elements of Mexican culture with those of the urban United States. Police officials and public media experts referred to the young males who embodied this subculture as "zoot-suiters," especially during and after a major confrontation between European Americans and Mexican Americans erupted into the 1943 "zoot-suit" riots (Mazon, 1985).

Mexican street gang style persisted until the late 20th century because of the continued immigration of Mexicans and the internal dynamics of gang subculture forged by street socialization. The earlier European American ethnic immigration largely subsided by the 1920s, allowing subsequent generations from these groups to adapt eventually to mainstream American ways of life. But the pace of continuing Mexican immigration and, later, that of Central and South American (Latino) immigration quickened. This situation, along with persisting racial barriers aimed toward a mostly indigenous people of non-European appearance, perpetuated situations and conditions that spawned gangs among immigrant populations, especially of the second generation.

Hence, gangs in Mexican American barrios (neighborhoods) persisted, and the gang subculture evolved over several generations. With continued immigrant adaptations and accommodations to conditions of poverty and marginalization, barrio youth learned to use gang life to cope with street pressures and realities. In time, each cohort contributed to new goals, norms, and values from street experiences, which became more or less institutionalized as a gang subculture. No longer was it a "boy gang," as in the earlier years, for now a subcultural dynamic had evolved to recruit, socialize, and turn out "gang kids." Coupled with the forces noted earlier, this subculture within the Chicano street population became a force in its own right (Vigil, 1990).

Female residents who share such multiply marginal backgrounds also had to contend with the gang subculture, but in ways that insured that the males controlled and dominated (Moore, 1991). The gang is and has been mostly a "man's" thing and developed largely as a result of each ethnic group's male socialization practices, which had fewer restrictions on seeking street adventures and excitement than those composed for females by family and community norms. The female variant counterpoint to the males' *pachuco* differed in that Mexican American cultural prescriptions prevented the full participation of young women in street life, especially involvement that suggested wayward, unladylike behavior. Males commonly called such women *putas,* or whores.

Urban, rural, and suburban enclaves that produce Chicano gangs are often of long duration; White Fence and El Hoyo Maravilla in East Los Angeles date from the first decades of immigrant settlement. Rural barrios, established next to the workplace, attracted citrus and vineyard workers and railroad section hands. Founded in the 1930s and 1940s, barrios such as Cucamonga, Chino, and Pacoima came to dot the greater Los Angeles basin. Areas that began as providers for the agricultural needs of the city of Los Angeles persisted as low-income niches. Both rural and urban enclaves bore definite turf boundary markers, often "across the tracks," with traditional gangs engaged in conflict, or gangbanging, with nearby rival barrios, and in drug use and abuse among themselves.

In the 1980s and 1990s, in addition to filling in some vacated *cholo* areas, the large influx of Mexican/Latino immigrants and their children spawned new enclaves where gangs emerged. Some of them quickly founded new gangs without undergoing the second-generation phase mentioned earlier—for example, Los Carnales in south-central Los Angeles, heretofore an African American area. In general, these new immigrant populations were large and densely concentrated, occupying wide areas of the city and undergoing an intense choloization that quickened the pace of street socialization. Coupled with the constant threats from established gangs nearby, these new immigrant children grouped together in gangs for defensive purposes. Moreover, because many of these youngsters had immigrated from large towns and cities in the Mexican interior—areas with their own sequence of multiple marginality processes—they had come to the United States precholoized and already familiar with street life. Quite prevalent in some Mexican border towns, through diffusion from the American side, were the beginnings of a sizable *cholo* youth population.

Suburban gangs in Los Angeles differ in many ways from their urban counterparts because their enclaves are peopled more by second and third owners of older, cheaper tract housing sections of greater suburban Los

Angeles. For example, a section of one of the first housing developments in Norwalk in the 1940s came to be known as barrio "Neighborhood" only in the mid-1970s. When the original, mostly European American working-class owners sold their property, they did so to Mexican Americans from established barrios in East Los Angeles who wanted to move but could only afford inexpensive housing. These socially mobile people left their earlier barrio space but, with their children, brought many barrio customs, including some knowledge of the gang subculture, to their new suburban locations in a type of diffusion or "hiving-off" process. Like the Mexican immigrant youth of today, these suburban youngsters had to form gangs to contend with established gangs already in the area, especially in the mostly rural barrios that had been engulfed by suburban developments. As spontaneously formed gangs without absolute barrio markers and experiencing sociocultural/psychological marginality, they developed a gang subcultural tradition that was less violent than that of their urban cousins.

Each of these gangs evolved goals, roles, and norms for their members as they strove to recruit and replenish their numbers. Some gangs became locally notorious barrio gangs, such as El Hoyo or the Cucamonga Kings. But not every gang carried such far-flung reputations; some barrios were more likely than others to produce consistently violent and deviant gangs.

African American Gangs

African American street gangs came much later, and avenues of proliferation and persistence differed from those for Mexican and Latino populations. After World War II, the African American population of Los Angeles increased through natural growth and internal migration from the south. Traditional ghetto pockets were enlarged, and new ones were created. For instance, the Watts area, made famous by the riots of 1965, had been home in the 1920s to two Mexican American barrios, Jardin and La Colonia. By the 1950s, Watts was rapidly becoming an African American neighborhood.

Gangs were not an issue in African American neighborhoods in Los Angeles until the late 1950s, when they were mostly of an incipient nature. By the mid-1960s, there had been some growth in the numbers of African American gangs and in gang membership. The Great Society and its social programs tended to undermine and curtail the expansion of gangs. However, political changes of the late 1970s withdrew many economic and social programs, and the gang problem within the African American population reached alarming proportions by the late 1980s (Hagedorn, 1988). The immediate change coincided with the contraction of the welfare state, which gradually at first and then in wholesale fashion was dismantled. For example, where there had once existed over 130 Teen Posts throughout the inner city area, by the 1990s only five remained.

Subsequent changes in the political economy magnified the gang problem as economic restructuring contributed to the growth of the underclass, already a sizable portion of the inner-city African American ghettos in the 1970s and 1980s. African American gangs underwent a major shift. Single-parent households, usually with the father absent, increased in number, as did youth unemployment rates. Heretofore, gangs had been mostly conflict oriented, but with even more limited economic and job opportunities, many street youth turned to drug trafficking, especially of "rock" cocaine (Taylor, 1990). The public eye, especially the attention of police and criminal justice officials in general, focused on this gang-drug association even though research showed that only about one third of gang members participated in drug sales and that nongang members account for most drug sales (Klein & Maxson, ND).

In the 1980s and 1990s, more youth in African American neighborhoods identified themselves by the external dress code of gang members. Wearing colors, such as blue for the Crips and red for the Bloods, became one of the distinctive habits of this ethnic group, and many an innocent adolescent and even child were shot and killed for sporting the wrong color.[3] As gang turf is more socially constructed in the ghetto, Crips and Bloods, among others, have been confederations that freely attract and recruit gang members from spatially scattered neighborhoods, unlike Mexican Americans, who generally reside in well-marked and held barrio enclaves. By the 1990s, African American gangs had spread beyond the ghetto to residential neighborhoods to recruit new members to establish affiliate gangs.

Vietnamese American Gangs

Vietnamese youth as a gang population can best be understood within the evolving, complex Southeast Asian refugee immigration sequence of the last quarter of the 20th century. The first wave of immigrants from Vietnam appeared in Los Angeles after the end of the Vietnam War in 1975. These were mostly American allies and collaborators of a relatively high social and economic status who were somewhat familiar with urban settings. With financial assistance from the United States government, these immigrants adjusted relatively smoothly and helped establish the Little Saigon ethnic enclave in Orange County. Meeting much resistance and rejection from local European Americans in the first years, they nevertheless eventually gained a strong foothold in the community. Although some organized adult criminal gangs, formed by former members of South Vietnamese elitist military and paramilitary organizations, accompanied this first wave, youth street gangs were absent.

When the second wave, known as the Boat People, began to arrive in 1978, the first indications of youth street gangs emerged. In contrast to the first wave, these newcomers generally were poor, were from agricultural communities, and had undergone various dislocations in the first years of the Communist takeover. With much less governmental assistance and with continuing anti-Vietnamese prejudice, many of these Boat People suffered immensely. The sequence of their arrival and integration was quite different from that of other immigrant groups.

Immigration for the later-arriving Vietnamese meant experiences with Communist relocation camps, dangerous boat trips always subject to pirate raids and atrocities, stays at overseas refugee camps, and finally the journey to the United States. Family networks unraveled, and only survival mattered. The United States government, responding to American public opinion, adopted a policy of refugee dispersal throughout the United States so as not to threaten any one community with this new "yellow peril." However, many of the dispersed refugees migrated again, seeking to reunite with relatives or simply with other countrymen. Finding their way to southern California with a climate and a resident Vietnamese population to their liking, children of the Boat People almost overnight began to experience the same sense of multiple marginality and breakdowns in social control that the Mexican American and African American groups had experienced before them. Family and school patterns were remarkably similar to those of these other ethnic groups, thus making gangs attractive to many as surrogate kin groups. Street gangs that were less territorial and conflict-ridden than African American and Mexican American gangs formed, and a criminally oriented lifestyle arose.

Although some gang conflict occurred, it was in the criminal realm that these youth gangs made their mark. The pattern of crime usually followed the following steps: grand theft automobile, home robberies (mostly of well-heeled Vietnamese), and extortions of business proprietors (Vigil & Yun, 1990). According to police officials, organized Vietnamese American crime networks began to recruit youth from these gangs by the late 1980s.

With the sometimes vast sums gained from criminal activity, these Vietnamese youth bought new clothes and cars and spent much of their social and recreational time at traditional coffee shops and pool rooms. Following a rational plan of securing money, they created fluid and mobile gangs, often traveling throughout the region or in nearby states to conduct their crimes. As wayward street children with hardly any semblance of family influence or control from authorities, they often teamed up with a group, including females, and went on a rampage of crime, with a motel room as their headquarters.

Female gangs surfaced later than their male counterparts but developed for similar reasons: Immigration and adaptation had so completely disrupted family life and traditional values in parts of the Vietnamese community that life was out of control. Thus, Vietnamese females occasionally formed their own groups in their adaptation to life in the United States.

The gang territory and gang membership of Vietnamese Americans differ markedly from those of other populations. Relatively new to the United States and to the Los Angeles area, Vietnamese groups spread into surrounding counties rather than centering only in Los Angeles for their criminal and gang activities. Little Saigon became a commercial and cultural center used regularly by Vietnamese of all ages and of both genders for socializing and eating at the many fast-food or restaurant establishments. Their gangs (the youths themselves prefer to say groups), although regionally based, offered fluid membership roles and often bore no specific name.

Drawing from various towns, this more impermanent and mobile gang structure allowed for and facilitated the criminal activities noted earlier. As for gang members, the range in criminal activities of the 1980s and early 1990s was based mostly on time and level of involvement, with older members leading younger ones in daring robberies and burglaries. Extortion and home robberies were conducted under the direction and supervision of the most experienced gang members, especially those with alleged ties to organized crime networks. The latter served as a source of intelligence and information on the persons or homes to "hit."

A Framework for Understanding Gangs: Multiple Marginality

Although with some ethnic variations and slightly different ways of incorporating females, all gang cultures in Los Angeles have revolved around how poor immigrants, migrants, or ethnic minorities and their children adapt to the city. The stresses and strains of this adaptation are manifold, and an assessment of them provides insight into what causes gangs and why certain individuals join them.[4]

Because barrios and ghettos and the living and working conditions of their residents stand as appendages to and facets of the remainder of society, this condition can best be characterized as multiple marginality. Applying this framework to the Mexican American case, one notes that there are ecological, economic, sociocultural, and psychological components of marginality. Although the sequence is clear, beginning with where people lived and worked and following with other adjustments, a dynamic action and reaction implicit in the construct account for the interaction among all of the sectors.

The barrio was founded in ecologically inferior areas adjacent to workplaces and separate from neighboring European Americans, which created a spatial and social distance alongside a visual blight of poverty that exacerbated Mexican American integration into society. Coupled with the low-paid, low-skill jobs that were available to barrio residents and the secondary labor market practices that affect permanent employment and retard social mobility, these conditions translated into substandard housing and crowded conditions that placed many families under stress.

Generational changes affected acculturation and the transition from Mexican to mainstream European American–dominated cultural norms. Some people sought total assimilation, while others selected paths in conformance with a bilingual-bicultural style. However, for many individuals, such assimilation was a very stressful, uneven affair, for neither Mexican culture was retained nor a new "American" mainstream culture acquired. Instead, a syncretic culture, midway in a hit-or-miss fashion between the two cultures, created the predicament of a *cholo* label defining the cultural marginals of the population.

With economic dislocations, culture change, and the effects of the streets came a loss of social control within traditional families. Under economic strain, adults lost firm parenting skills; in the family, gender roles shifted, especially when females found work outside the home and males did not. As families became less able to supervise their children and schools failed in developing appropriate learning programs for this population, a breakdown in the key sources of social control took place. Street socialization took over and brought youth into close, negative contact with police.

Because of the marginal, conflicting forces noted earlier, self-identification among barrio youth—especially during the adolescent "psychosocial moratorium," when a marginal status crisis emerged—led young people to street role models. Peers began to compete successfully with the family, school, and other authority figures. Age and gender clarification took on new forms and processes during this time, as a rigid sense of "masculinity" came to be embraced by gang members. Street pressures reinforced a code of toughness for survival.

In short, multiple marginality—combining, adding, and integrating different elements—worked to create disaffiliated, detached youths who grouped together into gangs. With the creation of the gang subculture, there arose a marginal street recruitment force with which youth had to reckon.

Because of variations in the degree and intensity of multiple marginality across barrios and ghettos, some poorer and more fragmented than others, different types of gangs as well as gang members emerged.

Street Realities as Socialization

Uniting all gangs, the crucible for the subculture, is the reality of the streets, especially in neighborhoods of older and more established gangs. On unsupervised streets, at-risk youth learn the ways of the gang, contending with new places, times, and modes of socialization. Most of the gang subculture activities occur in empty lots, hallway transits, the back or side porches of homes, alleyways, rooftops of apartments, out-of-view corners and crannies of odd-shaped public parks, and backsides of stores, apartments, and small industrial buildings. Much of the time spent in such locations is during the night. In the dark, symbolically, perhaps, when darker human emotions reign, such places—as well as unoccupied locations such as school yards and recreational facilities—are often taken over by gangs. Youngsters out at night also encounter winos, gangsters, molesters, the homeless, the criminally prone, and, of course, society's street social control specialists, the police.

In the course of such encounters, behavior is shaped by street realities. An attitude of awareness—one of wariness bordering on paranoia, looking over the shoulder, double-checking associates, watching friends, and avoiding danger as best one can by being streetwise—is cultivated.

It is in the context of the street that the gang subculture flourishes. Pervading this street reality is fear: fear of hidden places, fear of darker times, and fear of strange behaviors. For children entering street life, peers, older children, and young adults begin to affect their attitudes and shape their behavior in unconventional ways. Prominent in the curriculum of street socialization are how to talk, walk, think, and observe the rituals and ceremonies of the gang. Friendship and protection are important to gang subculture, for emotional security and physical defense from real threats are key to survival.

Gender socialization occurs under the strict auspices of the street codes. Girls are usually subject to male domination, sometimes including molestation and rape. Because of this, brothers and older male relatives of young females constantly admonish them for being "out in the streets," even when they themselves run the streets. Some girls and young women have rejected such supervision and advice and have established a street reputation of their own. However, most of the females reluctantly follow the male directives, avoiding the worst effects of the streets. If they do join the street gang, they usually do so as an auxiliary of the male gang.

Males are a different story. Traditional working-class male values extol the virtues of "masculinity" and showing that one "has balls." Many Mexican Americans and African Americans share this urban working-class background. For those who come from immigrant or migrant backgrounds, however, the changes forced by such street realities can be doubly difficult. Job and work paths for ethnic minorities in urban areas change traditional male maturation patterns from their former rural, small-town base. Coupled with high dropout and unemployment rates that further undermine male developmental experiences, the streets become the "only game in town." Being "a man"—tough, unfeeling, courageous, and daring—limits the role choices available to males forced to adjust and adapt to street realities. To resist this street subcultural requirement is to invite trouble; a person is left unprotected, unaffiliated, and subject to the wills and whims of others.

Street children have to deal with pervasive fear, and if their parents and other authorities cannot help, the gang steps in. Although the media and police reports emphasize peer gang member pressure and intimidation as principal means of recruiting new gang members, one cannot escape the observation that family and school voids—in short, social control breakdowns—are the main reason these children give for being in the streets. In their reality of limited choices, they feel almost compelled to join a gang (Klein, 1968). Many come from female-dominated, single-parent households and must learn to measure up to male rules and expectations in the streets. This socialization is a strange and unsteady arrangement, which gang initiation rituals partially address: Beating up a new gang member helps ensure that all the "femininity" is eliminated and also provides a public showing for fellow gang members to see how a "man" takes a beating.

Contrasts between African Americans' experience with deep-rooted racist and other structural developments and the refugee Vietnamese predicament make for different types of family structures and maladies. For one group it may be a permanently etched blemish, while for another a temporary arrangement that marks the first years of adaptation. Similarly, the Mexican American population's history shows that the economic relationship between two neighbor nations and incessant immigration from the poorer one create troublesome family dynamics. What follows is a general outline that provides a baseline for all of the ethnic groups whose youth are drawn to gang life.

Focusing on social control features is a middle-range analysis that acknowledges macrohistorical (e.g., immigration and racism) and macrostructural (e.g., secondary labor market, underclass, and poverty) causative forces but also attempts to spell out what these factors are and how they can be recaptured by societal efforts and programs in lieu of a major transformation of society or revolution. Four broad areas aid our understanding of the process: attachment, commitment, involvement, and belief.

Attachment emphasizes effective ties that youth form to significant others, such as family, parents, and other role models who become primary socializers for acceptable behavior. When these conventional ties loosen and voids are created, other social units serve this need. With commitment, the key point is aspiration for an acceptable status with well-defined future goals in the offing. Again, if possibilities for affiliation and achievement are missing, other avenues are sought or taught for gaining respect and prestige. Involvement is simply a category that highlights participation in conventional activities that lead to socially valued success and status objectives—in other words, the quality of a youth's time spent on prosocial activities. Finally, belief specifies acceptance of the moral validity of the core social value system, the social rules. The implications of this latter aspect of social control are obvious, especially if a youth recognizes dominant values but may feel disaffiliated because of weakened ties to them. Some researchers refer to "oppositional" culture, in which working-class youth subvert middle-class values (Willis, 1977).

With breakdowns in the social webs, which cause confusion around questions such as whom to look up to for direction, what to do to reach goals, how to spend spare time, and why to accept social rules, it is no wonder that the gang subculture has evolved for just these purposes (Cohen, 1955). A gang is established and persists because it continues to meet the needs of those who follow its creators. With choloization and street socialization frequent products of immigrant adaptation dynamics, the gang subculture serves several functions for many unconventional youths.

Gang members have troubles with school, strained families, and an excess of free, unsupervised time to follow the wrong leaders and actors. The gang fulfills important needs, both personal and social, because of the voids mentioned earlier. If we stretch our minds to say that involvement, attachment, commitment, and belief in conventional social control units have shifted to the gang, then we are better able to appraise what gangs actually do and what potential might lie in empowering and redirecting the energies of gangs. But first we have to ask directly: What does the gang subculture do?

Social Control and the Gang Subculture

One 16-year-old gang member who was asked "Why did you join the gang?" answered, "Fun, adventure, money." Summaries of gang culture have suggested the following as important features: (1) recruitment and initiation, (2) goals and roles, (3) striving for rank, and (4) positive self-concept (Cartwright, Tomson, & Schwartz, 1975). (As noted earlier, there are important gender differences in the manner in which these features are enacted. Here, the focus is on male gang members.) Attachment to significant others is a key facet in gang structures. Commitment is shown to attain status, but in a street-devised, gang-directed manner. Involvement is unconventional but approximates what street people consider "socially" acceptable status objectives and use of time. In the end, belief in social rules revolves around and is constricted by the limited horizons in which gang members find themselves.

The strongest role played by gangs is in offering friendship, emotional support, and a sense of security and protection in the face of unpredictable, "crazy" street pressures. Attachment to the gang and gang members is verified in what gang members do for one another, such as "backing up" each other, retaliating when a member is killed, providing a place to sleep, and sharing personal resources. Friendships may have started earlier if the youngsters grew up together, bonding on many different dimensions, but gang affiliation usually entails the use of fictive kinship terms. Mexican Americans, for example, refer to themselves as *carnales* (usually translated as brothers; the word more nearly approximates "of the [same] flesh"), "homeboys" (same gang or neighborhood), or *camaradas* (comrades) to verbalize, sometimes with great aplomb, the seal and pact that constitute gang membership. African Americans usually rely on "cuz" (cousin), "bro" (brother), "blood" (close relative), and homeboy, although in Los Angeles at least "blood" and "cuz" took on new connotations of particular gang names by the 1990s. Both Mexican American and African American groups feel and say on countless occasions that the gang is like a family (Vigil, 1988b).

The sociopsychological aspects of this attachment dynamic include ego, group, and role facets. Self-identification within the gang involves observing, mimicking, and following the attitude and behavior of peers, older relatives who have been in gangs, and *veteranos* (veterans, experienced gang members) or OGs (original gangsters, in the African American version). The latter provide examples for how to act, think, and feel about any number of street realities, such as how to group together for self-defense. A gang initiation ritual cements these relationships.

Commitment comes from attaining status with the gang goals as the individual learns to surrender himself to the gang or group. This type of dedication, or release of individual or significant-other choices, is possible because most gang members have weak or fragmented self-identities, which makes them particularly vulnerable and receptive to group pressures and concerns. The trade-off, protection and friendship from the group, encourages the individual to be loyal and supportive to the group. Showing care, sharing resources, backing up one's homeboys or *camaradas,* and making time and expending energies for all types of gang activities are also ways to attain status and reach goals designated by the gang.

One important gang goal is defense of the "turf" or barrio from transgressors' drive-by shootings of homes, cars, and people on the streets. To protect against such intrusions, there is a need for particularly tough and strong gang members. A valued gang quality specifically for members of the gang is *locura* (the art of acting or playing with craziness, or wild and unpredictable behavior). Locos are prized gang members, and there are some who are in fact loco (crazy). However, many more stretch into the role of loco. Usually, the ingestion of alcohol and drugs aids the role-playing required to demonstrate *locura,* often with one of the older or experienced gang members goading a novitiate into crazy action (e.g., a drive-by shooting). Status, albeit unconventional and antisocial, is striven for and attained by such loco activity. Even the gang initiation ritual is viewed as a public demonstration of one's *locura* capabilities: Can he take it and dish it out or is he a punk?

Street life directs what street children do and how they show their involvement in different types of socially valued successes and status objectives. Obviously, the quantity of time spent on the streets by gang members appears to be endless. However, most of their time is spent in very normal, adolescent youth activities covering play, socializing, love and dating arrangements, drinking and doing drugs, and being entrepreneurial (Taylor, 1990). Such activities are well-spent, quality time, but other, more publicly recognized antisocial, gangbanging habits also receive quality time. Homework or street work, for that matter, may take the form of learning how to plan and prepare a drive-by shooting or retaliation, to arrange a meeting place to "score" drugs or alcohol, and to listen at a gang hangout to *veteranos'* war stories of past battles lost and won.

Many peripheral, temporary, or situational gang members mix conventional and unconventional activities. Some compile fairly decent school records and successfully hold a job while continuing as a gang member. Eventually, many of these individuals mature out of the gang, typically through finding a good-paying, career-ladder occupation or a steady, stabilizing girlfriend or wife. They look back at their gang years as a crazy, disjointed period, sometimes with embarrassment, for they "weren't really themselves." The fact remains, however, that they did spend time on the streets and learned about the gang subculture. Also, for a time, they valued and dedicated their energies to other objectives.

Belief, the last of the social control facets, is very complex. Familiarization with the gang subculture most assuredly leads to a new belief system.

Implicit in choloization and street socialization is disruption of the socially acceptable value system and blurring of what constitutes correct values. The streets produce their own realities, which through human adaptation and creativity (or maladaption) lead to new values. Although it might be stretching matters to state that these street youngsters have consciously fashioned an "oppositional" culture to subvert society as rebels of one sort or another, it is clear that a life of instability and of fending for oneself has necessitated the creation of new ways to think, act, and believe. If there is a conscious choice in the matter, as the "fun, adventure, money" response mentioned earlier shows, it is more an ephemeral, spontaneous reaction to life as it is rather than how it should be. Some have suggested that *vatos locos* (crazy dudes who opt for and consistently follow *locura)* have taken an old Mexican and southwestern United States folktale character derived from Native American traditions, the Trickster, and corrupted it. Instead of being Trickster only 1 or 2 days of the year, the *vato loco* has reversed it to mean only 1 or 2 days for normal behavior.

The marginalization and street socialization that ethnic minority youth experience transforms conventional attachment, commitment, involvement, and belief dynamics. In large part integrating these dynamics, gangs have developed broad strategies of street coping. But can society recapture these functions, returning commitment and respect to the family, school, police, and other authorities? More critically, with the creation of a street gang subculture, there are new values and norms that did not exist before; can these new patterns be eliminated, curtailed, redirected, or co-opted or are they here to stay? This question raises another challenge, for any effort to alter these dynamics must of necessity address ways to use potentially functional elements of the gang subculture that street youth have fashioned. Is the subculture something new or really more a fractured, segmented facsimile of what existed previously?

Turning Gang Organization Around: Building on the Positives

In general, community approaches to resolving the gang problem must focus on role models that already exist on the streets: former gang members, streetwise counselors, and many poor and working-class parents, including single-parent household leaders, who have successfully reared their children under adverse conditions. Police, probation, community agency personnel, schools, and other public support services could provide many positive models for emulation if a communitywide, broader approach to the problem came about. As it is, every unit or agency protects its respective jurisdiction and resists outside meddling and, worse, can be reluctant to intersect and work with others. A blurring of the lines that demarcate public service roles goes a long way toward the creation of links of cooperation rather than conflict.

Training and remediation programs and multifaceted diversion efforts, such as sports, entertainment, and job/craft training, help reformulate youth's commitment to a higher status and future goals. Connections with private industry and corporate America become essential to this thrust, as training and education go hand in hand with jobs. Moreover, aware that much quality time is wasted in negative and destructive gang affairs, a concerted effort to steal time away from street routines can come with well-conceived, creatively formulated schedules infused with socially redeemable values.

And finally, if it is too late to have the current crop of street youth buy into the dominant moral value system and we begin to plan how to resocialize future generations, it might be advisable to examine and explore how to reverse street values or, better, how innovatively to reconstruct them to fit into established social ones. Friendship, protection, emotional support, desire for achievement and status, and acceptance and self-identity, among other characteristics of the gang, are youthful yearnings worthy of attention and respect. How do we channel these human emotions and needs in constructive and positive directions?

If we accept the premise that social control functions have moved out into the streets, then let us attempt to figure out two things: What social control functions has the gang taken over? Moreover, how can society use current community resources and programs to weave in and co-opt these gang patterns? The first response has been outlined already. The second begins with the natural motivations and predispositions that already exist in gang members.

Among the many positive qualities in the African American community, there is a deep-rooted oral tradition with many ramifications; spirituals, church orations, blues, and rhythm and blues are some of them. Street life has produced a variant that values speaking ability, especially the skill to "rap," including just being articulate in normal conversation. In earlier decades, as documented by notables such as Dick Gregory and Bill Cosby, "playing the dozens" (or "wolfing" as used on the West Coast) was a verbal game in which combatants one on one seized on the habits, flaws, and weaknesses of an opponent to make fun of him. This humor often entailed fabricating flaws or, better yet, magnifying minor ones to get onlookers to laugh. The winner was the one who could provoke more raucous laughs and thus fluster and derail the opponent. The repertoire of information to carry this out also included joking about a family member, mainly one's mother. The wolfing was almost always conducted in a rhyming and rhythmic fashion. Clearly, these language patterns had a strong influence on the development of modern-day "rapping" that crowds the radio stations.

Rap singing in its present form began to affect youth culture in the 1980s, with catchy tunes and meanings that many could mimic. Street gangs make up their own raps. If a street youth takes the time, energy, and creativity to dream up these raps, then it might be useful to marshall community resources behind this effort. For example, teachers of singing, poetry, drama, and public speaking could be enticed and hired to set up programs that structure and expand on this custom.

Also, with Mexican Americans as well as African Americans, the streets have instilled a great deal of fear in the youth population. The desire and motivation to acquire fist-fighting ability in part stems from this fear; the other part revolves around working-class culture's sports interest, which may indeed have evolved from the same street/fear beginnings among European American ethnics in the late 19th century. In any event, prize fighting, boxing, and, to a lesser degree, Asian martial arts present a window of opportunity to garner even more street energy. Boxing programs and clubs have for decades made an impact on ethnic minority communities. From the streets to the ring has been the rags to riches avenue for many of these young men. Because professional boxing has become so corrupt and bloody, it might be advisable to focus entirely on amateur boxing, with a new set of rules and regulations and the use of monitoring devices, or on "electronic" boxing (where no head blows are allowed and scoring to determine the winner is done by computer).

Art and artistic expression, strongly embraced by ethnic minority youth, provide another positive springboard for street life and youth activity if rechanneled with imagination. For example, in the Chicano/Latino population, widely circulated adolescent magazines, such as *Low Rider* and *Q'VO,* glamorize and caricature the street *cholo* and low-riding habits and customs. "Prison artists" quite commonly do such work for inmates who write letters to their loved ones, accompanied by these pencil drawings (often imitations of expert tattoos). Well developed in several barrios is the mural art found on various local buildings and walls, a genre sparked by the 1960s Chicano movement but with clear roots in the Mexican mural tradition. Similarly, in the 1980s, there emerged a "graffiti" mural style popular with some of the street youth who have been successful at avoiding gangs. They developed their own subcultural style that channeled frustration and anxiety born of the barrio into murals, even though some of them regularly put their "pieces" on buildings and walls without solicitation. In contrast, many local leaders in business and the community alike, as well as public agencies, began to commission and pay for such work.

In addition to these activities, there are the more obvious sports and recreational habits often associated with African American and Mexican American males. The former, of course, have had a profound effect on a variety of sports of every imaginable level and region in the United States: basketball, football, baseball, and track, for instance. Some cities, like Los Angeles, introduced Midnite Basketball to attract "night-owl" street kids away from the gangs, drug activity, and violence associated with the dark streets. Latinos, of course, have brought the world's most popular sport, soccer, to the United States. Since the 1980s, parks and quasirecreational space in the central Los Angeles area have been occupied by either soccer teams in competition or by families and small groups picnicking on the grass. Handball, often learned in prisons, is another popular activity, but few places for playing are available to young men.

One segment of the gang population deserves special mention: youngsters who are "slow" learners, perhaps untutored and too withdrawn to achieve academically, and "short and small" in stature. Both features affect attainment of status and respect within the requisites of the gang subculture. Not smart enough to excel in school or on the streets, not big enough to make the sports squad or fend off street toughs, these youngsters' limited choices lead them to join a gang. There, they become highly likely to carry out gang functions, especially the destructive and wanton ones, that the smarter and bigger gang members cagily avoid. Indeed, the latter gang members "use" these individuals to carry out such deeds. Quite often, these individuals are very gregarious types who want to please. Occasionally, some of them are leaders of sorts in engendering a socializing, festive ambience. In their efforts to please, they sometimes show ingenious ways to "hustle up" some food, drink, drugs, or other resources.

Because of these characteristics, such individuals could gain immediate benefit more from job training in skilled craft trades, such as carpentry, masonry, and electrical work than from academic instruction. This would especially be the case if coordination with corporate/business leaders included plans to redevelop, refurbish, and build up the decayed infrastructure prevalent in the inner cities. School learning programs and recreational and sports activities would affect them in the long haul, but it is the smarter and bigger—more academically and athletically ready—youth who would show progress from the beginning.

In both Mexican American and African American populations, in their rural, precity life, young children worked by helping out either with household chores or in the fields; children were taught and expected to contribute to the comforts and needs of the family. This changed in American cities under an industrial economy. Any form of child labor and "street" employment (such as shoeshine boys, newspaper vendors, and as incipient numbers runners for gambling enterprises) had almost disappeared by the second half of the 20th century. With the end of child labor and the "invention" of adolescence prolonging childhood and changing the acquisition of responsibilities, there remained only "street" jobs, which more and more were of the antisocial, criminal type. Ironically, by the 1990s, Mexican/Latino immigrants began to introduce new types of street jobs, such as ice cream and fruit vendors, but in a recession economy, adults became more likely than young people to hold these jobs.

By the time African American and Mexican American youth had a gang problem, relatively few street occupations remained and child labor was out of the question. In fact, the earlier changes, stretching childhood into adolescence and postponing responsibilities, were difficult enough. To compound matters, new technological replacements for human labor and the present economic restructuring made even fewer jobs available.

A major goal then is to generate jobs for children, of preteen ages preferably, given the traditional background of work and responsibility that has been part of their parents' socialization. Earning extra money, although an understandable goal for a low-income population, is a consideration secondary to the socialization power of jobs. At the base of this suggestion is the reintroduction of responsible activities that could occupy the time of youngsters and also reshape their attitudes toward work, providing them with skills and knowledge of a particular craft or trade—for instance, training as a carpenter's or mason's helper.

Innovating with Social Control

Clearly, eliminating social control voids would go a long way toward reaching a solution to the gang problem. Family life is where this process has to begin, because this is the first chance to get people to conform to societal rules and demands. Stresses and strains from historical and structural dynamics have resulted in a high percentage of low-income, single-parent, crowded households and uneven family socialization routines among ethnic minority populations.

A reversal in public policy and practice is needed, for all family safety nets must be furnished to ensure that children in such households receive some guidance and supervision. Many of the children in such households require additional supervision, because in African American families and increasingly in Latino households, the single parent is overwhelmed by other demands and comes up short in parenting duties. Affordable childcare centers would help immeasurably in this regard. Other families in the neighborhood who have had a modicum of success in raising their children, whether of a single- or dual-parent household, should be recruited and compensated in some way to help families under stress.

Schools, second in importance, should be supported not only to expand recognized successful programs, such as Head Start, but to begin pilot/exploratory efforts to follow through with elementary and junior high school enrichment and remediation curriculum changes. Programs, such as Get Smart (elementary) and Stay Smart (junior high), could ensure continuity for what was initiated in Head Start and could also allow teachers and school personnel to monitor over a period of time individual children who remain marginal and may fall between the cracks even with such special treatment. A key to maturing out of a gang has been attaining a meaningful career (Moore, 1978); early efforts toward such a direction might deter gang recruitment.

Although it sounds grandiose, street schooling might be an alternative, with the use of a local parent's home as the classroom or, more risky, a schoolmobile that visits hangouts and connects with students. Many incentives can be attached to these alternatives, such as paying street students for their leadership in school recruitment and curricular and disciplinary planning or providing other services for recreational events (Irby & McLaughlin, 1990). In Cleveland, Ohio, a new school policy in the 1990s put money in a bank account for the future college education of students with good school attendance and passing grades; this is an example of an incentive that returns so much for Cs, Bs, and As, thus teaching students that the harder you try, the higher the rewards can be.

Following the logic of the streets, where the dominant forces are gangs and the police, law enforcement and the criminal justice system have a large role to play in this scenario. The Los Angeles Police Department during the 1940s and 1950s had an expanded outreach program known as the Deputy Auxiliary Police (DAPS), which, just like the gangs, recruited and attracted youth from many different neighborhoods. The police officers who led this special program showed a gentler, kinder face to the barrio and ghetto communities back then. Today, we have Community Resources Against Street Hoodlums (CRASH) of the Los Angeles Police and Operation Safe Streets (OSS) of the Los Angeles sheriff's office—as we have increasingly noted, a narrow response to a complex problem (Boyle, 1991). A concerted expansion of the older activities could be appropriate.

Although religion and churches are seldom mentioned by gang members, for their personal and family lives have become disconnected from established social institutions in too many dimensions, it is important to note that church-operated programs have existed for some time. In earlier decades, for instance, the Catholic Church, to which the bulk of the faithful among Latinos claim at least nominal membership, operated a Catholic

Youth Organization settlement house/recreation center program in many different neighborhoods and made successful inroads among at-risk children. Since the 1970s, however, budgetary constraints have led to a very limited, skeletal replica of what existed before. With the exception of a few parishes, like the one in East Los Angeles pastored by Father Gregory J. Boyle in the 1980s and 1990s, the Catholic Church has done little to address gang life directly.

At the same time, especially after the 1992 civil unrest following the verdict in the trial of police officers accused of beating Rodney King, Protestant fundamentalist operations stepped up their activities in many barrios. One of these, Victory Outreach, has attracted a sizable following, especially among gang members and street drug abusers and dealers, toward whom it is particularly targeted (Vigil, 1982). Expansion of such efforts might add to the restoration of acceptable social control functions for at-risk and delinquent youths.

Conclusion

Friendship, protection, security, recreation, courting, and socializing are found within gang subcultural practices and habits. Even with the breakdowns in social control, gang participants still mostly carry out the normal functions and activities found among adolescents and youth. However, the negative and destructive patterns and the aggressions and intimidations are the most alarmingly felt and widely publicized acts of gang subcultural members. It is these deeds and actions that have drawn public attention to the gangs, even though such activities constitute a relatively small percentage of what gangs do every day.

Although the most multiply marginal communities and the most established individual gang members are probably responsible for the initiation and perpetuation of much of the violent and life-threatening activities, it is the fringe and casually connected gang members who get caught up in the momentum—the *locura* binge, if you will—that dominates street life. With nothing else to do except hang around with the *vatos,* making them easily available for gangbanging duties, they are regularly accessible to the influences of "significant others" to carry out deeds that they have not conjured up themselves.

To address this gang problem, our society must reevaluate the complex networks of social control. If family, school, and police goals and purposes have fallen short and have been undermined such that the gang subculture has taken them over, how do we recapture them? Simply stated, attachments, commitments, involvements, and beliefs have to be reengineered within the context of the gang subculture to reconnect with conventional norms and values. This strategy can begin with the understanding that most gang members eventually "mature out" of the gang and discover other sources of direction and support. If outgrowing the gang and ending the psychosocial moratorium commonly occurs, those who have matured out could operate as "shock troops" for social programs aimed toward shepherding and hastening the maturation process for other younger gang members.

The focus on maturation is important for several reasons. First, it is certainly the case that maturing out of the gang has been associated with finding a good job and a steady girlfriend to redirect a person's life (Cartwright, Tomson, & Schwartz, 1975; Moore, 1978, 1991; Sullivan, 1988). Similarly, female gang members often leave the gang through attachments to work and husband or boyfriend. So crucial to all members of society and especially wayward street youth, this act of starting a family and learning how to behave in responsible ways is a marked accelerator for maturing out of the gang. Instead of remaining a gang member well past the normal gang membership age (roughly the late teens and early 20s), a member can be thrust into a new role that requires more conventional habits.

Responsibility from the gang members must be matched by responsibility from society, however. If jobs and programs are lacking to expedite maturation, then only a dead end awaits the former gang member. Maturing out seems to have been stretched and delayed with the early 1990s because of economic restructuring and limited job opportunities; there are more "dinosaurs" (older gang members) today (Hagedorn, 1988; Moore, 1991; Sahagun, 1990).

It is from this group that identification and recruitment of former gang members are crucial. Getting such streetwise, experienced adults to help in turning the gang problem around constitutes a key element to a broadened, community-wide strategy. These individuals know both the attractions and the dangers of gangs. They can help provide community leaders with insights into and information on how gang entrance and exit unfold in particular neighborhoods and gangs. They can offer details to help the public to comprehend the processes and rules of such affiliations and dissociations. Advice from these individuals would help public leaders to focus on the strands of social control that need to be addressed. They could act as the most immediate role models and be empowered with connections to different community resources and agencies geared to hastening gang members' maturation out of the gang. With this leadership role and as members of the community who know the problem firsthand, they could help shape new commitments for status and goals and make arrangements for uses of time in activities that lead to positive, prosocial objectives. They could begin to challenge gang members just where it hurts most: the belief system of the gang subculture that maintains street life leads nowhere except to trouble.

Notes

[1]Although the discussion will be dominated by issues and examples from the Mexican American population, the author's ethnographic base of African American and Vietnamese youth experiences will also be included where appropriate. All of the data and evidence are based on fieldwork in Los Angeles and Orange County, a multiethnic metropolitan area with large numbers of street youth and a pervasive gang problem since the early decades of the 20th century.

[2]Most of the early work on gangs centered on Chicago; see, for example, writings of the Chicago School of Sociology in the 1920s (Burgess, 1925; Park, 1928; Thrasher, 1926). These and writings that followed after the 1940s consistently pointed to the deficiency of Chicago's social support services for inner-city youth (Cloward & Ohlin, 1960; Shaw & McKay, 1942; Whyte, 1943/1973).

[3]From the 1970s into the 1990s, social science studies of gangs have repeatedly documented their structural features, interdependence with economic conditions of their neighborhoods, and degrees of intensity of affiliation with particular ethnic memberships. Moore (1978) and Vigil (1988a, 1988b) document gang life for Latino males and females of Southern California. Moore (1991) describes major changes underway in Los Angeles and gives in-depth treatment to female gang members. In contrast to these social science accounts, journalistic books, such as that by Bing (1991) on the Crips and Bloods of Los Angeles, portray gang members primarily in terms of their relish for violence and criminality. Hagedorn (1988) details the underclass nature of African American gangs, and Taylor (1990) and Padilla (1992) provide more insight into the entrepreneurial business side of gangs in Detroit and Chicago, respectively. In fact, the latter makes a clear case for the organizational structure of a criminal subculture. Films of the early 1990s offer similar portrayals. "Boyz n the Hood" (on African American gangs) and "American Me" (on Latino gangs) drew sharp criticism for "celebrating" the brutality of gangs' males toward "their" females as well as toward their own communities' young.

[4]A previous work (Vigil, 1988a) elaborates a conceptual framework to highlight most of the elements that contribute to gang formation in barrios and how these elements converge and are reflected in the lives of particular gang members.

References

Bing, L. (1991). *Do or die*. New York: Harper Collins Publishers.

Bogardus, E. S. (1926). *The city boy and his problems*. Los Angeles: House of Ralston, Rotary Club of Los Angeles.

Bogardus, E. S. (1943). Gangs of Mexican American youth. *Sociology and Social Research, 28*, 55–56.

Boyle, G. J. (1991, January 9). Getting tough got us nowhere. *Los Angeles Times,* p. B70.

Burgess, E. W. (1925). The growth of the city: An introduction to a research project. In R. E. Park, E. W. Burgess, & R. O. McKenzie (Eds.), *The city* (pp. 47–62). Chicago: University of Chicago Press.

Cartwright, D. S., Tomson, B., & Schwartz, H. (1975). *Gang delinquency.* Monterey, CA: Brooks/Cole.

Cloward, R. A., & Ohlin, L. B. (1960). *Delinquency and opportunity: A theory of delinquent gangs.* New York: Free Press.

Cohen, A. K. (1955). *Delinquent boys: The culture of the gang.* Glencoe, IL: Free Press.

Hagedorn, J. (1988). *People and folks: Gangs, crime and the underclass in a rustbelt city.* Chicago: Lake View.

Huff, C. R. (Ed.). (1990). *Gangs in America: Diffusion, diversity, and public policy.* Newbury Park, CA: Sage.

Irby, M. A., & McLaughlin, M. W. (1990). When is a gang not a gang? When it's a tumbling team. *Future Choices, Fall*(2), 31–41.

Klein, M., & Maxson, C. L. *Gang involvement in cocaine "rock" trafficking.* Center for Research on Crime and Social Control, S.S.R.I., University of Southern California, Los Angeles.

Klein, M. W. (1968). Impressions of juvenile gang members. *Adolescence, 3*(9), 53–78.

Mazon, M. (1985). *The zoot-suit riots: The psychology of symbolic annihilation.* Austin: University of Texas Press.

Moore, J. (1978). *Homeboys: Gangs, drugs, and prison in the barrios of Los Angeles.* Philadelphia: Temple University Press.

Moore, J. (1991). *Going down to the barrio: Homeboys and homegirls in change.* Philadelphia: Temple University Press.

Padilla, F. M. (1992). *The gang as an American enterprise.* New Brunswick, NJ: Rutgers University Press.

Park, R. E. (1928). Human migration and marginal man. *American Journal of Sociology, 33,* 881–893.

Sahagun, L. (1990, November 11). Fight against gangs turns to social solution. *Los Angeles Times,* pp. A1, A3.

Sahagun, L. (1991, January 16). Sheriffs, officials, community leaders shift gang strategy. *Los Angeles Times,* p. B3.

Shaw, C., & McKay, R. (1942). *Juvenile delinquency and urban areas.* Chicago: University of Chicago Press.

Sullivan, M. (1988). *Getting paid.* Ithaca, NY: Cornell University Press.

Taylor, C. (1990). *Dangerous society.* East Lansing, MI: Michigan State University Press.

Thrasher, F. M. (1926). *The gang.* Chicago: University of Chicago Press.

Vigil, J. D. (1982). Human revitalization: The six tasks of Victory Outreach. *Drew Gateway, 52*(3), 49–59.

Vigil, J. D. (1988a). *Barrio gangs: Street life and identity in Southern California.* Austin: University of Texas Press.

Vigil, J. D. (1988b). Group processes and street identity: Adolescent Chicano gang members. *Ethos, 16,* 431–445.

Vigil, J. D. (1990). Cholos and gangs: Culture change and street youth in Los Angeles. In R. Huff (Ed.), *Gangs in America: Diffusion, diversity, and public policy* (pp. 146–162). Beverly Hills, CA: Sage.

Vigil, J. D., & Yun, S. (1990). Vietnamese youth gangs in Southern California. In R. Huff (Ed.), *Gangs in America: Diffusion, diversity, and public policy* (pp. 146–162). Beverly Hills, CA: Sage.

Whyte, W. F. (1943/1973). *Street corner society.* Chicago: University of Chicago Press.

Willis, P. E. (1977). *Learning to labour.* Farnborough, England: Saxon House.

Child Saving and Children's Cultures at Century's End

Gary Alan Fine
Jay Mechling

How have perceptions of youth and their position in society shifted since the 1950s? It was then that the baby boomers reformed somewhat their legacy from the late 19th century of the culture of youth to take into account suburban life, the influence of mass media, and the need to plan leisure time for youngsters. Youth organizations that served underprivileged youngsters diminished in importance as those that met the demands of suburban families grew. Inner-city youth increasingly came to appear abnormal to policymakers and, indeed, to see themselves as such in light of the images of the young life portrayed in the media. Drawing on fieldwork with a European American, middle-class Boy Scout troop and Little League team, the authors suggest features of these groups that meet needs common to youth across sociocultural groups. The challenge to youth policymakers is to ask: How alike are children? Only after informed deliberations on this question can youth leaders build organizations to meet needs that are common across cultures rather than molding children in images derived from values and ideals of earlier decades.

> We find ourselves more taken with the running up and down, the games, and puerile
> simplicities of our children, than we do (afterwards) with their most complete actions; as if we
> had loved them for our [own] sport. . . .
>
> *Montaigne*
> *"Of the Affections of Fathers to Their Children"*

Adults in the United States have difficulty thinking clearly about children. Our own childhood experiences and our particular lenses of gender, ethnicity, and social class lead us most often to "see" the child of our projected wishes and, sometimes, of our projected fears. This muddled thinking about children is bad enough when, as parents, we come to decide how we want to deal with our own children. Muddled thinking about children becomes dangerous in the debate about public policy concerning their well-being. And that, of course, is precisely the case in the waning years of the 20th century, as media and government attention turns increasingly to the "problems" of children, from homeless children to children with AIDS to the increase in suicide, alcoholism, and pregnancy among teenagers. As the American public panicked over the state of childhood in the 1990s, assigned blame everywhere, and wondered what was to be done in an economy that forced unpleasant choices, clear thinking about children's lives in the United States became increasingly challenging.

Still, to treat the child merely as a "text" of adult anxieties and politics falls far short of our adult responsibilities for the lives of children. Because we adults have such better access than children to the resources of society, we are faced with a version of what William James (1896/1984) called the "forced option"; we must choose how we shall intervene in the lives of children because not to choose is to choose neglect and to leave children as victims of that neglect of responsibility. Is there some way for the social critic simultaneously to keep alert to the gender, class, race, and other interests tangled in public discussions of children's problems and to act responsibly on behalf of children?

We ask in this essay how American adults in the 1990s can think more clearly about children's lives as a first step toward designing and reforming institutions for children, especially children identified as "at risk." We look first to the 1950s origins of our present images of and ideas about children and then at the class bias heightened by the 1960s and 1970s. Most mainstream institutions for the socialization of children, from the suburban junior high school and senior high school to the Boy Scouts and Little League, took their modern form in the 1950s and reflected those mid-century images and ideas. Our goal is not to present a full social history of the 1950s but to sketch the biases that may interfere with our understanding of the lives of children in the 1990s.

Next, we draw on our own investigations of two youth organizations (Fine on the Little League and Mechling on the Boy Scouts) to identify what "works" well in institutions with basically European American, middle-class, male pre-adolescents and adolescents. We than ask: Do gender, race, social class, and even age have such particular impact on children's lives that our generalizations from working with European American, middle-class males provide no clue to what would be successful for working with youth considered at risk? Finally, we ask how we would have to alter our list of the ingredients of a successful organization for European American, middle-class boys if we wanted to create a successful organization for, say, Latino working-class teenagers.

The goal here, in short, is to address how our research on the social interaction of children might contribute toward constructing neighborhood-based organizations that serve the needs of children and community. In what ways do the models that have been designed for majority, male youth apply to other children, and what dimensions need to be taken into consideration to change these structures to increase their effectiveness?

1950s Image and Ideology—and Beyond

Our 1990s' images and ideas about children, especially children at risk, arose primarily in the two decades after World War II, when defects of the legacy of youth policies that had originated in the late 19th century became increasingly evident. The baby boom that began in 1946 and lasted almost two decades had two important consequences for 1990s' thinking about children. First, the boomers themselves were a phenomenon around which American parents of the late 1940s and 1950s built a new, affluent, suburban, European American, middle-class way of life. The suburban home, the suburban school, the automobile, and the shopping mall were connected elements in this new middle class, in which men exchanged their blue collars for white and wives stayed at home to raise the children (Friedan, 1963). Part of creating this suburban, middle-class way of life was ensuring that children had all the "advantages" and the "security" that their Depression-reared parents did not have, from dance and music lessons to Scouting and Little League.

The proliferation of television sets in the 1950s also meant that this new middle class was exposed to a daily helping of mass-media narratives modeling their way of life. The suburban, middle-class boomers grew up with television versions of themselves, as portrayed in *Father Knows Best, The Adventures of Ozzie and Harriet, I Love Lucy, the Donna Reed Show, Leave It to Beaver,* and a dozen other domestic sitcoms. Thus, the actual lives of the boomers themselves, reinforced by mass-media images and narratives of 1950s' television, created a perspective of the "normal" American family. Historians and social scientists had good reason to believe that the "typical" middle-class family of the 1950s was an aberration, a quite new "invention" that departed from the normal pattern of American family lives in the 20th century. However, the facts of family form and function are less important to our analysis than is the image. Middle-class parents and their baby-boomer children believed they were the normal American family, and it is that 1950s' family that became the benchmark for judging "threats" to the family over the next four decades.

The second great consequence of the 1946 to 1964 baby boom is that the first cohort of boomers entering their 40s hold, or are about to hold in the 1990s, positions of power affecting the lives of children into the next decade. Boomers are now mayors and chairpersons of school boards, members of Congress and chief executive officers, widely read authors and senior professors, and powerful attorneys and physicians, as well as parents and occasionally grandparents. This simple demographic fact—that many adults raised as middle-class children in the 1950s could now profoundly affect the lives of all American children in the 1990s— suggested the importance of a phenomenon we label *symbolic demography,* that is, the tendency of people to act in the present according to images and ideas acquired earlier in a particular social, demographic location.

If we believe that 1950s' images and ideas about children are key impediments to clear thinking about children in the 1990s, how might we characterize the ideology from that period? First, that decade saw the *triumph of scientific psychology over religion* as the privileged system for understanding the person. Scientific psychology's assault on religion began at the end of the 19th century, as the nascent "social sciences" tapped into the strength and prestige of Darwinism. A sign of the victory was the shift from 19th-century talk about "character" and the moral connotations of that concept to 20th-century talk about "personality" (Susman, 1984). The prestige of scientific psychology received a boost from the Progressive Era's worship of expertise and the subsequent marriage of behaviorism and "scientific management" in American industry and bureaucracy. The social sciences, including psychology, thrived in the "natural social experiment" that was the Depression 1930s, and psychology came to serve the war effort in a range of matters, from analysis of propaganda to treatment of the mental traumas of war.

By the late 1940s, scientific psychology had established its credentials with the American public, who looked increasingly to experts for advice on rearing children. Various contemporary critics described the 1950s as an "age of anxiety" (Susman & Griffin, 1989, p. 23), so it is little wonder that the number of therapists increased dramatically in that decade. This is not to say that Americans were not "religious" in the 1950s; indeed, middle-class Americans expressed their religiosity conspicuously in the period. But the most successful religious figures wed their theology to psychology, relying on the latter's prestige. Thus, the 1950's legacy in our thinking about children tends to discount traditional religious perspectives in favor of psychology's explanations for children's behavior and attitudes.

Second, adults in the 1950s tended to *idealize* both childhood and play. Behavioral psychology supported the view of innocent childhood, and adults tended to view children's play as free, voluntary, spontaneous, and egalitarian (Sutton-Smith & Kelly-Byrne, 1984). The primary business of the child was to have "fun," which included learning to be creative and sociable. There arose what Wolfenstein (1955) called a "fun morality." Children were removed from the instrumental venues of society (Zelizer, 1985). Children's labor was unneeded, and even schooling was supposed to be made enjoyable, so that students should "want" to learn. "Fun" was the ideology that suggested that childhood was expected to be "expressive." Children were expected to be socialized into the morality of the social order, but this was to be achieved painlessly—like taking one's polio vaccine on a sugar cube.

On a fundamental level, of course, all young people desire to maximize their personal satisfaction ("fun") from their voluntary activities. As Goffman (1961) suggests, the only legitimate rationale for leisure (or, in his argument, for games) is fun, and activities that do not *as a minimum* provide this fun have no hold on participants, nor should they. Fun, however, is a phenomenological experience, and we have no inherent reason to believe that what one person will classify as fun another will, too. Yet the postwar period incorporated the desire for fun into the ideology of socialization.

There are cultural preferences in fun just as in other human endeavors. We should distinguish between values that persons choose by virtue of their cultural upbringing and values that rest in human potential. In the former, class and ethnic differences are readily apparent (e.g., different preferences in music, slang, and clothing styles). The depiction of racial and ethnic group value differences is much less clear. Indeed, one can argue that all groups have relatively similar values, as mediated by the expected probability of success and their structural position in the social order. In other words, the at-risk child who doesn't expect to do well in school and who doesn't expect success in school to translate into anything may share a middle-class value about the importance of education (Horowitz, 1983) but simply does not feel that the investment is worth the probable outcome. The worlds of voluntary organizations—perhaps more than the demanding, mandatory worlds of work or school—are dependent on personal preferences, and typically these preferences guide leisure-time choices. We do not suggest that leisure activities avoid morality, for they surely have moral components, as in the case of controversial leisure, such as hunting and sexual swinging (Olmstead, 1988). Rather, people feel that leisure is a personal choice. As with so many domains that involve children, however, adults feel that they have a right and a proper role to guide those choices. The guidance sometimes turns out to be closer to coercion. So, we return to issues of ideology and power, even when coercion is masked as "choice."

Third, the 1950s saw a strong cultural bias toward *individualism* that influenced adult ideas about children, from formal developmental theories to everyday conversations (Cosaro & Eder, 1990, p. 198). Americans were "worried" about individualism, in part because they experienced strong social pressures toward conformity. Yet passing through World War II and confronting the Cold War, our "enemies"—the Nazis, the Japanese, the Soviets, and the Chinese—were all stereotyped by their unyielding conformity. Conformity was mistrusted even while it was embraced. One of the great paradoxes of the 1950s is that the middle class eagerly consumed cultural narratives extolling the dangers of conformity—from books like Riesman's *The Lonely Crowd* (1950) or Whyte's *The Organization Man* (1956), to novels like *The Man in the Gray Flannel Suit* (1955), to films like *High Noon* (1952) or *The Caine Mutiny* (1954)—while pursuing consumer life-styles and opinions that would make them like and be liked by others. The consequence of this cultural ambivalence was a view that children should simultaneously strive to fit in and to be liked by their peers, learning sociability in schools and in organizations like the Scouts, *and* establish their own individual identities and talents.

Fourth, the suppression or *domestication* of boys' anger moved center stage in 1950s' advice literature and adult strategies of child rearing. Postwar feelings about violence only reinforced a larger 20th-century trend toward the domestication of anger in all children, but especially in boys (Stearns & Stearns, 1986). Boys' play at mid-century was also becoming more like girls' play, which is to say it was moving from being physical to being more symbolic and from being competitive to being more collaborative (Sutton-Smith, 1979). The evidence of children's play parallels evidence of parental behavior during the period, as middle-class parents tended to rely on symbolic measures, such as the withholding of love or material rewards, rather than physical punishment for controlling the child's behavior (Miller & Swanson, 1958). The ideal child of the 1950s, therefore, was well behaved, knew how to control his or her anger, and shied away from aggressive or violent play.

While the parents, psychologists, teachers, and other experts were working on this ideology of the normal child in the 1950s, they were also creating a picture of a threatening alternative: the juvenile delinquent. A recurring theme in parental worries about adolescents in the 1950s was that lower-class values and behavior were "infecting" middle-class youth (Gilbert, 1986). By distinguishing between "good" and "bad" adolescents and by blaming the mass media (comic books, films, television, and rock and roll music), parents and some experts worked at creating an image of a normal teenager to match the image of the normal, middle-class child. Ehrenreich (1989, p. 22) notes that part of the process of the professional middle class's defining itself in the 1950s was connecting juvenile delinquency with the lower classes. The "discovery" of poverty in the 1960s helped solidify the professional middle class's identity by clarifying what it *was not*—namely, poor, black, or brown, and uneducated. In addition, the 1960s' "war on poverty" helped institutionalize an infrastructure of professionals and organizations aimed at helping youth at risk.

This brief account of the rise of images and an ideology of normal childhood in the 1950s conveys in broad strokes the mind-set that American adults brought to dealing with issues of children's lives in the 1980s and the 1990s. Similarly, voluntary youth-serving organizations that flourished in the 1950s remained attractive models for neighborhood-based organizations in the 1990s. Let us now turn to two such organizations and see what might be learned from their successes and failures.

The Successful Voluntary Organization for Youth

Fieldwork among children and their voluntary organizations serves as a healthy reminder that the actual practices of children's lives arise out of a dynamic interaction between the formal organizations that adults design and the informal peer cultures that children bring to organizational settings. Fine (1987) intensively observed Little League baseball teams made up of preadolescent boys (aged 9 to 12) and their coaches, and Mechling (1981) worked with a Boy Scout troop of preadolescent and adolescent boys (aged 11 through 17) and their adult leaders.

Although these organizations were founded before the 1950s, both flourished and assumed their modern forms in the 1950s. The specific boys and organizations we studied were primarily European American and middle class; certainly most were not at risk, at least as conventionally conceived. These two organizations have been extremely successful in contributing to the personal, social, and moral development of their clients. Thus, it is worth asking whether any lessons learned from studying these programs designed for European American, middle-class, preadolescent and adolescent boys can be applied to our thinking about strengthening or creating neighborhood-based organizations for the ethnically and racially diverse clientele of today.

Three essential features characterize effective voluntary organizations for pre-adolescents and adolescents: (1) the maintenance of strong *identity structures,* which tie the individual to the organization in the face of multiple centrifugal forces; (2) the presence of strong and just *superego models* in both the youth and adult leaders; and, paradoxically, (3) the existence of a *robust peer culture* overlapping but not identical with the organization and sometimes actually resisting the organization's formal identity structures and superego models.

Irby and McLaughlin (1990) suggest that successful youth organizations might be modeled on the gang. A youth gang is a remarkable organization, given its enviable success in connecting children who are said to lack the ability to bind. The gang, in most respects, enjoys these three features. But it also has a fourth feature. As a successful *economic organization,* the gang is difficult to combat (Jankowksi, 1991; Padilla, 1992). Indeed, a crucial element in the success of the Jesse White Tumbling Team described by Irby and McLaughlin (1990) is economic: The young men get a share of the fees collected for performances by the team, and this means each boy gets $600 to $800 each month.

Seeing voluntary youth organizations as a source of income for the youths is an alien concept for middle-class organizations. The middle class has accepted the American *political economy of leisure and recreation,* the view that recreation is a universal human right—"the right of all people to have rich, diversified leisure opportunities and experiences as part of their quality of life, to contribute to their overall growth and development" (Kraus, 1987, p. 47)—and that the "psychic income" from participating in voluntary leisure activities is both its own immediate reward and an investment in the future "productivity" of the individual. The culture critic recognizes in this ideology the fusion of romanticism and capitalism found so often in late capitalism.

But this calculus of rewards is a luxury that children at risk can ill afford. The "rights" of an individual to leisure activities are little more than a philosophical nicety that pales in the face of economic necessity. We must abandon our class expectations, based on the belief in "universal prosperity," when thinking about adapting existing programs for diverse clientele.

Our discussion, then, describes the features of successful youth organizations as witnessed in our own fieldwork, in our broader readings in the ethnography of children's small-group cultures, and in our understanding of the current state of theory in the culture studies disciplines. Our aim is to generalize from these features to group life beyond the social location of the children we have studied. Few descriptive studies have addressed the attempts of these organizations to reach into poverty pockets, so much of our analysis will be based on speculation and the crumbs of data that are available.

Identity Structures

One of the remarkable parallels between fin de siècle American culture of the 19th and 20th centuries is in the set of worries adults have about children and in the rhetoric adults invoke to explain children's problems and to propose institutional solutions. The large number of immigrant children showing up in late 19th-century urban America—children largely unsocialized to American values and to middle-class style—became the occasion for "child-saving" reform movements in the public schools, in the playground movement (Cavallo, 1981), in the legal and penal systems (Platt, 1969), in labor practices (Zelizer, 1985), and elsewhere. Most relevant to the present discussion, adults in the 1880s and 1890s saw children's gangs as a significant threat both to the children's character and to the social order. Reformers who established the youth movements of the late 19th and early 20th centuries were quite explicit in their talk about creating organizations that would rival the boy's gang (Macleod, 1983). The reformers were relying on new Darwinian sciences, psychology and sociology, for guidance in this work. The Boy Scouts of America (founded in 1910), for instance, made its patrol composed of eight boys because those who studied the matter believed eight was the natural size of a boy's gang; the Boy Scout patrol was to be a wholesome version of the boy's gang. The psychology of G. Stanley Hall (Ross, 1972) pervades the rhetoric of the founders of these youth organizations, and from Hall's psychology the reformers drew the notion that preadolescent and adolescent boys were driven by strong instincts of loyalty and selflessness. For Hall and others, these instincts could be exploited in changing the boy's loyalties from the gang to more socially respectable groups.

Without drawing all the parallels, we note simply that this scenario strongly resembles the present. Hall's psychology is now outdated, seen as an interesting artifact of the intellectual and social history of the time (Ross, 1972), but this perspective should not prevent us from recognizing that we are seeing in gangs, in Little League teams, and in Boy Scout patrols the same behavior that Hall was seeing and fitting into his Darwinian mold. Put differently, we conclude from our own fieldwork that there is a strong need in American preadolescent and adolescent boys to belong to a group that provides them with a strong identity structure. We question if there is any biological, developmental necessity in this; our interactionist approach tends to minimize or dismiss those forces. Nevertheless, the anthropological perspective supports the near universality of a need for the group in adolescence.

In exploring this crucial feature of organizations for youth, we must excise our modernist language exalting the individual. Hall (Ross, 1972),

Puffer (1912), and others recognized that they were bucking a cultural tide when they spoke of the boy's need for establishing an identity through the group rather than apart from the group. Yet their belief in the centrality of the boy's group was unshakable. As Puffer put it: "The boy's reaction to his gang is neither more nor less reasonable than the reaction of a mother to her babe, the tribesman to his chief, or the lover to his sweetheart" (p. 7). Put this way, the remark seems sentimental claptrap, but there is some truth here, as is evident in the continuing presence of gangs, no matter the forms of social control arrayed against these groups. Gangs survive because they provide preadolescents and adolescents with a sense of place and of importance in a world that may seem out of their control. One of the first things that a group of boys does when they decide to "hang together" is to name themselves. They create a point of self-reference so that they can say, "I am an X." Often, along with this is the implied "other" reference: "I am an X and not a Y."

Youth organizations have learned the effectiveness of providing their members with *identity markers*. Merely providing youth with a place to recreate or an activity does not itself create the identity linkage between boy and group. Although it may be easier simply to provide a space for activity and then permit those interested to come and go at will (as in the settlement house or drop-in center model [Weber, 1972]), this may not produce the desired effect. The organization has not challenged and changed the youths' identities.

In contrast, successful organizations may establish uniforms as a crucial identity marker. The Boy Scout uniform is the most elaborate example of this strategy, and even in that case, troops and patrols within troops will find ways to alter the uniform so as to mark the unique identity of the boys' folk group within the organization (Mechling, 1987). We note as well the importance of the uniform to the members of the Jesse White Tumbling Team, based in a high-crime housing project of Chicago. The team labels itself a "supergang" and dresses its participants in red and white warm-up suits with team logos. These uniforms are meaningful to the boys, and the demand that boys wear the proper outfit is important not only to fostering discipline but to promoting the individual's identity (Irby & McLaughlin, 1990, p. 3).

As Fine (1988) has noted, the establishment of identity symbols is critical to tethering individuals to voluntary organizations. One reason for the remarkable success of Little League baseball is that participants belong to a team and wear uniforms that give public testimony to their membership. Players like to wear these uniforms for the same reasons that gang members show no compunction about wearing colors, despite the danger.

More complex group *rituals* also reinforce members' sense of belonging to the organization. Rituals usually include formal dramatic performances full of symbolism and magic (such as a Boy Scout troop's formal initiation ceremony), but equally important are what we might more properly call *routines*—brief, traditional, formulaic social exchanges or customs unique to the group. The troop that Mechling (1980a) studied, for example, is proud of the unique yells they perform at every campfire, and the organizational life at camp is full of small customs, such as the requirement that diners ask the cook (sometimes the youngest in the patrol) for permission to leave the table after eating. Several teams that Fine (1987) observed developed special cheers or styles of cheering that the boys felt differentiated them from their opponents.

In addition to such material and ritual identity markers, the successful youth organization provides program structures for the boy's expression of *loyalty*. In the Boy Scout troop studied by Mechling (1980a), the summer camp program provided the boys with opportunities to show loyalty to both their patrols (eight boys) and to the entire troop. After a day of particularly strenuous contests between patrols, for example, the troop used a campfire program to reintegrate the group toward a shared identity that superseded loyalty to patrols and to "best friends" in the patrols. Pre- and postgame meetings, with their distinctive rituals, serve the same purpose in Little League baseball, and, of course, most teams have some kind of collective outing at a key point in the season.

If G. Stanley Hall got things at least partly right, then adolescents have a strong drive to *serve others,* and successful youth organizations seem to find a way for the expression of this impulse. This point will shock those who think of adolescents as selfish, self-centered beings, but that may describe mainly privileged teenagers who have available to them no structured program for expressing their loyalty to the group through service to others. Mechling (1986b) discovered in the Boy Scout troop's game of capture the flag occasions for altruistic behavior, and the entire program of the troop is built around the principle that older boys teach younger boys the practical and moral lessons to be learned in the troop. Similarly, older baseball players instruct new players in the importance of team loyalty and may stress the importance of collective action in the game itself.

The expression of loyalty to the group through selfless rendering of service and even sacrifice for others amounts to a form of *moral education*. Successful youth organizations discover a program that permits youths to identify with each other and with the group while serving prosocial ends. The Boy Scouts, which models war and adventure (Mechling, 1984, 1986b), is an exemplary model of how activities enjoyed by boys can also provide moral instruction. The test for Scout leaders is to teach "morality" at the same time they permit the "wild" side of boys to flourish. This paradox is central to Scouting, but it is also at the heart of other successful organizations and programs. In Little League, the way that adult-sponsored sportsmanship is mediated through the players' interpretation of baseball ethics (learning to be "cool" and develop emotional self-control in supporting the team) exemplifies this peer-sponsored morality—set within the explicit moral teachings of adults (Fine, 1987, pp. 85–88).

A crucial element in a successful youth organization's identity is a set of needs clearly articulated as *goals* that, if they are effective, will appeal to the participants' motives as moral actors. Recreation and fun are not sufficient goals or motives for sustaining an effective youth organization. Americans feel a powerful need to *justify* their voluntary, leisure activities as morally and socially proper (Fine, 1983; Irwin, 1977; Mitchell, 1983; Stebbins, 1979). This may be a cultural inheritance from Calvinism, with an added dollop of American pragmatism. In any event, Americans seem to understand their voluntary, leisure lives best when they can articulate the important contribution those activities make toward a healthy, moral, social self.

Americans believe that leisure is not to be justified for its own sake (Peiper, 1963) but must be awarded the moral trappings of work. Much literature on leisure attempts to describe not just its particular delights but "the virtues that it breeds in men" (Bourjaily, 1963, p. 10). Consider, for example, a quotation from the Little League (1977) baseball book of rules and regulations that details the goals of the adult organizers:

> Little League baseball is a program of service to youth. It is geared to provide an outlet of healthful activity and training under good leadership in the atmosphere of wholesome community participation. The movement is dedicated to helping children become good and decent citizens. It strives to inspire them with a goal and to enrich their lives toward the day when they must take their places in the world. It establishes for them rudiments of teamwork and fair play. (p. 2)

The justifications are fully applicable to the leisure activities of at-risk youth, who no less than their wealthier comrades want meaning and purpose in their play. Gangs easily provide this real-world legitimation. Although gangs can provide significant amounts of enjoyment, they also are involved in enough goal-directed activity to satisfy any participant that what they are doing has lasting impact. Sports, although surely different from drug dealing, has this built-in goal direction. Any youth program designed for at-risk youth should take into account this "need to do." The aim is not simply to fill the "idle" time of these youths. From the folklorist's point of view, there is no such thing as idle time; standing around a street corner, "just talking," is an important activity accomplishing important ends. What is needed in an organization is not just "play" but meaningful play—play that serves a socially legitimate purpose and provides a basis for further growth and development.

Superego Models of Leadership

Our experiences in directly observing youth organizations for preadolescent and adolescent boys suggest that successful organizations have strong role models of moral guidance. If the Boy Scouts seems old-fashioned at times, it is because much of the organization's values and rhetoric are straight out of the 19th century, when the notion of "character" connoted moral content and a sense of duty to the community. But as we have shown, the rise of scientific psychology and the increasing secularization of children's organizations have made Americans somewhat uncomfortable with talk about moral training in schools and in voluntary organizations.

Several culture critics have commented on the "crisis of authority" in mid-century American society. We do not have the space here to examine the textures and variations of this observation, except to sketch some general ideas that provide a context for our point that successful organizations provide strong superego training.

The Depression's blows to fathers' traditional roles in the family and the large-scale absence of fathers during World War II set the stage for the more important postwar developments, resulting in a crisis in the superego training of American children, at least for the middle class. By Lasch's (1979) account, the shift from a production economy to a consumer economy, combined with the rise of the therapeutic model of the person, resulted in a pervasive narcissism devoid of moral content. Moreover, a result of the "feminine mystique" (Friedan, 1963) of the 1950s was the feminization of what little moral training middle-class children received. Fathers were largely absent from the home, and when they were home, they wanted to play the child's friend rather than the stern disciplinarian. The traditional mother's warning to mischievous children, "Just wait until your father gets home," increasingly lost its meaning in the 1950s and 1960s, as the middle-class fathers of the baby boomers strove to understand a new role that departed significantly from that played by their own fathers (Parke, 1981; Parke & Stearns, in press). These men were consumed by work, they rejected the harsh disciplinary role of their fathers, and they had never learned how to "father" young children. Some tried their best; others ignored the whole problem, making the children the domain of their wives. This was a generation in which fathers had an ambiguous relationship to the rest of the family. Much more so than their wives, they lacked role models whose behavior made sense in the context of the postwar era. At least their sons were able to model their behavior toward their children on the nurturing of their mothers! Fathers of the boomers lacked the tools of discipline, love, and even equal-status friendship, and their sons are now striving to redefine (yet again) what it means to be a husband and a father in the 1990s.

In the organizations we studied, the boys seemed to welcome *discipline* that was sure and just. Young people appear to have a more tolerant orientation to discipline than some adults expect. Although children may protest discipline, their protests are usually perfunctory or are really objections to "unfair" discipline. Consciously or not, children welcome discipline as a way of ordering their lives, and children are very orderly. Moreover, children welcome discipline as a clear signal of how significant adults want them to behave, and children want to please significant others. What children do not want are vague, inconsistent, and unjust signals about what is expected of them by adults.

Yet since 1945, we adults have come to question robust and severe discipline. There are complex historical, social, and ideological reasons for this change (Stearns & Stearns, 1986), and the effects have ranged from advice for parents to rules forbidding corporal punishment in the schools. Physical child abuse is intolerable in any case, but we wish to offer a brief in favor of rethinking discipline in youth organizations.

We have argued elsewhere (Fine & Mechling, 1991) that the elimination of options for informal discipline (for example, regulations against youth leaders' ability to physically punish their charges) changes the power structure such that children can be disciplined only if they choose to submit, an unlikely condition. The only option for adults in such a situation is to bring in an external system of control, such as the courts or state psychologists, transforming a situation that could be handled easily into one that is more complex and out of control. Just as unfortunately, concern about the possibilities of improper adult conduct and the legal liabilities of organizations for that improper conduct have limited the kinds of activities that adults can do with children. Such fears hit hardest the leisure groups in which a large number of active adult volunteers are not available, in which standards of discipline differ from the middle-class ideal, and in which the youth are not generally well behaved by the standards of adult volunteers.

Our ethnographic experiences with youth organizations support the view that children appear to prefer strict adult guidance. Fine found that preadolescents desired Little League coaches who were strict, who made them practice, who criticized when they played poorly, and who even made them run laps when they did not pay attention. This social control suggested to players that adults were taking the activity seriously and that the outcome mattered. Ironically, punishments indicated to these children that they were being treated like adults.

Mechling found a similar pattern in his fieldwork with a Boy Scout troop. The scoutmaster had a strong personality and was known to be capable of explosions of anger. In fact, some of the most enduring folklore in the troop came in the form of stories the boys told each other about past episodes of anger and punishment. These were "cautionary tales" through which the boys shared knowledge about what sorts of careless mistakes would lead to "getting your ass chewed." But the boys also knew that most of those episodes featured a careless act that somehow endangered the health or even the lives of other boys. Also important in the boys' acceptance of the scoutmaster's strict discipline was his Socratic approach to rules and punishments. Through a series of questions, the scoutmaster led the punished boy through a dialogue in which the boy himself saw the reasons for the rules. The result was that the boys in this troop were enormously fond of and loyal to this strict disciplinarian.

The most dramatic and probably the most effective form of social control in youth organizations is the threat of exclusion. This discipline is powerful when adults have the authority to make it stick (even if it is rarely necessary). The stronger the identity structures and the stronger the idioculture of the group, the more important is the group to the individual's sense of identity and belonging. Ostracism becomes a powerful threat, enough in some cases to impel individuals to give up powerful pleasures: drugs, alcohol, violence, or sexual intimacy. This makes a successful youth organization a powerful force for establishing communal virtue in communities that seem otherwise loaded with deviance. As Irby and McLaughlin (1990) commented on the Jesse White Tumbling Team:

> While . . . the tumblers are subject to top-down directives of authority, the majority of their personal behavior is guided through clear-cut registers of rules and sanctions that reinforce expected norms within the group. Rules maintaining exclusivity, reputation, and quality of work are strictly enforced. . . . Jesse is the sole authority of sanctions. As he tells them, "If you're . . . in trouble with society then you're in trouble with me, and I think you'd rather be in trouble with the police than with me if I catch you doing something that is in violation of our rules and regulations." (p. 3)

Of the approximately 950 youths who have participated in Jesse White's program over 30 years, only about 80 have been dismissed from the team for infraction of team rules or group norms, and only about 30 have ended up in real trouble, including poor academic performance and involvement with drugs or alcoholism. Considering the problems of the surrounding community, this is a powerful indicator of the positive effect of Jesse White's discipline.

In examining the literature of middle-class youth organizations, the absence of any discussion of the need for strict discipline is striking. These organizations appear to believe that there is no such thing as a bad kid—a child who cannot be reached through rational discourse—despite instances that suggest that there are at least badly behaved children. The willingness to believe that an organization should be open to everyone may decrease its effectiveness for everyone.

This discussion of leadership in a youth organization would be incomplete without addressing a potentially troubling dilemma, that of *charismatic leadership*. Can an organization create a successful identity through its program alone? The successful Little League teams and Boy Scout troops with which we are most familiar have single charismatic adult leaders whose personality and style become the center of meaning for the organization's identity. Certainly, the Jesse White Tumbling Team is defined in large part by the personality of Jesse White. Can these organizations survive the loss of their charismatic leader? We are not sure they can, and this may have important implications for the action component of our intellectualizing about youth programs. The evidence suggests that youth organizations without charismatic leadership are unlikely to succeed. This makes charismatic leadership an absolutely crucial resource. Unfortunately, it is a scarce resource.

A Robust Peer Culture

It is not enough that adults create an organization and program that provide strong identity structures for the young participant. Within a successful organization there grows an independent, *robust peer culture*. One of the paradoxes of organizational cultures is that the health of the organization depends equally on its official culture and its unofficial culture, which at times may be antagonistic to the official culture. The best-laid plans of adults go awry if the group never coalesces to create and sustain a small group culture, an *idioculture*.

Fine (1979, 1987) explains that an idioculture consists of a system of knowledge, beliefs, behaviors, and customs that is shared and referred to by members of an interacting group and that serves as the basis of further interaction. Through this culture, members recognize that they share experiences and that these experiences can be meaningfully referred to with the expectation that they will be understood by other members. This permits the group to become a social reality for participants.

The content of small-group cultures can take many forms, including nicknames, slang, customs, jokes, songs, gestures, narratives, ceremonies, and material artifacts (Bronner, 1988). What is critical in these forms is their symbolic meaning for the group. A robust idioculture in a small group signals for the folklorist the existence of intense, healthy bonds between members. Small groups that fail to develop robust idiocultures have usually failed to develop meaningful relationships.

Knowledge and acceptance of a group's idioculture distinguish members of a group from outsiders. Cultural traditions serve functions not only in their own terms, but also to exclude outsiders. As social psychologist Robert Freed Bales (1970) writes: "Most small groups develop a subculture that is protective for their members, and is allergic, in some respects, to the culture as a whole. . . . [The members] draw a boundary around themselves and resist intrusion" (pp. 152–154). The culture becomes valued in its ability to differentiate.

Studies of gangs (Fine, 1982; Thrasher, 1927) emphasize the elaboration of information found within organizations. A group that merely provides a staging area for an ever-changing array of individuals to engage in pleasant activity is rarely as effective as a stable team that can develop as a community committed to a project or season outcome. Rituals and symbols are critical in keeping the group together. The group emerges not merely to accomplish instrumental means but to accomplish the more humanly important expressive work of sharing, creating, shaping, and talking.

One of the most important pieces of personal and social business accomplished by the idioculture of a youth group is the exploration of the meaning of *friendship*. Children's friendships are a complex matter (Asher & Gottman, 1981). Fine (1987) applied the sociological method of sociograms to chart the patterns of friendship within the Little League teams he studied, and Savin-Williams (1987) employed the same approach in his study of dominance behavior in two summer camps. Fine and Mechling both have observed how preadolescent and adolescent boys use the organization as a sort of laboratory for making and testing friendships. For adolescents in particular, same-sex friendships pose significant challenges, not least of which is the task of becoming close without worrying about homosexuality. In male groups, a good deal of the joking and ritual insulting publicly scorns homosexuality and anything that might signal the "feminine" side of a boy's personality. This male behavior helps confirm for the boys that their feelings of closeness are decidedly not homosexual.

Constructing and sustaining female friendship in childhood and adolescence may be an even more difficult project. If girls' friendships really tend to be as dyadic as some research suggests, then girls in large youth organizations may be even less prepared than boys to build meaningful friendships with several others. The paucity of studies of children's friendships in natural settings makes it difficult to offer these generalizations with much confidence, and further research is necessary. We raise the question here, however, because we know how important friendships are in the groups we studied and because we consider it an open question whether youth organizations will be more successful if they are single sex or coeducational.

It is within the safety and acceptance of a group's idioculture that its members learn how to share and to *play*. Play performs a crucial role in the developmental and social lives of young people. Like friendship, play is far too complex a matter for us to examine here. We want simply to note that a group with a strong idioculture usually is the site of extensive play. Adult leaders sometimes seek play only on official terrain, and that expectation may be a mistake. Play is often antithetical and doubting, mocking and disrespectful—it is "dirty" (Fine, 1988). Even this play can be a sign of a healthy and robust idioculture and should not be seen as destructive.

The development of an idioculture in a group cannot be taken for granted. Those who organize a youth group, whether they be the adolescents themselves or adults, can take initial steps to create a meaningful idioculture. Thus, creating a name for the group is important not only for its ability to cement identity but also for its establishment of meaningful group ties. The "invention of tradition" is common in successful groups. Creating such tradition is a good strategy as long as members are involved and feel free to continue the process of invention. This creation should not be defined as something that is imposed from the outside. As one of Mechling's Boy Scout informants explained to him, "We have lots of C&Ts [customs and traditions] in our troop, but our most important C&T is always to invent new C&Ts!" In a certain sense, there is no *one* Boy Scout program or Little League program, but there are only *programs* that emerge in particular troops and teams, each with a unique collection of children and adult leaders.

Whereas adult leaders have a great deal of control over the design and operation of the *identity structures* discussed earlier as the first feature of a successful youth organization, adults will find that they have less control over the creation and sustenance of the idioculture of the group. This is as it should be. Idiocultures provide young people (especially adolescents) with important, symbolic means of *resistance* against the dominance of the adult leaders' definitions of the organization; along with a supportive culture, an organizational "counterculture" may develop (Martin & Siehl, 1983). Young people invent and share some elements of the idioculture as ways of taking power in an organization clearly dominated by adult power. The paradox of group life is that these symbolic traditions of resistance may strengthen the organization, giving the young people the sense that they are equal participants in and, accordingly, have an equal stake in the culture of the group. No doubt, adult leaders will be uncomfortable with elements of the idioculture invented or appropriated by young clients. This is true in organizations with a European American, middle-class clientele, and it is all the more true for organizations designed by middle-class leaders for youth who are at risk. Adults should tolerate these expressions of idioculture as much as possible, recalling that youth groups are competing against more deviant gangs with their rich lore and traditions.

How Alike Are Children?

From one perspective, all children—indeed, all humans—are alike. But from an equally reasonable perspective, each child is unique. Finding between these two extremes a way to generalize about children so as to make wise public policy is a considerable challenge, but generalize we must. Neighborhood-based, voluntary organizations for children necessarily fashion their programs for some general population, even if an important element of those programs is to try to accommodate the needs of the individual child. What is the appropriate level for making such generalizations, taking into account age, gender, ethnicity, race, social class, physical or mental disability, and even sexual orientation?

The symbolic demography of the parents of the children of the 1990s complicates this question. One dimension of the European American, middle-class world view from the 1950s and 1960s is that the poor and people of color are different from the rest of us, that the poor do not have normal family relations, and that juvenile delinquency is a sickness of the "culture of poverty." Media accounts of crimes by children in the late 1980s and 1990s helped confirm this view of a difference; all the more shocked were parents when "nice," European American, middle-class kids committed acts of violence usually associated with "others."

At the same time, the European American middle class believes that children, especially younger children, are more alike than different. Visual appeals from UNICEF or from various international "save the children" groups play on our sense that a child is a child, innocent until corrupted. Adults who work with voluntary youth organizations often work from the same assumptions and faith that kids are fundamentally alike and that kids can make anything of their lives if they can be rescued from the cultures of poverty, neglect, and abuse. Money, materials, concern, and care *should* be sufficient. Beneath this confidence lies a strongly held pragmatic belief that the wealthy and the poor have the same goals, the same values, and the same aspirations.

This belief is simultaneously true and false; understanding its truth and falsity is critical to understanding how neighborhood-based, voluntary organizations can be most effective in dealing with children defined as being at risk.

In reflecting on our experiences studying organizations and programs designed to serve preadolescent and adolescent males, we believe we see some general dynamics of children's cultures that we expect would be true in groups beyond the European American, middle-class male populations. This similarity derives from several grounds. First, our reading of folklorists' studies of children, especially children of color (Brady, 1984; Goodwin, 1990; McDowell, 1979), suggests that the dynamics of the folk cultures of children's groups seem rather constant across diverse ethnic groups. Ellis (1981, 1982), for example, observed in his fieldwork at Hiram House Camp, a summer camp serving disadvantaged African American children from Cleveland, folk cultural dynamics remarkably similar to those observed by Mechling at the European American, middle-class Boy Scout camp. (See also Heath [1991] and Mahiri [1991] for similar findings from a European American, middle-class Little League team and an African American work-ing-class basketball team.) In part, we are observing in children's group cultures versions of any culture's dynamics. Although each group has its own dynamics and its own distinct idioculture, some cultural similarities tran-scend groups.

Second, we believe that some of these dynamics of children's folk cul-tures are the product of developmental processes. All children face similar "developmental imperatives." Our social constructionist perspective does not deny that biological, developmental processes can be real conditions con-fronting both the individual child and the societal definitions and structures that adults have created. Hormones have their own logic, as anyone who works closely with adolescents knows. Each child—at each age period—has certain challenges to overcome. Whether or not one argues for a firm stage theory, such as that propounded by Erikson (1963), there are physiological, psychological, and social issues at each age. There seems consensus that the broad outlines of this development transcend group boundaries.

Third, we should not underestimate the powerful influence of school-ing, including Head Start programs, in socializing children to conform to middle-class norms (see chapters 7 and 8). Schools are the sites both of suc-cessful socialization and of resistance (Giroux, 1983), but even the resis-tance seems to fall into predictable cultural patterns that transcend race and class, although perhaps not gender. To the extent that schools may bring together children from different cultural backgrounds, teachers and students alike struggle to communicate at the borders of custom and language (Heath, 1983). In some cases, the children create a creole culture of the classroom and of the recess yard. In others, the confrontation of differences resegregates the children, even in the face of remarkable similarities in the dynamics of those segregated group cultures.

Fourth, children are shaped in the same mass or popular culture "fish-bowl." Although specialized media appeal to local segments of the youth market, in general, children are exposed to the same mass media and often share this exposure with adults (Postman, 1985). Children all bathe in "the American dream," as mediated through cultural institutions. We do not suggest that no racial, ethnic, class, or gender differences exist in media preferences, but there are considerable similarities, with television providing the base of this equality. The media provide a cultural pressure toward sameness.

Finally, other interpersonal channels (Fine, 1987), such as shared group membership or acquaintanceship ties, can also smooth out cultural differences as youth cultures spread. Children move from one neighborhood to another, from one school to another, and from one state to another, carrying with them jokes, folk beliefs, customs, and other elements of children's cultures. The children's folklorist knows that riddles and jokes, for example, transcend time and place, obeying broader cultural dynamics (Bronner, 1988; Fine, 1980; Mechling, 1986a).

None of these sources of similarity in children can eliminate the reality of group differences. Class differences do provide different access to culture, and resources do shape behavioral preferences. The lack of resources provides a sharp brake on the possibilities of some behavior and emphasizes others. Different expectations and channels for success (Sullivan, 1989) alter attitudes and behaviors. If we assume that all children are rational in maximizing their satisfactions as they understand them, then it follows that children in radically different circumstances will not have the same models of behavior or means of achieving their goals, even if we assume that their ideal goals are similar. Cultural traditions learned from parents and other adults in the community will have effects, and, as we noted, there are varying patterns of media usage.

The reality is that children are the same and different. This realization is challenging to discuss and to put into effect because discourse on group similarity and difference is politically charged. Few wish to be labeled racist, elitist, or sexist, even when they believe that treating groups differently may truly be in the best interests of the children. Too often, we pull our punches to protect our reputations, possibly at the expense of improved public policy for children. As the causes of group differences are unclear and connected to loaded ideologies and controversial public policies, such discourse will always be contentious. The best we can hope for is a sincere, well-meaning, and respectful debate.

Some Modest Recommendations

Our list of the essential characteristics of successful neighborhood-based, voluntary organizations for youth, along with our belief that the dynamics of children's cultures are remarkably similar, leads us to recommend the Boy Scouts and Little League as instructive models for creating programs for youth at risk. This means that the organization must provide a strong *identity structure* tying the individual young person to the group, that the older clients and the adult leaders must provide strong and just *superego models* who understand as one of their tasks the moral education of their youthful charges, and that the adult leaders should understand that a *robust peer culture* is usually a sign of health of an organization, not a sign that the children are getting out of control. Adults must tolerate the existence of peer culture and must understand that occasionally the peer culture will be antagonistic toward adult values and norms of behavior.

Of course, a youth organization can have all of these elements we see as characterizing a successful organization and still fail for lack of resources. Fine (1989) has argued that leisure activities need to be analyzed in terms of their ability to mobilize resources, what he has termed "provisioning theory." Successful activities will be those that are able to obtain and use sufficient resources for the satisfaction of their participants: material resources, resources of time and space, and primarily symbolic resources.

When gathering resources from within one's community, middle-class communities have an obvious advantage. In terms of the material side of resources, however, the divide may not be quite as wide as it first appears. Some youth organizations affiliated with the state (e.g., 4-H), with religious denominations, or with national organizations (e.g., Boy Scouts, Little League, or Boys and Girls Clubs) may benefit from the organizations' ability to transfer resources from one branch to another. Indeed, many of these organizations have a commitment to do precisely this as a means of meeting what they see as their mission. In some sense, the provisioning of resources may be the easiest challenge for those who wish to bring programs to the underprivileged, because there are material resources within the system. Obviously, when youth organizations are available to all rather than just to a handful of experimental, model programs, this may alter the financial picture. But for now, these opportunities are possible (Abreu, 1987; Bennett, 1980; Fairfax, Wright, & Maupin, 1988; Willis-Kistler, 1988).

Camp Fire, for instance, made a serious and sustained effort in the late 1980s to serve the needs of those they label "high-risk youth." Although the national office did not provide extensive resources to this project, they did provide suggestions for local Camp Fire councils. In attempting to develop programs for high-risk youth, they emphasized that local groups must have a commitment to provide resources (Camp Fire, 1990, p. 10). They noted, not coincidentally, that often such programs had a strong likelihood of receiving external funding—certainly more than would be true for programs that served youth not defined as social problems. Thus, although resources need to be gathered for these programs to be operated successfully, because those for whom they are provided lack discretionary resources for leisure, these resources are available under certain circumstances.

Funding and other material resources, however, are only one segment of the needs of such organizations. Personnel count for something. The program must be staffed by individuals who have the ability to successfully motivate high-risk youth. This frequently poses a significant barrier for the sponsoring organization, because the standard ways in which an organization measures a resume may not apply. These organizations have very talented individuals, but often they are not suitable for the task. Camp Fire (1990) suggests a need for individuals with multiple, cross-cutting talents: an ability to identify with the audience of the program, an ability to work within the system and within the structure of the agency, an ability to handle conflict, and the ability to convey a "professional" image, all of which amount to a person comfortable in several cultures (p. 15). To find all of these skills in the same person is rare. The text blandly notes that such a person "probably will not be found among the persons currently associated with Camp Fire" (p. 15). Just as we take into account the diversity and limits of the children and concentrate on their real strengths, we must do the same for their guardians, bracketing our desire to uncover perfect adult specimens.

In our ruminations on the character of successful youth organizations, we are struck by the absence of *religion* and of religious organizations in much of the public discourse about programs for youth at risk. This secular bias is completely understandable, given the symbolic demography of the baby-boomer generation, but the bias may be leading parents and youth workers of the 1990s to neglect a sort of organization that already understands the importance of group identity, moral education, and constructive uses of peer culture. Returning to his earlier work on "children of crisis," Robert Coles (1986, 1990) was struck by the importance of religion as a source of moral guidance and courage in children. The European American, middle-class baby boomers tended to mistrust organized religion from the 1960s through the 1980s, but it was significant that many of those boomers returned to religious congregations to introduce their children to the moral education of those congregations. Moreover, some of the most successful congregations have been those that have built strong youth programs. Public policy can and should recognize the important role of religious congregations in creating neighborhood-based, voluntary organizations for young people.

We have argued that successful organizations for youth at risk need to take into account several key features that we found in successful organizations for European American, middle-class, preadolescent and adolescent males. Youth organizations with these qualities will function effectively as "mediating structures"—as midrange institutions with the strengths of a family and the strengths of a public institution (Berger & Neuhaus, 1977; Mechling, 1979, 1989).

All our philosophical and social scientific sophistication leads us to understand how "child saving" is an ideological act, explicable with reference to historical and social forces. Child saving movements arise at particular times and among people in particular social locations. In short, our social constructionist perspective enables us to fully deconstruct and make relevant the American child-saving movements of the 1980s and 1990s, just as we have the child-saving movements of the 1890s and 1890s.

Still, we are parents and citizens, and when all the relativizing work is done, we must ask ourselves: What can we do for the children? We shall never see children clearly; we always see the child we construct. Our lens is covered with nostalgic, fearful, and hopeful hazes. But that should not prevent us from taking active steps to build organizations meant to serve children as best we can know them, limiting European American, middle-class, romantic biases. We are inspired by the moral courage of William James, who understood that we always act with incomplete knowledge. We owe the children this much: to remain open to the fact that demographics, economics, cultures, and gender relations change. Organizations must do the same—never fixing in their structures, philosophies, or perceptions of children a final product and never assuming that child saving rests in any narrow vision of institution or program.

References

Abreu, J. A. (1987, December). Leisure programming for Hispanics. *Parks and Recreation,* pp. 52–54, 75.

Asher, S. R. & Gottman, J. M. (Eds.). (1981). *The development of children's friendships.* Cambridge, England: Cambridge University Press.

Bales, R. F. (1970). *Personality and interpersonal behavior.* New York: Holt, Rinehart and Winston.

Bennett, J. T. (1980, June). The Youth Council approach: An alternative to the street. *Parks and Recreation,* pp. 34–36.

Berger, P. L., & Neuhaus, R. J. (1977). *To empower people: The role of mediating structures in public policy.* Washington, DC: American Enterprise Institute for Public Policy Research.

Best, J. (1990). *Threatened children: Rhetoric and concern about child-victims.* Chicago: University of Chicago Press.

Bourjailey, V. (1963). *The unnatural enemy.* New York: Dial.

Brady, M. K. (1984). *"Some kind of power": Navajo children's Skinwalker narratives.* Salt Lake City: University of Utah Press.

Bronner, S. J. (1988). *American children's folklore.* Little Rock, AR: August House.

Camp Fire (1990). *Programming for high-risk youth: A guide for Camp Fire councils.* Kansas City, MO: Camp Fire.

Cavallo, D. (1981). *Muscles and morals: Organized playgrounds and urban reform, 1880–1920.* Philadelphia: University of Pennsylvania Press.

Coles, R. (1986). *The moral life of children.* Boston: Houghton Mifflin Company.

Coles, R. (1990). *The spiritual life of children.* Boston: Houghton Mifflin Company.

Cosaro, W. A., & Eder, D. (1990). Children's peer cultures. *Annual Review of Sociology, 16,* 197–220.

Dornbusch, S. M. (1989). The sociology of adolescence. *Annual Review of Sociology, 15,* 233–359.

Ehrenreich, B. (1989). *Fear of falling: The inner life of the middle class.* New York: Pantheon.

Ellis, B. (1981). The camp mock-ordeal: Theatre as life. *Journal of American Folklore, 94,* 486–505.

Ellis, B. (1982). "Ralph and Rudy": The audience's role in recreating camp legend. *Western Folklore, 41,* 169–191.

Erikson, E. (1963). *Childhood and society.* New York: Norton.

Fairfax, J. L., Wright, L. A., & Maupin, M. L. (1988, December). At-risk youth: Special needs. *Parks and Recreation,* pp. 40–43.

Fine, G. A. (1979). Small groups and culture creation: The idioculture of Little League Baseball teams. *American Sociological Review, 44,* 733–745.

Fine, G. A. (1980). Children and their culture: Exploring Newell's paradox. *Western Folklore, 39,* 170–183.

Fine, G. A. (1982). The Manson family: The folklore traditions of a small group. *Journal of the Folklore Institute, 19,* 47–60.

Fine, G. A. (1983). *Shared fantasy.* Chicago: University of Chicago Press.

Fine, G. A. (1987). *With the boys: Little League baseball and preadolescent culture.* Chicago: University of Chicago Press.

Fine, G. A. (1988). Good children and dirty play. *Play and Culture, 1,* 43–56.

Fine, G. A. (1989). Mobilizing fun: Provisioning resources in leisure worlds. *Sport Sociology Journal, 6,* 319–334.

Fine, G. A., & Mechling, J. (1991). Minor difficulties: Changing children in the late twentieth century. In A. Wolfe (Ed.), *America at century's end* (pp. 58–78). Berkeley, CA: University of California Press.

Friedan, B. (1963). *The feminine mystique.* New York: Dell.

Gilbert, J. (1986). *A cycle of outrage: America's reaction to the juvenile delinquent in the 1950s.* New York: Oxford University Press.

Giroux, H. A. (1983). *Theory and resistance in education: A pedagogy for the opposition.* South Hadley, MA: Bergin and Garvey Publishers.

Goffman, E. (1961). *Encounters.* Indianapolis, IN: Bobbs-Merrill.

Goodwin, M. H. (1990). *He-said-she-said: Talk as social organization among black children.* Bloomington, IN: Indiana University Press.

Heath, S. B. (1983). *Ways with words: Language, life, and work in communities and classrooms.* Cambridge, England: Cambridge University Press.

Heath, S. B. (1991). It's about winning! The language of knowledge in baseball. In L. B., Resnick, J. M. Levine, & S. D. Teasley (Eds.), *Perspectives on socially shared cognition* (pp. 101–124). Washgton, D.C.: American Psychological Association.

Horowitz, R. (1983). *Honor and the American dream.* New Brunswick, NJ: Rutgers University Press.

Irby, M. A., & McLaughlin, M. W. (1990). When is a gang not a gang? When it's a tumbling team. *Future Choices, 2,* 31–39.

Irwin, J. (1977). *Scenes.* Beverly Hills, CA: Sage.

James, W. (1896/1984). The will to believe. In B. W. Wilshire (Ed.), *William James, the essential writings* (pp. 309–325). Albany: State University of New York Press.

Jankowski, M. S. (1991). *Islands in the street*. Berkeley, CA: University of California Press.

Kessen, W. (1979). The American child and other cultural inventions. *American Psychologist, 34*, 815–820.

Kraus, R. (1987, December). Serving ethnic minorities: A submerged issue? *Parks and Recreation*, pp. 46–50.

Lasch, C. (1979). *The culture of narcissism*. New York: Norton.

Macleod, D. I. (1983). *Building character in the American boy: The Boy Scouts, YMCA, and their forerunners, 1870–1920*. Madison, WI: University of Wisconsin Press.

Mahiri, J. (1991). Discourse in sports: Language and literacy features of preadolescent African American males in a youth basketball program. *Journal of Negro Education. 60*, 305–313.

Martin, J., & Siehl, K. (1983). Organizational culture and counter culture. *Organizational Dynamics, 12*, 52–64.

McDowell, J. H. (1979). *Children's riddling*. Bloomington, IN: Indiana University Press.

Mechling, J. (1979). Myths and mediation: Peter Berger's and Richard John Neuhaus' theodicy for modern America. *Soundings, 62*, 338–368.

Mechling, J. (1980a). The magic of the Boy Scout campfire. *Journal of American Folklore, 93*, 35–56.

Mechling, J. (1980b). "Playing Indian" and the search for authenticity in modern white America. In J. Salzman (Ed.), *Prospects* (pp. 17–33). New York: Burt Franklin.

Mechling, J. (1981). Male gender display at a Boy Scout camp. In R. T. Sieber & A. J. Gordon (Eds.), *Children and their organizations: Investigations in American culture* (pp. 138–160). Boston: G. K. Hall.

Mechling, J. (1984). Patois and paradox in a Boy Scout treasure hunt. *Journal of American Folklore, 97*, 24–42.

Mechling, J. (1986a). Children's folklore. In E. Oring (Ed.), *Folk groups and folklore genres* (pp. 91–120). Logan, UT: Utah State University Press.

Mechling, J. (1986b). Male border wars as metaphor in capture the flag. In K. Blanchard (Ed.), *The many faces of play* (pp. 218–231). Champaign-Urbana, IL: Human Kinetics Press.

Mechling, J. (1987). Dress right, dress: The Boy Scout uniform as a folk costume. *Semiotica, 64*, 319–333.

Mechling, J. (1989). Mediating structures and the significance of university folk. In E. Oring (Ed.), *Folk groups and folklore genres: A reader* (pp. 339–349). Logan, UT: Utah State University Press.

Miller, D. R., & Swanson, G. (1958). *The changing American parent: A study in the Detroit area*. New York: John Wiley & Sons.

Mitchell, R. (1983). *Mountain experience*. Chicago: University of Chicago Press.

Olmstead, A. D. (1988). Morally controversial leisure: The social world of gun collectors. *Symbolic Interaction, 11*, 277–287.

Padilla, F. M. (1992). *The gang as an American enterprise*. New Brunswick, NJ: Rutgers University Press.

Parke, R. D. (1981). *Fathers*. Cambridge, MA: Harvard University Press.

Parke, R. D., & Stearns, P. (in press). Fatherhood: An interdisciplinary examination of historical trends. In G. H. Elder, Jr., J. Modell, & R. D. Parke (Eds.), *Children in time and place: The intersection of developmental and historical perspectives*. New York: Cambridge University Press.

Peiper, J. (1963). *Leisure: The basis of culture*. New York: Random House.

Platt, A. M. (1969). *The child savers: The invention of delinquency*. Chicago: University of Chicago Press.

Postman, N. (1985). *Amusing ourselves to death: Public discourse in the age of show business*. New York: Penguin.

Puffer, J. A. (1912). *The boy and his gang*. Boston: Houghton-Mifflin.

Reisman, D. (195). *The lonely crowd*. New Haven: Yale University Press.

Ross, D. (1972). *G. Stanley Hall: The psychologist as prophet*. Chicago: University of Chicago Press.

Savin-Williams, R. C. (1987). *Adolescence: An ethnological perspective*. New York: Springer-Verlag.

Stearns, C. Z., & Stearns, P. N. (1986). *Anger: The struggle for emotional control in America's history*. Chicago: University of Chicago Press.

Stebbins, R. (1979). *Amateurs*. Beverly Hills, CA: Sage.

Sullivan, M. L. (1989). *Youth crime and work in the university*. Ithaca, NY: Cornell University Press.

Susman, W. I. (1984). *Culture as history: The transformation of American society in the twentieth century*. New York: Pantheon Books.

Susman, W. I., & Griffin, E. (1989). Did success spoil the United States? Dual representations in postwar America. In L. May (Ed.), *Recasting America: Culture and politics in the age of the Cold War* (pp. 19–37). Chicago: University of Chicago Press.

Sutton-Smith, B. (1979). The play of girls. In C. B. Kopp & M. Kirkpatrick (Eds.), *Becoming female: Perspectives on development* (pp. 229–257). New York: Plenum.

Sutton-Smith, B., & Kelly-Byrne, D. (1984). The idealization of play. In P. K. Smith (Ed.), *Play in animals and humans* (pp. 305–321). New York: Blackwell.

Thrasher, F. M. (1927). *The gang: A study of 1,313 gangs in Chicago*. Chicago: University of Chicago Press.

Weber, W. J. (1972, September). The case for drop-in centers. *Parks and Recreation*, pp. 86–87.

Whyte, N. (1956). *The organization man*. New York: Simon & Shuster.

Willis-Kistler, P. (1988, November). Fighting gangs with recreation. *Parks and Recreation*, pp. 44–49.

Wolfenstein, M. (1955). Some variants in moral training of children. In M. Mead & M. Wolfenstein (Eds.), *Childhood in contemporary cultures*. Chicago: University of Chicago Press.

Zelizer, V. (1985). *Pricing the priceless child*. New York: Basic Books.

6

Collaborate or Go It Alone? Tough Decisions for Youth Policy

Juliet Langman
Milbrey W. McLaughlin

*Organizations, as well as communities and individuals, take on identities
linked in various ways to ethnicity and gender, and they have their stories
to tell of how and why they have come to be as they are. Any collaboration
of personnel, services, and resources threatens an organization's sense of
self and raises defenses against adaptation to the exigencies of limited
resources and shifting demographics. Primary consideration can shift
away from youth populations when youth organizations value their own
identity over beneficial collaborative efforts; on the other hand, top-down
mandates for collaboration often omit consideration of both gender needs
in general and the cultural needs of particular ethnic groups. This nuts-
and-bolts chapter considers several cases of collaboration—some successful,
some failed, and others moderately successful—in three major metropolitan areas. The authors elaborate on the factors that enabled organizations
to cut through barriers of ethnicity and gender, often to reshape and redirect the very identity of the youth organizations so that they might create
environments in which youth populations could find new opportunities for
self-definition and self-expression.*

> Not everything that is more difficult is more meritorious.
>
> *Saint Thomas Aquinas*

Among youth organizations and those that fund them, pressure grows to forge collaborative relationships. At a time when demands for youth activities or services far outstrip availability and when the fiscal and human resources necessary to support youth organizations are in short supply, collaboration becomes politically correct and practically compelling. It makes sense.

By the early 1990s, the appeal of collaboration grew particularly salient in agencies of inner-city communities because these agencies had for the previous decade steadily been losing public financial support while facing an ever-larger, younger population in need of support. Moreover, funding organizations traditionally the major source of funding for all social service agencies seized on collaboration as a way to combat their own financial instability, as well as to accommodate the ever-increasing number of community-based agencies that looked to them as their sole support.

Images of ethnicity and gender, politically unpredictable and ambiguous in the late 1980s and early 1990s, often stood in the way of collaboration, however. Roadblocks developed from misperceptions on the part of both those making youth policies and those leading youth organizations; they learned that collaborative efforts often polarized groups into positions more isolationist or separatist than before such efforts began. Those who made youth policies often pushed for collaboration, with the unspoken but frequently displayed attitude that "all those people" ought to learn to work together. Individual civic and business leaders justified calls for collaboration across ethnic and gender boundaries through reminders of the shortage of available funds, often evoking the national metaphor of the "melting pot" or building on the national political agenda of integration and multiculturalism.

Individual differences among youth organizations faded in the minds of policymakers, who now equated all organizations in the simplistic view that their goals were to solve the problems of urban youth. Thus, when individual organizations indicated reasons why collaboration between their unit and another with a very different ethos, set of activities, or operational style might not work, policymakers and funders viewed these groups as uncooperative and excessively enveloped in their own sense of mission. Youth organizations with considerable support from religious groups or with an ethos that promoted group cooperation, respect for community, and codes related to "proper" language and dress met particular resistance from funders. Organizations committed to building a sense of family and downplaying competition faced charges of being "out of touch" when they resisted suggestions that they collaborate with organizations dedicated to the promotion of individual competition, winning, or the building of athletic prowess. Single-sex youth centers found it difficult to convince policy boards that collaboration with coeducational groups or institutions composed of youths of the opposite sex would take special planning and could call for an entirely new set of activities and events.

Youth centers in areas historically linked to a particular ethnic group but currently serving a highly diverse population often remained ethnically labeled by policymakers and funders that had not kept pace with changing demographics in particular urban areas. Often, such centers had worked hard to arrange times when their facilities could be used by youths of different ethnic groups so as to avoid conflicts from local gang rivalries that washed over into youth organizations. Therefore, when collaborative proposals brought in yet other groups or tipped the balance of power among the groups, organizations faced the harsh reality that cooperation could actually endanger the lives of young people. Similarly, when one center had not felt the spillover of community rivalries while another organization across town had, bringing the two groups of youths together could actually spread violent behaviors and increase tensions. Within inner cities with powerful gangs, sensitive youth leaders had constantly to consider even the slightest details so as not to provoke attacks by gangs.

The Case for Collaboration

When ethnic, gender, and community loyalties, as well as youth organizations' differing approaches, clash in collaborative efforts, one must ask why policymakers promote collaboration. The theoretical benefits of collaboration are multiple. Collective action can respond to problems beyond the scope of any single agency. Collaboration can produce economies through pooled resources, shared specialization, and integrated activities. Collaborative action can reduce the disorder and inefficiency that sometimes result when agencies act in independent and often conflicting ways. Collaboration among agencies can enhance the legitimacy of one or more partner organizations. In the best of all possible worlds, collaboration allows for agencies and organizations to combine their resources—financial, human, and material—to provide youth with a bigger and better set of program options and possibilities.

Given the projected benefits and ideological appeal of collaboration, it was not surprising in the early 1990s that many funders acted to "strongly encourage" or require collaboration as a condition of funding. Apple Community Grants, for example, gave preference to proposals submitted by "networks" of organizations. Traditional funders of neighborhood-based organizations, most notably the United Way, encouraged if not insisted on collaboration. Increasing numbers of private foundations concerned about youth and community-based organizations also mandated collaboration as a way to reduce the number of contact points in a community and to provide evidence that broad community support existed for a proposed initiative.

The Case for Localized Options

Amid this enthusiasm for collaboration, the costs of collaborative relationships and the differential value of collaboration dependent on context remain relatively unexamined. By the late 1980s, within the youth policy community, the assumptions were that collaboration is a good thing and that more collaboration is better. But is collaboration necessarily the best course for organizations to take, and are collaborative arrangements always in the best interests of youth? As the following case examples show, successful collaborations are exceedingly difficult to accomplish, and the costs of collaboration may outweigh intended and expected benefits. To begin to answer this question, we must look at definitions of collaboration. To think of collaboration in terms of a working together of any set of groups, organizations, and individuals with the goal of improving service to youth is too simplistic. There are differences in both the nature of collaborative *activity* and the *structural relationship* between partners. These two aspects of collaboration, moreover, are always played out in a local context that uniquely defines the collaboration for partners, recipients, and the larger youth organization community.

In our field sites—River City, Lakeside, and Big Valley—as elsewhere, four general categories describe the nature of collaborative activities: coordination of services, sharing of services or resources, joint planning, and joint action.[1] Collaboration may involve one or more of these forms.[2] For example, coordination of services may involve joint planning and joint action or it may mean little more than "parallel play," in which recreational services and social services, for example, are scheduled so as not to conflict with each other in a particular community. Sharing of services or resources may involve only making facilities available to other organizations or individuals or may require extensive planning for integrated services. Each form of collaborative activity presents its own advantages as well as its own difficulties. Each also has its own limits and potential costs.

In major metropolitan areas in the 1990s, a number of structural relationships commonly exist that define collaborating partners.[3] The minicases
that follow describe a number of successful and unsuccessful collaborations
that involve three different types of collaborating partners: collaborations
that involve two equal partners with traditions of youth service; collaborations that pair youth service organizations with expert organizations in particular areas, such as education; and collaborations that bring together large
numbers of organizations into a type of umbrella organization. In each case,
ethnicity, gender, race, and community affiliations play key roles in determining the nature and the outcome of collaboration.

Equal Partners: Two Local Chapters of Two National Organizations

To help increase use of a Boys and Girls Club facility and to allow Girl
Scouts to participate in activities not available to them within the confines
of once-a-week Girl Scouts meetings, the special projects director of the Girl
Scouts of the River City regional area and the director of a local River City
Boys and Girls Club forged a collaboration. The Boys and Girls Club gave
each registered Girl Scout a Boys and Girls Club membership. The Girl
Scouts provided transportation for the girls to the Boys and Girls Club once
every 2 weeks. At the Boys and Girls Club, the girls could swim and use
computers. As a result of this programmed introduction to the Boys and
Girls Club, a number of girls and their families began to use the Boys and
Girls Club on their own, thus increasing the range of recreational activities
open to them. This collaboration further allowed residents of the public
housing community in which the Girl Scout troop was located to see that
the Boys and Girls Club had "good things to offer" and began to counter the
accepted belief among public housing community residents that the Boys
and Girls Club was a "white" institution and that they were not welcome
there because they were African American and poor. (This had, in fact,
been a valid perception in the past, and one that the new leadership of the
Boys and Girls Club was trying to change.) This affiliation similarly bene-
fited the Girl Scouts, an organization actively trying to involve African American girls living in a River City public housing community and working hard
to counteract views of Girl Scouts as a white, middle-class organization.
This successful collaboration expanded participants' views both of effective
community resources and of organizational identification for Boys and Girls
Clubs and for Girl Scouts. According to the Girl Scout director, "[This collaboration with the Boys and Girls Club] was a very positive step in our
efforts to integrate the girls into the neighborhood structure and to change
the myth that Girl Scouts is for the white, middle-class girl." Collaboration
with the Girl Scouts aided the political agenda of the River City Boys and

Girls Club executive director, who had been pushing hard for equal services and attention to girls: "The Archie Bunker types who sat on the board of the Boys Club didn't think that services for girls were important." Collaboration with the Girl Scouts provided good evidence to the contrary.

Not all collaborations between local affiliates of national organizations have been so successful. In each of our field sites, collaborations between Girl Scouts and Boy Scouts have been problematic, especially from the Girl Scouts' perspective. Collaboration between these two national organizations was, in all cases, a forced marriage that was required either by United Way or by the schools and that involved Girl Scouts and Boy Scouts in jointly offering an in-school scouting program for youth. Girl Scout leaders in all three cities complained about the clash of program objectives and operating philosophies and about the reactive role in which they felt themselves placed regarding activities. A Lakeside Girl Scout administrator echoed the words of colleagues in our other sites when she said:

> There are a lot of things wrong with the [In School Scouting] program.
> Collaboration was at the instigation of the schools, and not either
> scout organization. We still feel like second sisters. We are notified late
> about important program decisions, have to push to see a detailed
> budget. The Boy Scouts still dictate program.

Although programs in the schools offered collaboratively by Girl Scouts and Boy Scouts operated relatively smoothly, both organizations viewed the product of their shotgun marriage as departing from their "core" philosophy and as a funding requirement rather than an elective response. The fundamental problem the Girl Scouts encountered was that the Boy Scouts, a stronger and more economically and politically powerful organization, was, in their words, unwilling to "truly collaborate." The Boy Scouts, for their part, felt the pressure for collaboration as a relatively unwelcome intrusion into their own operations and planning. Without demands from funders or schools, each partner would prefer to go it alone or to seek relationships with organizations more compatible with their philosophies and perspectives on gender and appropriate youth activities.

Youth Organizations Team up with Professional Organizations

Although the previous examples describe collaboration between two local branches of national organizations, a different type of collaboration was established between a major league baseball team and a grass-roots sports association in River City. The public relations arm of the River City Rangers formed a collaboration with the Hillside Athletic Association (HAA), an organization that held the charter for Little League in the Hillside area of River City.[4] HAA was in the process of expanding its programs into the winter with a baseball skills and homework project for which they were seeking funding. HAA was also involved in lobbying the city for the designation of an official Little League field so that they might expand their volunteer base by having games after 6:00 P.M. The Rangers donated Rangers' souvenirs, equipment, a batting machine for rookie ball, and use of the batting cage at the stadium, as well as time from their staff. Increased service and increased visibility were common goals of both the Little League and the Rangers. Together, they achieved a far broader set of programs in the winter and reached a larger number of youngsters than they had previously. This successful collaboration built on shared goals for youth, common activities, and a shared commitment to sports. This relationship also provided "high-status" links to the broader community for African American youth who lived in the Hillside area, youth traditionally underserved by both public and private agencies.

Mayfair Craftsman's Association (MCA), a River City arts and training center, provided the locus for two large institutions—a state arts fund and the local school board—to collaborate. Together, these three groups provided ceramics and photography classes to a broad range of students both in area high schools and in after-school classes at the MCA. While in the schools, the artists acted as teachers and role models to the students and also provided a link to MCA, where youth could work on their own, watch artists work, and develop relationships with positive role models. Through this collaboration, established artists with educational training had the opportunity to work with youth, the school system was provided with quality art education at no fee, and the students received the value of working with artists. MCA coordinated the funding and programming and supervised the artist staff to present a cohesive goal for this art-related, youth-empowerment work.

Like this arts program, River City's Harmony House had a central goal of providing an opportunity for personal development through goal-directed activities in an environment with easy access to experts who served as positive role models. This collaboration involved the Harmony House, a community center with literacy programs, and researchers from the Center for Language and Literacy at a nearby university. Both researchers and graduate students from the Center for Language and Literacy worked with the adult staff and teen writers. The program provided a place for researchers to share their expertise with practitioners and students in nonschool settings while engaging in research on writing methods at the same time.

This collaboration marked a major shift in programming and identity for Harmony House, which had been a place for African American youth to be involved in recreational programs. A primary goal of the new program was to provide youth both from their traditional neighborhood and from neighboring, predominantly European American areas with activities that would be self-enriching, while providing a forum for African Americans and European Americans to work together. Moreover, through the writing projects, the goal was to offer another image of youth in the neighborhood: an image of youth who cared about their neighborhood and actively sought productive avenues for their energy. Through the collaboration with the university, Harmony House could provide a program in which teens gained experience in self-expression, evidence of their value as writers and observers, and opportunities to see their home environments with a more analytical as well as appreciative eye. Youth also encountered many role models and adult mentors in the graduate students and researchers who worked with them at Harmony House. These relationships, the young people reported, expanded both their horizons and their sense of self.

Communitywide Coalitions

Unlike the collaborations outlined in the previous sections, which involved two or three partners, the Latino Youth Network (LYN) drew together a large number of Lakeside organizations with a common goal. LYN, which was established in the late 1970s as social service organizations attempted to deal with gang problems, has evolved into the largest Latino youth–serving coalition in the state. Founding members included a national organization dedicated to Puerto Rican culture and youth, a settlement house located in a Latino community, a local group working with gangs, and the YMCA. By the 1990s, LYN membership included hospitals, schools, community organizations, health services, colleges, and universities. "Full members" were geographically located in the Thomas Park area, historically a Puerto Rican neighborhood, but increasingly ethnically mixed in the 1990s; "affiliates" were from Lakeside or the greater Lakeside area. As a political voice, LYN successfully lobbied in several arenas of youth policy, most especially health and education. LYN led Latino community efforts in school reform; the organization worked locally and in the state's capital to pass a school reform measure with a substantial role for community involvement and direction. According to LYN's executive director:

> The major thrust of the coalition is different from other youth organizations. We do not provide direct services, but locate unconnected youth and refer them to agencies. We are recognized most for our role as a clearinghouse for information and efforts in Latino advocacy.

LYN worked to eliminate the "isolationism" of member agencies, and several joint activities developed as a result. Hospitals that used to be "territorial," for example, joined together to support conferences on teen pregnancy and suicide; the LYN-supported alternative school and training activities drew on the resources of many members. But, the executive director said:

> [Internal] competition is a major shortcoming of the network. All of these different agencies are competing for the same dollars, and I often receive requests for support letters from different agencies applying for the same funds. But the big problem is that they think that the LYN is also competing against them. We're not. The word now for funders is "partnerships," "collaborations," "coalitions." Funders have to be more aware of the difference among coalitions and why they exist. Also, they don't know the territory.

Despite these shortcomings, LYN's collaboration succeeded in blending diverse institutional forms. Accomplishments of this collaboration based on ethnicity and concerns for youth demonstrate the political power of minority voices united in purpose and strategy. LYN created and solidified a prominent place at the bargaining table, both locally and at the state level and in public policy debate. Indeed, Lakeside African American leadership admired LYN's strength and the voice it provided Latino interests and blamed their own relatively weak political position on the absence of such a coalition.

In contrast to LYN, the Neighborhood Youth Coalition (NYC) in River City proved to be a disheartening failure. This coalition involved 10 neighborhood groups with social service and youth agendas from 10 communities that together make up the Hillside neighborhood. These groups came together initially to write a grant proposal that would focus on youth in the community. Although the original proposal did not receive funding, the group found that they gained strength and enthusiasm in talking about their common vision and their common problems.

After 1 year of informal meetings, they applied for a second grant with the specific goals of establishing a network/referral service among their organizations and of developing youth councils to work with the community councils in smaller neighborhoods. These two goals were designed to bring more youth into organized activities and to develop a forum in which adult and teen members of the communities could meet in a productive manner. NYC was successful in securing funding as their networking goals corresponded with a local foundation's new focus on collaborative efforts in social service.

Having secured funding for 2 years, NYC ran into problems related to staffing, goal definition, and organizational structure. After 2 years, the funder was no longer willing to fund the coalition and asked for one member organization to take over programming. As no one organization was willing to take the risk of failure and possible damage to future funding opportunities, the final year of funding was returned to the foundation. At subsequent meetings, board members came to the conclusion that their collaboration worked well only when no funding and no program were involved. They had been successful in formulating problems they saw in their community and in proposing potential solutions, but they were unable to carry those solutions out cooperatively. They blamed personnel shortages in their own organizations and a lack of leadership and procedural planning on the part of the board of the collaborative effort. Failed efforts that stemmed from inadequate capacity, such as one organization's inability to get out the flyers they committed to produce, soured the coalition's exchanges; uneven commitment to coalition goals was even more divisive. Said one disappointed and somewhat bitter proponent of the initiative:

> The failure of the coalition is primarily due to the fact that some orga-
> nizations who joined didn't serve youth and didn't want to serve
> youth. They joined primarily for political reasons. There were a few of
> us who really wanted to work with youth and knew what we wanted
> to do. The others didn't know and they didn't care. They really were
> not in the youth business. They threw up all sorts of roadblocks and
> tried to manage the coalition.

Some members of NYC also attributed its failure to the management style of the director. One said:

> The director moved her own agenda and then complained when the
> board wasn't active. But she did nothing to activate it. These people
> have their own organizations to attend to . . . it was her job to push
> the coalition agenda, and she didn't do it. She failed to solicit the
> views of members and then act on them as the coalition agenda. So it
> all fell apart and really soured everyone on the idea of a coalition—
> participants as well as funders.

NYC had no strategy for blending neighborhood-based interests held by local or grass-roots members with the broader agenda of community-level or national organizations. Accordingly, many activists associated with neighborhood-based organizations felt that NYC competed with and eroded rather than supported their ability to work with their constituency.

Factors That Affect Collaboration

In the abstract—and often in local realities—collaborations make sense. They can enable the efficient distribution of services to the greatest number of clients—in this case, youth—by drawing on the expertise and commitment of a large number of youth agencies. They can enhance the services available to any particular group by pooling specialized resources or capacity. They can reduce wasteful duplication of efforts and promote integration. Given the successful collaborations described here, one might further argue that they are feasible and therefore highly desirable given the ever-increasing need for and ever-shrinking size of available resources.

But metaphorical benefits that claim "strength in unity" or a "salad bowl" approach are often difficult to achieve in practice. All those involved in successful collaborations indicated how tough their collaborations were to achieve and to maintain. Furthermore, efforts to collaborate carried potential costs to organizations and their constituencies, even when the collaboration was successful in terms of its joint objectives. In particular, the time and commitment necessary to establish and maintain new working relationships across the boundaries of one's own organization made heavy demands. A program director for a park and recreation department complained about endless meetings "where no one seems to be in charge; everyone just seems to assume that someone knows what the goals of the meetings are. I really wonder, with all the hassles, if the costs of trying to collaborate don't outweigh the benefits."

Pooling of resources across neighborhoods often raised difficult issues of racism or institutional stereotyping for many leaders of community-level organizations. One Boys and Girls Club executive director, outraged at the reluctance of a local board in a European American neighborhood to invite African American youngsters to use the facility, acknowledged the difficult tradeoff between a local sense of support and of neighborhood ownership and the social values of fairness and equality.

Some agencies may lose breadth, as well as distinctiveness of services, through collaboration. Girl Scout leaders in all sites felt the threat of having their service population subsumed by Boy Scout Explorer groups. They also worried about losing the special focus on girls' special needs and interests under certain collaborative requirements. Those involved with the Girls Clubs expressed deep concerns that the programming for girls—most especially programming focused on sexuality, personal health, and careers—would be lost in the newly defined Boys and Girls Clubs.

Collaborative arrangements can also impose costs in terms of diminished client access or services because of new layers of bureaucracy or administrative arrangements. What used to be an easy procedure may become daunting because of the new procedures required by a collabora-tive relationship. For example, the consolidation of the local Boys and Girls Clubs into the Boys and Girls Clubs of River City in the 1970s brought with it central fiscal management. The goal was to pool resources and increase the efficiency of accounting. An unexpected negative effect, however, of removing local control was the loss of local incentive for fund-raising from a number of communities that had previously regarded the local Boys and Girls Clubs as "their organization"; what used to be perceived as belonging to the neighborhood was perceived as "lost to downtown."

Some constituencies or organizations may also lose priority or familiar arrangements with powerful organizations because of the compromises necessary to forge collaborative relations. The Girl Scouts in River City, for example, lost their priority funding from the United Way when they began to receive funding through United Way-mandated collaboration with the Boy Scouts.

Grass-roots and minority groups have been particularly susceptible to this loss of institutional individuality, special mission, and attention to cul-tural norms and goals. A newly formed coalition of Christian churches wor-ried about a loss of identity as seen by their African American constituents as the coalition bent to a United Way demand to collaborate with better known and more politically powerful social service organizations, such as the YMCA:

> The new thrust on collaboration is very confusing, and it does nothing
> to alleviate our identity problems [or to support our efforts to
> strengthen black churches]. Nevertheless, I see that collaboration is
> necessary. As people, we just recognize that—but it exacerbates our
> problem of getting folks in the community to know which organiza-
> tions are providing what services [or to develop an ongoing relation-
> ship with their neighborhood church].

Leaders in African American and Latino communities expressed concern about the program components of traditional groups, such as Campfire, Girl Scouts, and Boy Scouts, which could conflict with their community's cul-tural backgrounds or norms. Camping programs pose a particular concern because they represent a foreign and often frightening situation for inner-city African American or Asian American youngsters and an unacceptable environment for the daughters of Latino families.

Finally, some organizations and clientele may be deeply disappointed as initial promises and commitments turn out to be merely symbolic or largely rhetorical, as was the case with NYC, described earlier.

Aspects of Organizations That Affect Collaborative Relations

Certain organizational features can help overcome the barriers to collaboration discussed earlier. Five aspects of organizations appear to affect collaborative relationships and to enable groups to override boundaries that may arise from gender, race, ethnicity, or community concerns. These aspects range from concrete operating needs to abstract assessments of ability to work together; they range from the effectiveness of day-to-day operations to actual and perceived roles in the larger political arena. The aspects of organizations that affect the nature of collaborative relations are:

- structures and routines
- capacity
- domains
- belief systems
- power and legitimacy

In the collaborations described earlier, quite different sets of organizational aspects were brought together. In one set of cases, local branches of different organizations operated at approximately the same level of power and control, and each was accountable within the hierarchical structure of their national organization, as well as at the local site. In the next cases, businesses, universities, and grass-roots organizations each had fundamentally different structures and lines of accountability, as well as different orientations to the local youth-serving community. Finally, in large collaborations that involve numerous partners, issues of the sheer number of communication links were added to issues of coordination of both operations and agenda.

Organizations able to establish effective collaborations take all of these aspects into account and focus on those that can cause difficulties in their particular collaboration. As these aspects are integral to the functioning of any organization, one does not always realize their importance until clashes or inconsistencies develop in a collaboration. As successful organizations appear to operate without controls, detecting the influence of various organizational aspects on success is difficult.

Organizational Structures and Routines. By structure, we mean the manner in which an organization and, by extension, a collaboration, carry out day-to-day operations. Three general issues apply to an organization's operations: authority, routines and procedures, and bureaucratic requirements. An organization's authority structure, or hierarchy of control, determines the game plan—that is, who is in charge of what. In most effective organizations, there is a clear sense of who the leader is or who is in charge of what. Moreover, an organization operates with a set of routines and procedures that explains "how things are done around here," how programs are started, how they are run, how accounting procedures are carried out, and how staff relations are negotiated. From outside of the organization come bureaucratic requirements that dictate how an organization must operate to stay in compliance with rules of functioning. These requirements cover such areas as health and safety, employee benefits, and personnel policies.

The failure of NYC to establish organizational structures and routines came as a surprise to the participating organizations. Each thought that the collaboration would naturally, almost by osmosis, conduct its operations just as their own organization did. NYC failed to set up either clear authority structures or routines and procedures. In more than 2 years of operation, NYC never established clear lines of hierarchical control and accountability, nor did it establish a set of routines that were written and agreed on. Moreover, it failed to meet the bureaucratic requirements that the funding agency set for it. As a result, NYC lost its funding. Not only had it failed to comply with the terms of the proposal, but it also could find no effective way of remedying that lack of compliance because it had no clear lines of authority or operating procedures.

In contrast, MCA addressed potential conflict about routines and practices, or "how things are done around here," in their collaboration with schools. As large and established institutions, schools have a very clear set of routines and practices that centers around discipline and scheduling. After some discussion with school personnel, the artists were able to create for themselves a unique position in the schools: that of "artists in the school." The schools' organizational and disciplinary routines and requirements ended upon entrance to the studio, where the rules and regulations of the artist and of the studio took over. In exchange, the artists were respectful of and supported the schools' rules and regulations outside of the studio. This arrangement ensured that teachers would not interfere with the looser disciplinary arrangements in the studio and that artists and students would not infringe on teachers' control in other parts of the school buildings.

In all three sites in our field, the Boy Scouts, the YMCA, and the schools were singled out as particularly difficult partners due to their codified authority structures and organizational routines. The YMCA was viewed by many youth leaders as "just too bureaucratic, they are just out for the numbers" and as "out of it in terms of meeting the needs of kids, especially inner-city kids; they are locked into facilities, their programs are determined by their buildings." This apparent rigidity on the part of the YMCA had turned away other organizations, especially grass-roots organizations that valued flexibility in program and use of facilities.[5] But even city officials cited problems collaborating with the local YMCA—for example, a program director for a parks and recreation department complained:

> It's been difficult. The Y wants to use the rec facility's activity rooms in the summer to get their kids out of the heat. This ends up undermining rec programs because they use our numbers and programs to get funding. The Y is very aggressive. They are a United Way agency; they deal in body counts. They have a very different focus than we do, numbers versus service.

In some cases, the age and venerability of the YMCA set up perceptions that they would not work as equal partners with other organizations. (The fact that the YMCA serves both youth and adults further complicates the issue. Youth programs typically suffer when their needs conflict with potentially lucrative adult recreational programming.)

The public schools came under similar criticism as too bureaucratic, narrowly focused, and unable to move across professional turf. A member of a large communitywide collaboration in Big Valley sees major problems ahead as the collaboration explores new projects that join education and social services:

> There are difficult problems with collaborating with the schools. Administrators don't want to let go of control; they are nervous about what partnership means to the district. There are fundamental issues that have to be worked out: Who is going to provide the services, the agency coming in or the schools? Who will come into the building? Who will use the building? Will it be disruptive to the educational program? Who will have authority over the folks coming into a school? Principals have pretty traditional concerns. Principals see a tight connection, a triangle, between students, teachers, and parents—"our primary job here is to educate." Everyone else is, in their view, outside of this. Well, a lot of us, especially health professionals, are going to have a lot of problems with this. There is a lot of room for conflict here about what the primary job is . . . this is what principals are worried about. . . .

Incompatibility in organizational structures and routines can, in short, frustrate even the best intentioned collaboration. They almost certainly will derail a mandated relationship. This was the case for the mandated Girl Scouts–Boy Scouts collaborations, in which the Boy Scouts' hierarchical structure and commitment to standard routines in all settings differed fundamentally from the cooperative and adaptive styles of organization of the Girl Scouts. Meshing diverse structures and routines present extremely difficult challenges to youth leaders, especially in the case of traditional national organizations, whose practices are rooted in the need to manage a dispersed system of local affiliates in a way that gives local meaning to national goals and objectives so as to "standardize" and provide predictable services.

Such institutional requirements conflict with local needs to be flexible and responsive and to tailor programs to the particular and changing needs of local youth. Hence, collaboration between traditional youth organizations and the grass-roots agencies with loyalty to cultural or neighborhood particularities must resolve difficult dilemmas of competing institutional needs (standardization or flexibility and predictability or adaptability), organizational agenda (inclusive or specific constituency), or organizational requirements (professional staff or local individuals knowledgeable about the neighborhood). The grass-roots organizations, for their part, are often criticized by national organizations as being too disorganized and unprofessional, factors that run counter to national emphases on professionalism in youth services.

Organizational Capacity. Although the organizational structures and routines define the framework in which activities take place, it is the organizational capacity of an organization that will determine the degree and types of program activity it can carry out. Central here are the resources an organization can bring to bear in terms of money, knowledge or expertise, staffing, and facility. An effective organization develops a program that takes into account its current set of resources and works to plan growth that falls within the foreseeable capacity of the organization.

An example of an effective collaboration in terms of organizational capacity is that of the Girl Scouts and the Boys and Girls Clubs. The club had the facility and the staff, as well as time available when their facility was not being used to capacity, and the Girl Scouts had the money to pay for the membership fees for the girls and to transport them to and from the club. They did not, however, have the expertise of the Boys and Girls Clubs staff to provide swimming and computer instruction. The capacity of each organization was enhanced by collaboration.

In the case of Harmony House, collaboration came as the result of a desire to shift to a new form of service. The challenge was to develop a new capacity in the staff so that they could work effectively with university staff and youth on literacy programs. This retraining of the old staff was, moreover, to be done in such a way that they would maintain their successful positive interactions with youth and be able to persuade those youth who felt disenfranchised in the schools that Harmony House's new focus on literacy was not designed to shut them out but rather to provide them with new opportunities. This shift in capacity was achieved through intensive workshops and group meetings between the core staff and various members of the university collaboration.

Capacity also determines, in many instances, the organizations invited to take part in collaborative efforts or even to come to the table. Salient here are procedures established by such gatekeeper organizations as the United Way. Small, grass-roots organizations are often excluded because they lack the capacity to prepare detailed proposals, install approved accounting schemes, or comply in other ways with United Way's criteria for funding. One United Way director commented: "We have set standards that an agency must meet and follow before we will fund them, and many of the grass-roots organizations do not have the means to accomplish this. So they are left out." A United Way director in another city acknowledged that "efficiency in some of the older organizations, such as the YMCA, is rewarded, but the fire of some of the newer ones is not." Excluded most often for reasons of capacity are minority organizations and grass-roots groups that serve local youth. Yet the success of River City's HAA shows what support of a grass-roots organization can accomplish when this support allows the grass-roots organization to use its own capacity in its own way.

Organizational Domains. While capacity covers what an organization can do in the area of programming, domain marks where the organization carries out its programming—the institutional field in which an organization's service falls and in which it has developed expertise. An organization's activities may fall in social work, education, recreation, or in a combination of these domains. Related to domain is the concept of turf. Turf encompasses both the geographic space in which an organization has traditionally provided service and the psychological space related to the type of youth traditionally served. Domain and turf are concerned with the ownership or rights to clients and types of services.

The success of the collaboration between the Boys and Girls Club and the Girl Scouts shows how turf issues were effectively addressed. These issues involved both the gender and the race of the traditional clients: European American boys for the Boys and Girls Club and African American girls for the Girl Scout troop. Although the traditional "clients" differed, the domain of recreational and educational service along with the goal of personal growth was shared by both organizations. The success of this collaboration lay in the ability of staff to allay concerns on the part of adults involved in both programs—particularly with reference to racial issues—

and in the accommodation, already in practice at the Boys and Girls Club, of having girls' night and boys' night for various activities.

The unsuccessful NYC failed to take into account the different domains in which the various organizations operated. Some saw themselves and, by extension, the coalition as education oriented, while others saw it as social service oriented and still others saw it as community service oriented. As a result, the coalition developed two somewhat incompatible goals: to provide programs and to broker information as a tool to recruit youth into existing programs. In addition, each organization had worked traditionally with a particular, often competing neighborhood and with particular groups, some with African American youth, some with European American youth, and some with youth and adults. The coalition's goal of bringing together youth from these competing neighborhoods was hampered by their inability to find neutral turf in which to carry out joint activities.

LYN, in contrast, forged a successful collaboration across domains by defining itself as unbiased, staying out of program except when agreed on by membership, and effectively filling an advocacy role for youth generally and an educational function for member organizations as well as policymakers. Their power came from collective voice and broad agreement on ends, if not means.

Organizational Belief System. A belief system has to do with the expressed and unexpressed goals that an organization and the individuals within it have for youth programming. Organizational belief systems drive both the goals of the programs and the manner in which the organization works to achieve its goals. This aspect encompasses questions that range from whether young men should remove their hats on entering a building as a sign of respect (cultural factors) to whether the value of providing tutoring specifically geared to school work outweighs that of educational development courses designed to augment problem-solving skills (educational factors). Issues concerned with beliefs also revolve around goals for hiring staff (does your organization hire exclusively "certificated" individuals or exclusively from the neighborhood?) and recruiting youth (girls only, boys only, girls and boys? ethnically diverse or ethnically homogeneous?) and the effect that such choices have on the nature of programs and the nature of the relationships that develop between staff and youth.

An example of the convergence of belief systems and goals between two very different organizations is seen in the case of Harmony House and the university. Both had the overall goal of developing educational programming for youth that focused on problem-solving and writing skills. Yet the university had as a primary goal conducting research on the problem-solving strategies youngsters developed, while Harmony House staff wanted their programming to make a difference in the lives of youngsters and, by extension, their community. The success of the collaboration came in that each organization's secondary goal matched the other group's primary goal.

A contrast in beliefs can lead to different ways of increasing membership and thereby funding, differences that lead to incompatibilities when collaborations are required. The Boy Scouts have traditionally held that low-income boys should adjust to the Boy Scout way of doing things, including the purchase of uniforms, badges, and handbooks, as well as participation in standard Boy Scout activities such as camping. In contrast, the Girl Scouts have, especially since the 1970s, encouraged local programs to adapt to the specific community of girls they serve. Hence, their programs in low-income neighborhoods address issues of teen pregnancy and self-esteem earlier than in other areas, and their meetings often include more literacy-oriented activities to ensure that girls can benefit both from traditional Girl Scout activities outlined in the handbooks, which are provided cost free, and from other educational opportunities. These different approaches to a similar goal make it difficult for these two organizations to work together.

Organizational Power and Legitimacy. Organizational power and legitimacy draw an organization into a broader sphere of influence, namely the local political space. In that arena, each organization is an actor that is both compared with and competes against other organizations. Organizational power and legitimacy affect the currency that an organization has among the power elite who have the funds and other resources to support programming for youth. Central among these players are organizations such as the United Way; foundations; branches of local, state, and federal government; and, in some instances, the local school board, businesses, and community members. Here, the networking ability of members of the organization, as well as its history of service or its track record, can determine the extent to which it is seen as viable, legitimate, and trustworthy.

In the case of River City's HAA and the Rangers, the power, legitimacy, and visibility of the Rangers helped HAA to establish links with wealthy supporters in the city. What HAA was unable to achieve on its own because of its lack of political or economic clout, it was able to achieve in collaboration with the Rangers. Although HAA was a grass-roots organization that had operated on a shoestring for most of its 20 years, it had a long track record of excellent service to youth, a currency that the Rangers' connection could parlay into increased funding. Through the collaboration, HAA succeeded in having the city designate a playing field as an official Little League field, a goal that they had been pursuing with little success for a number of years. Moreover, their increased visibility led to their success in securing a broader base of financial and volunteer support.

A story with the opposite ending is seen in the relative political power and influence of the Boy Scouts and the Girl Scouts. While the Boy Scouts had almost exclusively chief executive officers on its board of directors— individuals who could raise funds easily for Boy Scout activities—the Girl Scouts had no chief executive officers and few individuals with political power on their board and thus have had a much more difficult time rais- ing funds. As a consequence, Girl Scouts were in a weaker position as an individual organization and, by extension, a weaker position within the collaboration with the Boy Scouts in In-School Scouting. They were as a result much more dependent on United Way funding and thus believed they could not refuse to collaborate if the United Way instructed them to do so.

Grass-roots organizations everywhere complain about the power of the United Way or foundations "to jerk us around through their 'priority of the year' style of operation." Comprehensive service organizations located in impacted, high-poverty neighborhoods are able to reach into their limitless bucket of needs to respond. For example, the director of a neighborhood organization located in one of the nation's most desperate high-rise housing projects said: "In order to keep the funding for youth in place, we have to present the program under the guise of the current 'hot topic.' Since almost all of the kids fit into these categories, we can just rewrite." But not all neighborhood groups can accommodate these demands from powerful funding groups so easily, and thus opportunities for funding and for col- laboration are lost. Or when programs change their activities in response to funders' guidelines, relevance for local youth is often the cost. For example, to respond to United Way priorities and retain funding eligibility, a River City neighborhood organization scaled back its successful basketball activ- ity to add a tutoring program. The group retained its United Way funding but lost the participation of neighborhood youth as a result. The priorities and needs of local youth or neighborhood loyalties are often eclipsed by the priorities and procedures established by more powerful institutions.

The Local Context Revisited: Factors That Promote Successful Collaboration

Implicit in this discussion of organizational aspects that affect collaboration was the importance of the local context in determining what is salient to a given collaboration in terms of the needs of the organizations and the com- munity involved. Local context becomes even more crucial in understand- ing the strategies for managing and maintaining potentially successful collaborations over a longer period of time. The local context consists of four primary elements. First is the history of an organization, as well as that of others in the same service and geographic area. Equally important are needs as expressed by the community and the organization's ability to respond to those needs, as well as resources available for particular kinds of service based on the current politically popular funding tracks. Finally, the capacity of an organization to provide good service puts all of these other elements into action.

The local context for a specific collaboration, moreover, encompasses the appropriate interaction between partners in their shared local context. Organizations bring different levels of expertise, power, and capacity to a collaboration. They also bring different assumptions about practice or service, goals, ways of doing business, or different domains, all of which can potentially reflect a heavy influence of perceptions of ethnicity or gender. After all, these differences define them as individual agencies. Thus, it is not surprising that the same organization can be involved in both unsuccessful and successful collaborations at the same time—as, for example, in the case of the Girl Scouts in River City.

The interplay between organizations in collaboration requires differing types of response to different organizational aspects. On the one hand, there is a need for consistency and consensus in organizational structures and routines, as well as beliefs and goals. On the other hand, in terms of organizational domain, capacity, and power and legitimacy, effectiveness is most likely when each organization brings to the table unique and nonredundant skills and resources and when each organization can, by virtue of that unique contribution, act as an equal in the partnership. The sense of "equal" as used here is not direct equality but rather equality weighted by the question of the unique services that each partner can offer.

Ensuring that the organizational aspects of a collaboration are compatible represents the first step in designing a successful collaboration. Managing and maintaining successful collaborations, however, require attention to additional local factors—in particular, those related to interpersonal interaction at the level of staff, clients, funders, and community. These factors roughly divide into two overlapping areas: day-to-day operations and collaborative goals. Central to each of these factors is the communication between individuals who work in the collaborative. Such communication includes both regular planned interactions at the level of the organization and one-on-one communication among staff members. Factors that center on communication that can be planned are related, finally, to a number of intangible factors that can be neither mandated nor planned, factors without which collaboration is doomed to failure. These intangibles consist of personal compatibility, trust, consensus, and awareness.

Maintaining Day-to-Day Operations

At the level of day-to-day operations, a number of factors help initiate and sustain a successful collaboration. Successful relationships begin with formalized relations and continue with active administration, open channels of communication, and visible victories. Moreover, strategies for conflict resolution and problem solving must be instituted at the outset to head off potential arguments about operations, which draw attention away from the goals of a collaboration.

Formalized Relations. A joint construction and a clear understanding of the "rules of the game" are central to a collaborative's ability to work together. This is especially true when individuals and organizations have had little previous experience in cooperative ventures with one another. Clarity at the outset is also particularly important on issues pertaining to organizational self-interest and institutional responsibilities that may be sources of potential conflict. A decision that is important for collaborators and their staff to make at the outset, then, concerns the extent of formalization necessary to support the day-to-day activities of their collaboration. Hence, the HAA and Ranger partners clearly agreed at the outset that one key individual would serve as advisor to the board and liaison with the Rangers but would not be centrally involved in decision making or service. Furthermore, it was agreed that his role as advisor and his role as liaison would be kept separate: His advice on the optimal way of conducting an activity did not amount to acceptance of it by the Rangers.

Active Administration. As collaborations grow beyond relatively simple agreements about shared facilities, administrative leadership becomes an important element in the extent to which a collaboration functions well and achieves its goals. The experiences of organizations noted here and of collaborations elsewhere highlight a number of features important to effective administration. One is that the administrator be hired as staff to the collaborative and not "borrowed" from a participating organization. Second, collaborative administrators need to be dedicated to fulfilling the collaborative's agenda, not their own individual agenda. And third, administrators must actively solicit the views of participants and respond to them in a visible way. Active collection and integration of participant perspectives are essential to building and maintaining trust; they provide the glue that holds the organization together. NYC provides an example extraordinaire of failure to set up such an active administration. In contrast, MCA as an organization had a clear set of operational structures and goals. Moreover, MCA was given the contract to administer the art program in the schools, thus ensuring that there would be active and clear administrative functioning.

Open and Active Channels of Communication. Communication about activities, successes, disappointments, and problems is essential to a healthy collaboration. Channels not only have to be open; they have to be used frequently and be accessible to all members. The significance of frequent and clear communication lies in more than the information it carries; it provides assurance to "junior partners" that their interests are being addressed and that behind-the-scenes agreements among more powerful members are not steering the objectives and investments of the collaborative. The failure of NYC lay partially in the fact that communication was infrequent and selective. Each board member assumed that others were keeping track of activities, a situation that resulted in no one knowing or checking on the progress of the organization. The executive director for her part regularly communicated with individual board members on issues of personnel, youth councils, or programming activities, while giving the impression that she was communicating to everyone equally. When conflicts arose or decisions needed to be made, board members had differing amounts of information on which to base their views. In direct contrast to this was Harmony House, where all staff and advisors participated in planning meetings throughout the program and where, moreover, personal friendships among members extended contact well beyond the bounds of the working day.

Visible Victories. The energy and soul of a collaborative demand more than vision; they require achievement and visible victories. Selection of issues that are "winnable" and goals that can be met is essential to the continuing health of a collaborative. Reluctant members especially need to see that together the partnership is accomplishing more than individuals could alone. Small victories also build organizational confidence, a track record, and legitimacy. Although NYC had some victories, they were never visible to the members of the board, to the community, or to the funder. Reported victories, moreover, do not have the same strength as visible ones, as seen in the final sessions of the Harmony House projects. There, youth presented their findings to their parents, community members, funders, and members of the university team. These victories were also reported occasionally in neighborhood and city press.

Conflict Resolution and Problem Solving. An effective collaboration requires established procedures for addressing conflicts and problems as they arise. Agreed-on strategies need to be put in place at initial stages of the development so that disagreements will not fester, problems can be addressed quickly, and organizations with divergent interests or concerns about self-interest feel they have a forum. Control over decision making was lost by the Girl Scouts in their collaboration with the Boy Scouts, and the Girl Scouts were unable to negotiate effectively with the Boy Scouts because no mechanism for dealing with problems was put in place. In contrast, at Harmony House, although the executive director held final power over all decisions and potential conflicts, his consensual style of management ensured that all staff and advisors to programs were informed of potential and actual conflicts and participated in developing solutions.

Keeping Track of Collaborative Goals

In addition to establishing strategies for the clear operation of a collaborative on a day-to-day level, strategies to keep a focus on the goals of the collaborative—goals that are unique to the collaborative and newly formed with the establishment of that collaborative—are also crucial. To allow the collaborative's goals to remain clear and effective, partners in the collaborative need to *embrace diversity, reaffirm joint goals,* and allow for *active reflection* on the process of collaboration.

Strategies That Embrace Diversity. Youth organizations typically have an identity in terms of clientele—gender, ethnicity, race, or locale; in terms of focus—health, education, sports, or character development; or in terms of institutional affiliation—church, national organization, public service agency, or grass-roots association. Loss of distinctive institutional identity, legitimacy, and self-interest represent significant impediments to collaboration. Successful collaborations identify ways to acknowledge diversity while at the same time supporting the unique goals of an organizational collaboration. Protection for diversity becomes particularly salient for members with less power, influence, or visibility than other members. Effective strategies for providing that organizational assurance include explicit attention to individual or institutional self-interests, fair distribution of credit, and assurance that all participants benefit explicitly in some way from the collaboration. Unity or integration are brought to this diversity by agreement on a common or unifying theme, something owned by no member but instead particular to the collaboration. The most successful collaborations were ones in which the resources each organization could offer were unique and nonredundant, thereby allowing each organization to develop its strengths in a broader arena.

Strategies That Reaffirm Shared Mission and Responsibilities. If collaboration is to be more than a paper exercise or symbolic communion, strategies that reaffirm shared goals and responsibilities of membership are essential. Collaboratives are neither self-managing nor self-winding. Frequent gatherings and communication support this goal. Many successful collaborations have used such devices as retreats to focus specifically on goals and requirements. Participating members, especially the more advantaged or powerful partners, need occasional renewals of rationale for the collaboration and of the responsibilities of membership. Otherwise, the demands and day-to-day pressures of one's own organization can eclipse the requirements and interests of the collaborative. This was clearly the case with NYC, where members were required to come to monthly board meetings that had no explicit agenda and at which little decision-making or consensus took place. As a result, members regularly missed meetings whenever there was a conflict with an activity at their own organization.

Strategies for Feedback and Reflection. An effective collaboration requires information on an ongoing basis about its performance, about problems that may arise regarding collaboration specifically, and about adherence to collaborative goals. Shared purpose can breed shared delusions in the absence of credible, critical feedback. Such information enables a collaboration to make adjustments, repairs, and amendments—to learn from experience. The contrast between the board meetings of HAA, with its Rangers' connection, in which leaders checked continually on whether they were meeting everyone's different needs—HAA's need for resources and the Rangers' need for visibility—ensured that they stayed on the same track. Each party felt that the collaboration was meeting its needs. In contrast, individual NYC members set up separate and private lines of communication with subsets of the board to ensure that individual goals not necessarily compatible with NYC goals were met. Reflection and feedback were wholly absent until the final meeting of the NYC board, when funding had already been cut. Before that time, board members chose to "trust" what the others were doing, because they did not want to invest time in reflection and communication.

The Intangibles

Whether an organization receives benefits in excess of costs as a result of collaboration—whether collaboration "works"—depends finally on whether collaborating organizations achieve certain proximate and less tangible outcomes: awareness, consensus, trust, and personal compatibility.

Awareness. One important consequence of effective collaboration is a high level of familiarity with the goals, services, personnel, and resources of participating agencies. This knowledge of partner organizations enables successful adaptation over the course of a collaboration, as plans are revised, as the unexpected arises, and as the collaborative is required to respond to crises in the environment. Insufficient awareness of organizational partners can cripple plans made or plans anticipated.

Consensus. Consensus is another essential outcome of an effective collaboration. Successful collaborations require a degree of agreement among agencies about the services and goals of each others' organizations and about the collaboration itself. Conflict among agencies about either ends or means can derail collaboration. Consensus builds on awareness and on compromise; it does not assume complete agreement, but rather a shared understanding of the issues and the options available to support optimal benefit for all parties.

Trust. Related to but somewhat different from the previous factors is trust. Trust is both an institutional and an individual issue. On paper, the partners in a collaboration are the agencies and organizations. But, in fact, the individual staff members will be carrying out the collaboration. Here, the central issues are trust in one another on a personal as well as a professional level. Trust among individuals is especially salient in the context of up-close collaborations among community-based organizations as opposed to sometimes faceless coalitions of national organizations. However, even in the case of coalitions between national organizations, trust is essential for the members of organizations who will work together at the local point of delivery. Trust means confidence that various institutional self-interests will be respected, that promises will be fulfilled, that services will be provided competently and professionally, and that harm to individual or institutional concerns will be avoided.

Personal Compatibility. A fact of life for successful collaborations, especially at the local level, is personal compatibility. The right personalities are necessary to forge agreements, build trust, and move the collaboration forward. Institutional calculus will amount to little if the individuals involved cannot get along, do not respect one another, or cannot be an effective part of a team. So, in the case of the Girl Scouts' two collaborations, the director of special projects was able to establish a good working relationship with the director of the local Boys and Girls Club, as well as with the executive director of the regional Boys and Girls Clubs. This relationship was based on mutual trust and respect coupled with a clear agreement on how they could work together. In contrast, the special projects director was unable to establish a relationship with her counterpart at the Boy Scouts, who was unwilling or unable to spend time meeting with her to arrange their joint projects.

Without awareness, consensus, trust, and personal compatibility, few if any of the benefits of collaboration will be realized. These essential and proximate consequences of collaboration can neither be mandated nor guaranteed. Instead, they are a joint product of the characteristics of participating organizations and the strategies selected to manage and support the collaboration.

Tough Decisions for Youth Policy

Evident from the cases we have presented here is first and foremost that collaboration is *not cost free*. Aside from the obvious failures, there is also the risk of loss of distinctiveness—of gender, race, and ethnicity, as well as community identity—even in successful collaborations. Moreover, in every collaboration, considerable time and energy costs must be carefully evaluated, particularly within organizations that are not very powerful and influential. They have more to lose than to gain from collaborating and must therefore carefully assess the costs. Funders and organizations interested in collaborating must also assess the larger costs of failures. Organizational memories and histories will have long-term effects for individual organizations, the organizational pool, and the community as a whole if a collaboration results in failure.

Second, we have seen that the question of whether to collaborate or go it alone must be seen in context. The context that is particularly important here is the individual organization within its community setting—its lines especially to gender and local community needs—as well as contexts encompassing the other organizations within the community. Thus, a collaboration should aim toward bringing together nonredundant services that can complement and increase each organization's goals. In addition, the potential collaboration must assess carefully whether the goals of the collaboration are needed and desired in the community. There is a balance in youth organizations between stability and the ability to change with the changing environment. Is the organization too much as it is to be anything else? As neighborhoods do change with time, funders and collaborating partners need to be prepared to adjust to contingencies that result from shifts in the environment.

Yet no one can mandate what matters in a successful collaboration. Of central importance is the issue of trust. If we draw from the concept of the strength of weak ties, we see that individuals and not larger institutions or organizations are central to either the success or failure of a collaboration. Funders must be aware of this point, as well as of the difficulty and fragility of coalitions.

To be successful, organizations considering a collaborative enterprise must start small and not overreach in initial efforts to collaborate. Each organization must pay attention to organizational arrangements and, where necessary, provide for technical assistance to ensure that all organizational aspects that affect collaborations are taken into account. This is not an insignificant problem, because differences in organizational style rarely surface unless there are conflicts, and these types of conflicts can cripple the most ambitious and potentially successful program goals.

And finally, the possible benefits and costs of a collaboration must not be weighed in terms of key metaphors, a map drawn for political reasons, or even a map based on common targets for service. Benefits and costs must be weighed from the perspective of community and organizational needs. Assessment must, moreover, be substantive and therefore consider philosophies, activities, and norms of practice that can ensure collaboration with the "right" players in every sense of the word. These players must share common goals, especially around issues such as ethnicity and gender and around the salience of these considerations in the mission of the collaboration.

Acknowledgments

The work reported here was supported by a grant from the Spencer Foundation to Shirley Brice Heath and Milbrey W. McLaughlin for a 5-year research project entitled "Language, Socialization, and Neighborhood-Based Organizations."

Notes

[1]River City, Lakeside, and Big Valley are pseudonyms, as are all names of the organizations and neighborhoods mentioned in this chapter. Except where otherwise noted, all quoted comments were made by respondents in the course of our fieldwork. To preserve the confidentiality of sites and individuals, we identify respondents only in terms of their community role.

[2]Many organizational theorists and policy analysts treat collaboration and offer categories of institutional relationships. This typology follows that developed by Wistow (1982), but see also Gray (1985).

[3]The W. T. Grant Foundation's Education and Human Services Consortium *Series on Collaboration* contains publications focused on specific aspects of collaboration. This work expands and elaborates on the observations and analysis presented here.

[4]The River City Rangers also formed a collaboration with River City Parks and Recreation Department. Through that collaboration, they worked in two other neighborhoods in the city.

[5]There are YMCAs among our field sites that belie this description of bureaucracy, rules, and building-based programming. What these YMCAs have in common are directors committed to providing programs and an environment that attracts and engages inner-city youth. As seen in chapter 2, those YMCA directors also have "bent" or overlooked bureaucratic strictures to offer activities defined in terms of the needs of local youth.

References

Education and Human Services Consortium. (Multiple dates). *Series on collaboration.* Washington, DC: W. T. Grant Foundation.

Gray, B. (1985). Conditions facilitating interorganizational collaboration. *Human Relations, 38,* 911–936.

Wistow, G. (1982). Collaboration between health and local authorities: Why is it necessary? *Social Policy and Administration, 16,* 44–62.

7

The Winnowing of Organizations

Thomas James

How did early 20th-century concepts of youth, cultural assimilation, and adaptation to the work force mold current youth organizations? Settlement houses, playgrounds, and youth clubs took many of their cues from schools and bureaucracies that dictated a process of selection for youngsters based on norms and practices of standardization. Routines, predictable tasks, and efficient management marked the youth organizations that philanthropists, civic authorities, and public funders chose to maintain. Youth organizations that did not expose their young members to structures and values compatible with those of compulsory schooling and adult employment were winnowed out. This chapter explains how this history accounts for the low survival rate of grass-roots groups that attempt to meet local needs of youth by remaining adaptable to shifting demographic and socioeconomic conditions.

> The fault of "youth" lies, then, not in youth at all but with those to whom it has been asked to look: to its elders, the leaders, the professors who, when they are honest, acknowledge that they really know next to nothing at all.
>
> *William Carlos Williams*
> *The Embodiment of Knowledge*

The Columbian Exposition of 1893 at the Chicago World's Fair could not have come at a stranger moment. Visitors marveled as they strolled through the vast, hastily constructed buildings, ersatz caricatures of classical design. They found there an array of technological ingenuity like none they had ever seen, all the shiny stuff of industrial progress and popular culture. So great was the impact of this fair on public consciousness that, for many decades to come, it and later events like it symbolized the American dream, a belief in advanced technology, mass consumption, and middle-class comfort as the self-evident truths driving the nation's growing influence in the 20th century (Rosenberg, 1982; Trachtenberg, 1982). Looking at the same scene, however, Jane Addams (1910/1960) saw the pathetic contrast in "that terrible winter after the World's Fair, when the general financial depression throughout the country was much intensified in Chicago by the numbers of unemployed stranded at the close of the exposition." The fair remained gorgeously inviting as temperatures dropped, but when it ended, the police stations, even city hall itself, "were crowded by men who could afford no other lodging."[1]

The social conditions of the 1890s were so harsh that they set the tone for reform in the early 20th century, firmly establishing the undercurrent of dread that made reform appear indisputably necessary. Depression, labor insurgency, agrarian resistance (Goodwyn, 1978), racial violence, and swelling zones of poverty faced a crumbling party system in national politics. For the urban masses, socialism grew in appeal as a political alternative. A staggering variety of new immigrants, rising in number to more than a million a year at the dawning of the 20th century, intensified a public sense of urgency about the need to Americanize the newcomers. The public discourse of the respectable classes carried numerous signs that an unprecedented crisis in moral order and political control was fast approaching.[2]

Jacob Riis captured the degradation of social life in his popular book of 1890, *How the Other Half Lives,* which exposed the appalling conditions of tenement slums in New York City. Similar perceptions emerged from many quarters. In 1893, Stephen Crane's novel, *Maggie: A Girl of the Streets,* took its readers into the sweatshops and soup kitchens in which young women like Maggie were driven to brutal excesses by poverty while their male counterparts found no way to alter either their destiny or that of the women and children around them. One senses in the literature of reform a fear that the land of opportunity might be in danger of becoming uninhabitable by "civilized" beings. Alongside this foreboding was a conviction that drastic steps must be taken: first to redouble voluntary and charitable efforts on behalf of the poor and then to revamp social institutions, including—and perhaps especially—those aimed at the young. Commenting on the dimensions of the predicament for children in "the homeless city" (p. 206), Riis (1902) said in a later book: "There was, in the whole of Manhattan, but a single outdoor playground attached to a public school, and that was an old burial-ground in First Street that had been wrested from the dead with immense toil."[3]

As reformers organized to confront proliferating needs, their work coalesced into various strands of progressive reform in the early 20th century. They set about creating new organizations and services for the young, who, in their poverty, their ethnic and racial differences, and sordid representations of their gender, seemed to hold back achievement of the American dream for society as a whole. Forming political coalitions, the reformers took on municipal governments and produced lasting changes in the politics of American cities. They also worked to build intricate webs of professional control over key institutions, such as those of schooling, medical care, poor relief, and legal services. The institutional reforms of that era not only shaped but set the terms of survival for the subsequent histories of organizations that endeavored to help young people.[4]

This chapter reflects on the social meanings and enduring legacy of such reforms for youth-serving organizations. The aim is to explore the transition from informal to bureaucratic organizations of services for young people in the United States during the early 20th century. The very notion of creating organizations to "serve" youth was interwoven with larger institutional changes that defined young people as a client population and specified aspects of their development that were to fall under expert influence beyond familial and communal institutions. Justified as necessary at the time because of the need for order and efficiency, bureaucratic reform brought with it social assumptions that contributed to enabling and hampering the advancement of different groups in a changing social order. After suggesting a historical perspective for relating developments in mainstream institutions, especially public schooling, to the growth of youth-serving organizations (even to those that were avowedly unbureaucratic in their orientations), the chapter briefly considers the implications of such a perspective for reformers and youth-serving organizations today as they work to improve the lives of young people.

Institutional Reforms

The persistence of organizational changes that came between 1890 and 1930 appears most notably in their legacy of tacit rules to which later reforms conformed as a matter of course. This point is crucial in the evolution of specific organizations and service traditions, for it is abundantly clear in retrospect that administrative reformers and professional groups succeeded during those years in altering the fundamental norms underlying laws and policies that regulated social services. Offering plausible arguments for institution building in the face of widespread anxiety about social disorganization in the United States, reformers introduced formal standards, bureaucratic controls, and professional culture as dominant frameworks for the organizational expansion that subsequently proceeded at all levels of government, for all kinds of service providers, and across both public and private sectors. Even those working to complement and counter such influences found little alternative but to respond in kind with more highly structured and integrated organizations of their own.[5]

The number and types of youth-serving organizations grew dramatically in the early years of the 20th century. To an extent never realized in the reform movements of the 19th century, the ideology of reform became the lingua franca of public policy in educational and social institutions, as well as in other fundamental categories of social life such as taxation, economic regulation, and reorganization of local governments. The efforts of individual reformers such as Jacob Riis and Jane Addams on many fronts of human need brought a flowering of creative efforts in the organized and highly dedicated voluntary sector. Equally important, such efforts created momentum and focus for the dramatic expansion of public, legally sanctioned intervention into the lives of all citizens, but especially the poor, young, and immigrant. This latter development in turn spawned new structures and institutional relationships that channeled and regulated the activities of the voluntary sector. The interaction of public and nonpublic interests, including the competition of schooling, nonschool organizations, and governing agencies, helped to demarcate opportunities for the rising generation, authoritatively "structuring the meritocratic contest" of the young.[6]

The "search for order" brought expansion of public authority, philanthropic efforts, and middle-class professionalism to try to meet the needs of young people.[7] After 1890, a profusion of movements, organizations, programs, and methods set out to improve the lives of children and to smooth their transition to adulthood. These reform organizations enshrined "the economically 'worthless' but emotionally 'priceless' child."[8] The life of the young shifted from work roles during adolescence toward guided development under the care of organizations designed for that purpose—a trend accelerated by the passage of child labor laws and greatly intensified by the tightening enforcement of compulsory school attendance laws.

Schools were central to the drift toward institutionalized adolescence, as evidenced by the dramatic increases in enrollment at higher grade levels for school-age children with each passing decade of the early 20th century. Schools played a leading role in absorbing the anxious hopes of parents and reformers, but in so doing, they also helped to standardize both explicit and tacit rules for organizations that saw themselves as caring for the young. Schools moved briskly toward a scientific understanding of human development, a professional elite to control that understanding, and bureaucratic systems of control to maintain mass institutions of compulsory education. *Adolescence,* unknown and virtually inconceivable in the previous century, took form through a complex interplay of institutions, exclusion from the labor market, and changing attitudes toward the status of the young in American society.

G. S. Hall published his two-volume work, *Adolescence,* in 1904, offering the central message that adults must raise the young to be moral, patriotic, and wholesome; otherwise, the future of society could be in doubt. Gradually, over the next decades, adolescence and its synonym *juvenile* came to be linked with deviance, danger, and a need for control. Youth culture seemed to challenge the core of American ideology about the family; the young resisted rather than appreciated their parents' admonitions, expectations, and norms. Youthful deviance and delinquency strongly suggested that the family had lost its expected coherence and that society was suffering as a result.[9]

There was widespread evidence that young people could and did respond to both family and institutional efforts to restrain and reform them. They responded with an inventiveness of their own as they attempted to lay claim to their self-made experience. They created, among other things, distinctive youth cultures, language habits, rituals, self-generated strategies of resistance and accommodation, and unique patterns of consumption. (See, for example, Vigil's description in chapter 4 of the evolution of urban gang life in the early 20th century in Los Angeles.) Young people built a rich social history shaped but never entirely controlled by that evanescent collective consciousness imposed on them by mass institutions that separated and concentrated them together in increasing numbers. Yet despite the irrepressible capacity of young people to pull their habits and self-identities away from those of organizations designed by adults to shape them, formal institutions for adolescents strongly influenced public norms and expectations for the safe and "normal" development of the young.[10]

Bureaucratic, professional, and social-scientific advances after the turn of the century perpetuated the contrast discerned by Jane Addams in 1893. The public accepted a technologically refined vision of social progress for all that worked subtly to maintain the widely disparate opportunities available to different people in the social order. Even the most ostensibly meritocratic of advances, holding forth the promise of connecting social opportunities fairly with individual capacities and preferences, turned out to be reflections of, rather than countervailing forces against, preexisting inequalities. Such was the case in the vision of democracy espoused by the leading test developer Lewis M. Terman, whose pioneering work in psychometrics proceeded in close collaboration with the implementation of ability grouping or tracking in public schools.[11] The result was a framework of social advancement that constituted the most salient institutional reality confronting young people in the United States through their years of compulsory schooling. Social science, allied with bureaucratic expertise, carried a message that the distribution of educational resources grew out of a natural order based on divergent but justifiable human needs. Reinforcing the social order even as they proffered the hope of mobility based on individual differences, objective tests and tracking as conceived by professional elites were fundamentally antidemocratic. They condoned—indeed, reinforced—the contrast of fortunes, and they subordinated to one prevailing mode of evaluation all the myriad cultural intelligences and creative approaches that supported learning among diverse peoples and social groups.

The idea of legitimate disparities in social opportunity became central to schooling in the 20th century, despite reforms that attempted to develop a vision of distributive justice and substantive equality in educational policy. In both policy and practice, the ideal of common schooling shifted to one of variable opportunities according to presumed occupational destiny. The change also took root across the gamut of organized efforts to help the young. Playgrounds and settlement houses, as well as clubs, associations, and institutions of juvenile justice and rehabilitation, reflected a view of legitimate disparities. To some extent, organizations in the voluntary sector worked to maintain an egalitarian framework of social development within local communities for the young people they served; nonetheless, the organizations most likely to thrive were those able to channel the young into mainstream institutions of education and employment. Business and educational interests recognized that these institutions provided the socialization and sorting they viewed as necessary to allow them to continue their competitive selection procedures.[12]

The Child-Savers' Quest: Then and Now

Bureaucratic reforms in the name of efficiency, standardization, and competition injected demands into youth services that remain as salient at the end of the 20th century as at its opening. Publicly endorsed programs connected the aspirations of different groups in society with increasingly consolidated spheres of institutional control and cultural influence. The control that youth-serving organizations came to exercise over their environment, as well as the power they could wield on behalf of the individuals or groups they served, sprang in large part from tacit connections they made to education and employment. Even settlement houses and other organizations that sometimes honored the cultures of immigrant and minority groups, such as churches, subtly promoted assimilation into the dominant culture's institutional norms of time and space usage, concepts of ownership, language habits, and belief in progress as "getting better."[13]

Youth organizations found it difficult, therefore, to "save" children without taking on the goal of shaping them to predetermined images of what they "should" contribute to a productive society that valued efficiency, standardization, and conformity. Certain social, cultural, and linguistic habits of some groups more than others "fit" with behaviors most valued for socioeconomic advancement. To some youth, most visibly African Americans, the effect of social science and professional control over social institutions made racial isolation more permanent and justifiable through a manifest ideology of accommodation to subordinate roles in society (Anderson, 1988; Stanfield, 1985).

The winnowing of organizations became, then, an unspoken process of selection and destruction of programs and services for youth. Throughout the 20th century, this process has depended on the capacity of organizations, whether recreational, rehabilitative, or vocational, to engage and make use of underlying assumptions embedded in bureaucratic structures and procedures. Assumptions that shaped the institutional lives of young people have not only remained relevant to elementary and secondary schools; they constitute the most pervasive rationale and modus operandi for the sector of organizations that serve young people today. Society invests heavily in schools and other youth institutions, and the public view remains that all youth organizations should work together toward common goals and in complementary ways to save the young.

Prevailing Norms

The reasoning that undergirds structures and procedures of both formal education through schooling and youth organizations beyond the school have revolved around five prevailing norms.

The Psychologized Adolescent

In the late 19th century, it was fashionable to induct wayward and delinquent boys and girls into manual or domestic training, give them a skill, and prepare them for at least minimal productive activity in the world of work. The straightforward, moralistic views of the reformers and charitable organizations that led the way in this effort can be found in the records of these groups and state-sponsored institutions, such as the Massachusetts State Industrial School for Girls (Brenzel, 1983). After the turn of the century, progressive reformers grappled with the problem of capturing a larger portion of the inner life and motivation of misbehaving youngsters. Social scientists obliged by offering concepts that could be used institutionally to identify mental and social characteristics thought to be intertwined with deviant behavior, thus offering leverage for the rehabilitation of those in need of help. One result was an urge to deepen the emotional grasp or purported "love" of such institutions as they entered the lives of the young, while simultaneously increasing the control exercised.[14]

Despite this increasing concern with engaging the inner life of the young in an attempt to rehabilitate them, the living and socially embedded identities of the young as they came from community and family loyalties, ethnicity, and gender failed for the most part to enter into the performance of such organizations. To the degree that youth did not respond to or actively resisted interventions, they felt the punitive aspects of youth organizations progressively grow in intensity. Dissenting or recalcitrant individuals became more marginal to mainstream institutions, while conforming youth often found themselves separated from their families and community friends. Just as one finds today a "hunger of memory" among those who conformed to mainstream expectations and a hierarchy of cultural values that places their own ethnic heritage at a disadvantage, so, too, in the past, groups as diverse as Japanese American students heading for college (James, 1985) and Native American adolescents undergoing the trauma of boarding schools (Szasz, 1985) faced a wrenching choice: lower status in concentrated enclaves where ethnic identity continued its primary role in shaping their growth or potentially higher status and economic rewards although dispersed into mainstream institutions, demanding a disavowal of ethnic identity in favor of conventional norms and expectations.[15]

Concepts of social scientists both reflected and influenced racial assumptions, ethnic biases, and middle-class conceptions of appropriate male and female behavior during adolescence (Milofsky, 1989; Sokal, 1987). Such concepts were applied universally with little or no attention to the early age by which many young people took on adult responsibilities or to the power of religion, music, or language to reinforce a sense of ethnic connection for the young. The prevailing ideology of adolescent development tended to select ethnic minorities, as well as nontraditional women, into forceful interventions aimed at neutralizing their culturally specific behaviors and adapting them to society's mainstream norms. At the same time, this ideology supported freer and more spontaneous spaces for those whose background and behaviors favorably matched underlying norms of complex public institutions, especially those of schooling and wage labor. As public institutions increasingly dominated the landscape of programs for young people defined as "problems," tacit forms of selection set a frame of reference for youth organizations that attempted to supplement and improve services provided to such youth.[16]

When imported into bureaucratic organizations, psychologized conceptions of young people became preferred paths of development on one hand and defective types of personality on the other. But such conceptions also persisted as more than that. They infused locally initiated activity with presumed social meanings and expectations. They framed spontaneous effort with intentions linked to institutions beyond the local scene. Norms grounded in home and neighborhood expectations often lost force as youth organizations and upwardly aspiring families defined what was "best" for their children in adherence to the package of traits, attitudes, and skills defined institutionally in relation to professionalized knowledge and powers.

Americanization: The Assimilation Imperative

The period from 1890 to 1924 was one of virulent xenophobia and ideological cleansing in American society. Groups that had traditionally dominated the political and economic institutions of American society struggled to regulate the symbolism of public culture in all its forms. The intensity of the struggle during this era reflected much more than the diversity and growth in numbers among those who were not native-born Protestants of European American background. Diversity had been present before, but now the growing interdependence of communities in the larger society, as they became less segmented and localized, heightened the clash of differences. Paradoxically, the era gave rise to the idea of pluralism, the notion that groups as well as individuals have rights to identity and equal treatment in the public sphere. Yet the idea of pluralism also brought pervasive concerns about exclusionary rules and cultural consolidation into the mainstream of American society (Higham, 1978, 1984). All this social strain and the categories of thought it produced were closely interwoven into the growth of policy and institutions that could be controlled from afar through technical and bureaucratic accords. It was a constructed, contested reality— ultimately leading to widely shared and, for young people, strongly enforced views of what it meant to achieve membership in the nation.

Intensive peer-group socialization to inculcate a corporate conscience in place of ethnic parental authority came to be a central strategy of Americanization. From the playground movement of the progressive era to settlement house movements, cultural assimilation in youth programs was tied to consolidation of national identity and expansive agendas of liberal reform.[17]

An interest in child-centered and nurturing strategies came to be considered the "soft" or "romantic" side of progressive reform. On the hard side, iron-clad forms of Americanization carried imagery that not only defined national citizenship but specified cultural attributes and ideological aims to be reinforced by local youth-serving organizations. And administrative reform generally reduced the active representation of people—especially those from less affluent social groups—in local communities vis-à-vis mass institutions and social service agencies.

Catholics, Jews, and other groups modeled their youth programs on the Americanization drive in the second two decades of this century so as to avoid exclusion. Some reformers in this country flirted with totality—both with ideologically closed systems of thought and occasionally with total institutions in the realm of schooling, camps, and other organized efforts to govern conscience. Yet the drive for ideological consolidation floundered by the end of the Progressive Era, both in education and in national politics. Granted, the lessons of civic unity thundered with pious certainty in Americanization programs and in the xenophobic rhetoric of 100% Americanism. Standardization was celebrated on a massive scale, reflected not only in bureaucratic school reforms but in legislation that prescribed the inculcation of values.

Still, the lessons of national citizenship remained fragmentary in their effects. Perhaps only a historian's conceit could suggest that there was any thoroughgoing program of ideological consolidation in the United States after the turn of the century. Like schools, youth-serving organizations retained abundant constraints and fragmentation—primarily, no doubt, as a result of the sheer intractability of the challenges they faced. Even a strong susceptibility to social engineering did not eliminate all institutional differences in purposes and practices: The Boy Scouts of America emerged as distinct from the youth groups of churches or the YMCA. Yet like schools, most of these organizations gradually brought their norms of leadership and criteria for success in line with the dominant assumptions of mainstream educational institutions and with the predominant folklore about early socialization experiences that led to individual achievement as adults.

Elite Knowledge and "Associationism"

The leading organizations and interests involved in serving youth frequently welcomed greater systematization and hierarchical influence within their own sphere of operations, but they fought consolidation of authority in the political sphere. They wanted instead to retain what might be called a rationalized private influence (Lagemann, 1989). Such a pattern of influence could be wielded indirectly but in culturally authoritative ways through professional networks and institutions that produced reform ideas and technical knowledge and through coordinating agencies such as the Community Chest (Trolander, 1975). To the extent that organized nonpublic interests not only achieved but permanently institutionalized such influence, it may be that the limits of ideological consolidation sprang in part from the nature of organized social action within the private nonprofit sector itself. Complementing that action and perennially reinforcing it were the incapacities of the public sector: the inability to generate policy ideas, to create a foundation of authoritative information for rational action, and in short, to lead.[18]

In advancing such an argument, one must acknowledge the explanations usually offered for this country's lack of organic solidarity in public life: an unparalleled influx of immigrants, the disjointed policy worlds of American federalism, the deepening class divisions of industrial capitalism, the failure of the progressive movement as a political solution and challenge to the party system, and so forth. These explanations are, however, profoundly connected to the nature of voluntary action to influence public policy in the provision of services for young people. No action is more telling in this regard than the limits placed on public policy by strong expectations that the voluntary sector could and should furnish essential knowledge and services in the public interest.

In their scope of activity during the first three decades of the 20th century, youth-serving organizations in the private sector can be viewed within the larger motif of associationism, the use of private forms of association to meet the needs of public policy. In education as in other human service fields, the motif is far from consistent. Associationism can embrace antagonistic as well as common aims among groups organized in the private sector—just as is true, for example, in the relationship of business and industry to public policy that regulates commerce. The concept of joint private action in the public interest can also refer to vastly different aspects of public policy. These may range from surveying needs to establishing institutions to elaborating training procedures to evaluating the effectiveness of services provided.

This historical concept is still useful today for understanding organized private interests that claim to represent the public good on behalf of the young. What it suggests is that disparate groups can act independently to achieve aims that coalesce in a policy vision, one that reinforces the tacit rules and assumptions that shape youth-serving organizations and set terms for their survival in the various organizational fields where they operate.[19]

What must not be forgotten, however, is that private or voluntary networks are by no means disorganized. Not only are they highly organized after their own fashion, but they function in close communication with key figures within social and economic elites, as well as with strategically important gatekeepers in public policy and philanthropy, to maintain the status quo. Thus, these networks are able to transmit consistent messages about what is and is not acceptable in the funding of social programs, for example, or about the priorities for organizational development in relation to groups perceived as needing social services. Perhaps most important, the world of voluntarism in youth services is steeply pyramidal in its governance, dominated by men of wealth and high social standing but structured in layers of authority and involvement to provide high levels of participation for middle-class leaders while also attracting a mass constituency of young people.[20] As different as that world might seem on its surface from the overtly bureaucratized environments of public schools, these institutions are remarkably parallel and highly compatible.

Professionalism as a Way of Life

The reformers, social science experts, and appointed officials who sought to dominate urban social policy during the first three decades of the century created a fabric of voluntary affiliations outside the public sector. Moving in and out of the formal governance systems they worked so successfully to influence, they were far more mobile than local administrative hierarchies created in the late 19th-century phase of bureaucratization in urban institutions. These people formed an aspiring "private government" drawn from the increasingly nationalized culture of university and professional elites. To a large extent in many American cities, they realized their hopes of supplanting local political bosses with professionalized "social efficiency" in the control of urban social institutions by the end of the 1920s.

Organizations that sought to influence the lives of the young were forced to work in an environment increasingly dominated by bureaucratic procedures—surveys, evaluations, formal labeling and record keeping, and institutional criteria for promotion from one institution to another. The national reformers who led in organizing such changes were instrumental in presenting local reformers, public officials, and community groups with a coherent plan for the development of youth in relation to the demands of schooling. Yet it was a design that, over time, retained essential knowledge and powers of decision outside of the local sphere of public control. The pattern of school governance that prevailed in American cities set maturing bureaucracies against innovative leadership developing from within the ranks and at the grass roots. It created organizational disincentives against encouraging the bubbling up of new ideas from the work force and local community. Perhaps most of all, this pattern removed effective bureaucratic control from schooling organizations at the community level and frustrated strategies of youth development attuned to local and culturally specific conditions.

This emerging structure of administrative control in schooling presented local youth-serving organizations with a set of expectations of how schools would select and treat young people in the course of their formal education. Such practices derived from a strong emphasis on *social efficiency*—the power to allocate individuals to probable destinies in the occupational order. In addition, schools could determine *individual differences* on the basis of instruments developed by social scientists to scale human traits and sort young people into tracked opportunities. These, in turn, led to *differentiated programs and curricula* devised by professional educators who had the power to codify knowledge and experience in discrete subject areas and curricular sequences and to develop organized professional interests permanently around the transmission of such knowledge. *Supervision* ensured all of the preceding by giving full rein to the power of administrators—viewed as scientific managers separated from the process of production—to exercise the authority of the state over teachers and youth workers and to measure their performance according to administrative criteria of evaluation. The control of evaluation and its use are especially potent aspects of mainstream institutions in their dominant influence over marginal programs and countervailing strategies for working with young people.[21]

Consolidation in the Public Sphere

The incorporation of youth-serving organizations into a larger system of corporate/bureaucratic channeling and selection, as indicated broadly in the previous paragraphs, has been a lively topic of scholarly debate over the past 20 years. One of the key developments—the politics of the nonpublic-to-public shift in governance and priorities—deserves closer scrutiny. We can see the shift, for example, in the early development of vocational guidance after the turn of the century. Frank Parsons, whose Vocation Bureau in Boston was the prototype for the entire vocational guidance movement in the United States, did not live to see his idea conveyed fully from its philanthropic origins into the public bureaucracy. The story is a personal one marked by intellectual idiosyncrasies and a strong penchant for social criticism of the emerging industrial order. Parsons believed that working people could learn to analyze their lives and careers more thoroughly. This process of self-analysis, aided by expert counselors when necessary, would help people to make wise vocational choices. His writings and institution building, closely intertwined with the settlement house movement in the 1890s, proceeded independent of public-sector legal and institutional development (Davis, 1969; Mann, 1954).

After his death in 1908, the ideas of Parsons continued to influence others to launch nonpublic, community-based programs in vocational guidance and counseling. Much more important in the long run, his ideas entered into the larger policy debate taking place over vocational preparation for young people, and something called guidance became part of the standard institutional recipe for school-based social services that followed in school systems across the country. To leap ahead in time, by 1930, the function of vocational guidance had become part of the sorting and selection functions of public secondary schools. Ironically, this guidance had become more attuned to decisions about courses and schooling options than to the external exigencies of the labor market.[22] Strongly imbued with applied social science, vocational guidance began as an independent movement to serve youth, but it came to mean something closer to prediction and control of choices by professional educators. Guidance lost its primary goals, which lay beyond the schoolhouse walls, and was instead subsumed within the institution that took it over. After its bureaucratic metamorphosis, vocational guidance came to mean the expert handling of problem students within the school itself rather than open-ended counseling for rational decision making about jobs, as Parsons had envisioned (Stephens, 1970).

A similar process of principled, humanitarian initiative, followed first by incorporation into mass institutions, then by professionalization of standards and subordination to bureaucratic controls, and finally by inexorable shifts in original intent and social meaning, can be observed across numerous arenas of youth services as private, voluntary efforts coalesced with the normative structures described in this chapter.

Concerns for the Future

What can be learned from such a historical exploration that spans decades far removed from the present? Many people today are trying to reactivate the voluntary sector, partly in reaction to the perceived failure of mass institutions and partly in attempts to generate choice, initiative, and alternative approaches at the grass roots. Others are proposing ways to loosen bureaucratic authority in the public sector, aiming to stimulate greater variety and inventiveness in the creation of social services. These are significant developments in public policy, but the springs of social discord run much deeper than the current rhetoric of reform. The grinding contrast of 100 years ago is still with us: the high tech and the homeless. It may be true that the public sphere and its institutional world have become more elaborate and diversified than the most prescient progressive could have foreseen on the threshold of this century, but the dread that sustains bureaucratic control remains fully intact. It is most evident among mainstream institutions that serve the masses of people who cannot afford the cost of privileged organizations and educational self-determination.

It is specifically evident in the frequency of behaviors that seem to tear at the most fundamental of societal values, as the young enter boldly and publicly into "adult" arenas of behavior: producing offspring; establishing commercial enterprises (often underground and crime linked); and defying schools by defacing and ignoring them, declaring adult-controlled institutions irrelevant, and openly using schools as places from which to operate their own social and economic activities. Whereas gender and ethnicity were once thought to be good predictors of certain behaviors, today interethnic gangs and young women in criminal and drug activities make clear to school and police authorities that older norms and expectations no longer hold.

One important lesson from the historical experience is that small-scale and voluntary efforts are not enough to meet the needs of youth in the face of a pervasive institutional structure that operates to select youth programs into the mainstream or to push them toward oblivion. Indeed, small successes can be misleading without a concomitant drive to change the basic rules and assumptions of mainstream institutions in their treatment of young people. History suggests that if the most promising experiments in organizing the lives of the young "succeed" splendidly, they are all the more likely to become incorporated into institutions whose tacit rules and underlying social assumptions will transform them further. In addition, such experiments might—like new methods and organizational forms that sprang from the progressive education movement during the first half of this century—retain their originality to some degree but move into the arena of fee-based voluntary associations, patronized largely by those with enough money to make the choice. This, too, would arguably compromise their social vision.

Furthermore, a look back at youth organizations in this century reminds us that formal schooling and informal organizations for youth are interconnected agents of socialization. Out-of-school organizations cannot be treated merely as alternatives to dysfunctional schooling practices. They are part of a combined reality with mainstream institutions. To be understood in all their complexity, both must be viewed in relation to institutional norms that neither school reformers nor those who offer alternatives through youth-serving organizations have managed to overcome. To help young people find some place for themselves in family, community, workplace, and public bureaucracies, youth organizations must reexamine the highly problematic but powerful nexus of institutional rules that supports or impedes the growth of particular types of organizations. It may well be that rules that overtly support primary goals of academic achievement, college attendance, and "getting ahead" will find greatest favor with funders and public officials. Overlooked as lacking "vision" may be organizations that acknowledge "second-chance" educational institutions as appropriate for some young people and that celebrate youth who set feasible employment goals for themselves while they support families and delay further education or choose to study only part-time.

Creating acceptance for a range of youth organizations to meet the needs of those with a host of varying definitions and timetables of becoming "better off" is difficult but not impossible. Changing the institutions that set the terms for organizational growth and survival often seems impossible, but it is necessary. The latter challenge will offer struggles other than those engaged in by most reformers and advocates of change in the past. The first step is to realize that the conditions of organizational survival are constructed and actively maintained by coordinated networks of institutional control that have been granted longstanding legitimacy in law and public policy. But these are subject to change through political action.

The structure of mass institutions such as public schooling and other social services is grounded in the dread unleashed by this nation's swift passage from traditional and agrarian communities to an industrial society. Deep change requires a recasting of underlying categories, not just temporary new players among youth-serving organizations. That means more than restructured, high-performance grass-roots or local organizations to serve the young based on client or consumer preferences. The supreme task is to construct new values in the nation's public life, a phalanx of understanding robust enough to open the way for democratic, collective action unmediated by present institutional norms that govern social services for the young.

Notes

[1]Addams (orig. 1910, ed. 1960:121–122). On the cultural impact of the fair, see Rosenberg (1982) and Trachtenberg (1982).

[2]Boyer (1978); on agrarian resistance see Goodwyn (1978).

[3]Riis (1970); the quote is from Riis's *The Making of an American* (New York: Macmillan, 1902), p. 202, and "the homeless city" appears on p. 206.

[4]Reese (1986); for a perceptive essay on the meanings of progressive reform, see Rogers (1982:113–132).

[5]A fuller treatment of this subject and review of the pertinent literature appears in James (1991:167–222); on the bureaucratization of schooling, see Tyack (1974).

[6]For one major American city, Labaree (1988) traces this interaction in a study of the changing structures of educational opportunity in the transition from the nineteenth to the twentieth century.

[7]Wiebe (1967) traces this search for the years between 1877 and 1920 and underscores its interdependence with shifts in the organization of both the private and public sectors.

[8]Zelizer (1985) examines this shift in American society's vision of and approach to childhood.

[9]Several studies of twentieth-century views of adolescence indicate the close interweaving of societal integrity, family coherence, and adolescent control. See especially Gilbert (1986); and Kett (1977).

[10]The social and institutional change that redefined the lives of young people from the late nineteenth to the early twentieth centuries is well depicted by Kett, 1977 and Nasaw, 1985. On the changing shape of adolescence and youth culture, see Modell (1989) and Fass (1977).

[11]See Minton (1988) and (Chapman) 1988 on the connection of testing and tracking.

[12]On the changing conceptions of equality over time, see Coleman (1990).

[13]Lissak (1989), Carson (1990), and Crocker (1991) offer descriptions of settlement house life and its occasional brushes with pluralism.

[14]Schlossman (1977) and Sutton (1988) document ways that institutions worked to create "caring" images while trying also to reshape the young, even when such efforts brought alienation and displacement from families and communities. On the Massachusetts State Industrial School for Girls, see Brenzel (1983).

[15]See Rodriguez, 1981. On the cultural conflicts of Japanese Americans, see James (1985:155-174); on Native Americans, see Szasz (1985:209-218).

[16]On the ideology of social science and its influence on institution-building after the turn of the century, see Sokal (1987); for a current study on the bureaucratic uses of professional social science in schools, see Milofsky (1989).

[17]Compare, for example, Cavallo (1981) and Lissak (1989) on processes of Americanization in these different settings. Carlson (1975) and Olneck (1989) underscore the subtle, yet comprehensive, programs for conformity that touched immigrants, especially their young.

[18]For a perceptive study of private influence, see Lagemann (1989). The role of the Community Chest in "winnowing" local organizations after the 1920s is well explored by Trolander (1975).

[19]Details of these processes in specific decades appear in Hawley (1974). On private (specifically philanthropic) power and the bureaucratic organization of social planning, see Karl (1976).

[20]For a pertinent study of leadership in the Boy Scouts and the YMCA as character-building organizations, see Macleod (1983).

[21]A recent study (Stake, 1986) of the ways in which formal evaluation undermined a promising youth program offers a reminder that the chilly relationship between bureaucratic control and creative program development in youth organizations is of more than historical interest.

[22]Kantor (1988) reveals this development in his account of vocational reform in California between 1880 and 1930. On the development of the profession of vocational guidance, see Stephens (1970).

References

Addams, J. (1960). *Twenty years at Hull House.* New York: New American Library.

Anderson, J. D. (1988). *The education of blacks in the South, 1860–1935.* Chapel Hill: University of North Carolina Press.

Boyer, P. (1978). *Urban masses and moral order in America, 1820–1920.* Cambridge, MA: Harvard University Press.

Brenzel, B. M. (1983). *Daughters of the state: A social portrait of the first reform school for girls in North America.* Cambridge, MA: MIT Press.

Carlson, R. A. (1975). *The quest for conformity: Americanization through education.* New York: Wiley.

Carson, M. (1990). *Settlement folk: Social thought and the American settlement movement, 1885–1930.* Chicago: University of Chicago Press.

Cavallo, D. (1981). *Muscles and morals: Organized playgrounds and urban reform, 1880–1920.* Philadelphia: University of Pennsylvania Press.

Chapman, P. D. (1988). *Testers as sorters: Lewis M. Terman, applied psychology, and the intelligence testing movement, 1890–1930.* New York: New York University Press.

Coleman, J. S. (1990). *Equality and achievement in education.* Boulder, CO: Westview Press.

Crane, S. (1893/1960). *Maggie: A girl of the streets.* New York: Fawcett Premier.

Crocker, R. H. (1991). *Social work and social order: The settlement movement in two industrial communities, 1890–1930.* Urbana, IL: University of Illinois Press.

Davis, H. V. (1969). *Frank Parsons: Prophet, innovator, counselor.* Carbondale, IL: Southern Illinois University Press.

Fass, P. S. (1977). *The damned and the beautiful: American youth in the 1920's.* New York: Oxford University Press.

Gilbert, J. (1986). *A cycle of outrage: America's reaction to the juvenile delinquent in the 1950s.* New York: Oxford University Press.

Goodwyn, L. (1978). *The populist moment: A short history of the agrarian revolt in America.* New York: Oxford University Press.

Hall, G. S. (1904–05). *Adolescence.* Vol. 1 and 2. New York: Appleton.

Hawley, E. W. (1974). Herbert Hoover, the commerce secretariat, and the vision of an "associative state," 1921–1928. *Journal of American History, 81,* 116–40.

Higham, J. (1978). *Strangers in the land: Patterns of American nativism, 1860–1925.* New York: Atheneum.

Higham, J. (1984). *Send these to me: Immigrants in urban America.* Baltimore: Johns Hopkins University Press.

James, T. (1985). "Life begins with freedom": The college Nisei, 1942–1945. *History of Education Quarterly, 25,* 155–174.

James, T. (1991). State authority and the politics of educational change. *Review of Research in Education, 17,* 162–222.

Kantor, H. A. (1988). *Learning to earn: School, work, and vocational reform in California, 1880–1930.* Madison, WI: University of Wisconsin Press.

Karl, B. D. (1976). Philanthropy, policy planning, and the bureaucratization of the democratic ideal. *Daedalus, 105,* 129–149.

Kett, J. F. (1977). *Rites of passage: Adolescence in America, 1790 to the present.* New York: Basic Books.

Labaree, D. (1988). *The making of an American high school: The credentials market and the Central High School of Philadelphia, 1838–1939.* New Haven: Yale University Press.

Lagemann, E. C. (1989). *The politics of knowledge: The Carnegie Corporation, philanthropy, and public policy.* Middletown, CT: Wesleyan University Press.

Lissak, R. S. (1989). *Pluralism and progressives: Hull House and the new immigrants, 1890–1919.* Chicago: University of Chicago Press.

Macleod, D. I. (1983). *Building character in the American boy: The Boy Scouts, YMCA, and their forerunners, 1870–1920.* Madison, WI: University of Wisconsin Press.

Mann, A. (1954). Frank Parsons: The professor as radical. *Yankee reformers in the urban age.* Cambridge, MA: Harvard University Press.

Milofsky, C. (1989). *Testers and testing: The sociology of school psychology.* New Brunswick, NJ: Rutgers University Press.

Minton, H. L. (1988). *Lewis Terman: Pioneer in psychological testing.* New York: New York University Press.

Modell, J. (1989). *Into one's own: From youth to adulthood in the United States, 1920–1975.* Berkeley, CA: University of California Press.

Nasaw, D. (1985). *Children of the city: At work and at play.* New York: Oxford University Press.

Olneck, M. R. (1989). Americanization and the education of immigrants, 1900–1925: An analysis of symbolic action. *American Journal of Education, 97,* 398–423.

Reese, W. J. (1986). *Power and the promise of school reform: Grassroots movements during the progressive era.* Boston: Routledge and Kegan Paul.

Riis, J. (1890/1970). *How the other half lives: Studies among the tenements of New York.* Cambridge, MA: Belknap Press of Harvard University Press.

Riis, J. (1902). *The making of an American.* New York: Macmillan.

Rodriguez, R. (1981). *Hunger of memory: The education of Richard Rodriguez.* Boston, MA: D. R. Godine.

Rogers, D. (1982). In search of progressivism. *Reviews in American History, 10,* 113–132.

Rosenberg, E. S. (1982). *Spreading the American dream: American economic and cultural expansion, 1890–1945.* New York: Hill and Wang.

Schlossman, S. L. (1977). *Love and the American delinquent: The theory and practice of "progressive" juvenile justice.* Chicago: University of Chicago Press.

Sokal, M. M. (1987). *Psychological testing and American society, 1890–1930.* New Brunswick, NJ: Rutgers University Press.

Stake, R. E. (1986). *Quieting reform: Social science and social action in an urban youth program.* Urbana, IL: University of Illinois Press.

Stanfield, J. H. (1985). *Philanthropy and Jim Crow in American social science.* Westport, CT: Greenwood Press.

Stephens, W. R. (1970). *Social reform and the origins of vocational guidance.* Washington, DC: National Vocational Guidance Association.

Sutton, J. (1988). *Stubborn children: Controlling delinquency in the United States,*

1640–1981. Berkeley, CA: University of California Press.

Szasz, M. C. (1985). Federal boarding schools and the Indian child: 1920–1960. In N. R. Hiner & J. M. Hawes (Eds.), *Growing up in America: Children in historical perspective* (pp. 209–218). Urbana, IL: University of Illinois Press.

Trachtenberg, A. (1982). *The incorporation of America: Culture and society in the gilded age.* New York: Hill and Wang.

Trolander, J. A. (1975). *Settlement houses and the Great Depression.* Detroit: Wayne State University Press.

Tyack, D. B. (1974). *The one best system: A history of American urban education.* Cambridge, MA: Harvard University Press.

Wiebe, R. H. (1967). *The search for order, 1877–1920.* New York: Hill and Wang.

Zelizer, V. A. (1985). *Pricing the priceless child: The changing social value of children.* New York: Basic Books.

8

Misperceptions of Gender and Youth: Learning Together, Learning Apart

Elisabeth Hansot

Does separate mean equivalent in what youth organizations do for young women and men? This chapter looks at misperceptions of gender that, since the end of the 19th century, have influenced the provision of coeducational learning opportunities for the young in schools and youth organizations. These institutional views of what early learning conditions mean for males and females later in their lives are derived from mainstream traditional ideals of childhood and adolescence as periods of getting ready to be a man or a woman. Yet many young people currently take up adult activities and roles early in life and move primarily in gender-segregated peer groups. They resist institutions that regard it as their duty to prepare the young to be grown-ups. This chapter suggests that youth organizations— particularly those in inner cities—need to look beyond the matter of gender mixing to discover ways of building cross-generational learning contexts for young men and women.

Home is the only place where you can go out and in. There are places you can go in to, and places you can go out of, but the one place, if you do but find it, where you may go out and in both, is home.

George MacDonald

During the 1980s, youth-serving organizations came under considerable pressure to become socially inclusive, to mix boys and girls, and to integrate young people from different ethnic groups. The implicit or explicit premise for such pressure was that if young people learn to live with social differences, they will become more tolerant adults. However, some commentators on society questioned a policy of social integration. In the 1990s, many feminists who once sought to open all-male youth groups to girls advocated benefits in all-female organizations. Leaders of some neighborhood-based organizations expressed their belief that ethnic homogeneity might assist them in better adapting youth services to diverse communities. Integration or separatist pluralism—which policy should guide practice?

This policy debate, of course, was hardly new in a society as pluralistic as the United States. In fact, one strand of policy and practice of social integration extends over more than 150 years: coeducation in public schools. In the mid-19th century, Americans called public schools "common schools"; the term illustrates the ideal (often violated) that public education should mix all the children of all the people. The common school was to teach together rich and poor, native born and immigrant, Catholic and Protestant.

But the term *coeducation* designated a special kind of mixing by gender. By the 1850s, when the word coeducation was invented, it had already become standard practice to mix girls and boys together in classrooms and to teach them basically the same subjects. A curious relationship developed between policy talk and practice in coeducation. When the practice of coeducation began, silence reigned; few people bothered to discuss it. Once coeducation had become embedded in schools—part of the institutional grammar of the institution—it proved to be exceedingly difficult to dislodge, despite repeated attacks from its foes. Practice deflected policy talk as a rock does the rain.

A long history—a full storehouse of experience—enables us to look at the rationale and practical operation of coeducation in public schools, institutions that have wielded strong influence on other youth-centered institutions over the past century. Are there perhaps conclusions or questions that arise from this history to inform current debates about gender and ethnic integration and separatism in youth-serving organizations? This chapter sees *gender* as a social construct, the array of cultural meanings that become attached in any sociocultural group to the biological division of the sexes. But mainstream institutions, public media, and public policies also play a part in constructing gender, and the creations of meanings around behaviors that mark one's gender are highly interdependent with other forces at both the local and national levels. The focus in this chapter is first on how gender differences have played themselves out in schools and then on the ways peer groups operate when they are not part of adult-driven organizations such as schools. Finally, this chapter suggests how, in the face of what appeared at the end of the 20th century to be the increasing isolation of some peer cultures, the need to reconnect these peer groups through achievement and affiliation with adults from across generations emerged as a more important issue than ethnic or gender integration.

Ways of Seeing Coeducation in Public Schools

For most of the history of the United States, most advocates of coeducation did not believe that boys and girls would or should follow the same paths in later life. In other words, social integration in school was not designed to produce identical career paths in adulthood. Schooling was intended to prepare girls to become better mothers and boys to become citizens and efficient workers. (See Tyack and Hansot [1990] for a history of coeducation in U.S. schools, especially chapter 6 on expectation paths for males and females.)

Most supporters of coeducation did not argue that boys and girls were basically alike in aptitude or behavior. Instead, they contended that the sexes should learn together because their differences were complementary, and the result of coeducation would be that both would become educated in a more well-rounded way than through separate education. This "contagion" model of education clearly served coeducation; its proponents never seemed to consider it odd that they expected only what they might regard as "virtuous" behavior to spread from one gender to the other.

In general, boys and girls had far more similar experiences when under the control of teachers in the classroom than they did when they were more on their own, on the playground or within extracurricular events. When not under adult jurisdiction, younger children typically segregated themselves by sex and pursued different activities. Peers—not adults—played an important role in teaching children and youth distinct norms of behavior and in producing gender segregation. (See chapters 3 and 4 in Tyack and Hansot [1990] for discussion of such peer-orchestrated segregation.)

Gender segregation and preparation for distinct adult roles, such as homemaking and other occupations, increased in coeducational schools as students grew older. In elementary schools, children studied basically the same subjects together. In high schools, particularly in urban areas that could afford it, as children approached adulthood, they more often pursued sex-segregated courses in vocational subjects and participated in certain sex-distinct activities, such as sports. (For discussion of similar patterns among contemporary children, see Anyon, 1983, and Maccoby and Jacklin, 1987.)

But gender expectations established in the 19th century differed greatly from discussions of gender in schools a century later. Liberal feminists argued for equal education of girls and boys because they wanted schooling to produce equal opportunity in work and in public life for adult women and men. These feminists saw girls and boys as intellectual equals and pointed to discrimination in classrooms as the source of differences in achievement, especially in science and mathematics. Following a hierarchical model in which influence flowed from adult to child, these feminist reformers focused not on peer groups so much as on parents and teachers. When feminists spoke about "patriarchy," they envisaged a common pattern of male domination in all institutions and distinct gender identities created by sex-role socialization that operated in essentially similar fashion in all contexts. Male domination was part of a seamless web found everywhere. They had great faith in the power of consciousness-raising as a way to bring individuals in line with what they saw as appropriate mainstream norms. (For evidence of sexism and sex bias in schools of this era, see Frazier and Sadker,1973, and Pottker and Fishel, 1977.)

If, in the 1970s, gender mixing was seen as a prerequisite for adult equality, in the 1980s, the opposite premise gained currency—namely, that adult equality could best be achieved by an earlier experience of gender separateness. By the 1990s, a new generation of feminists advanced ideas quite different both from those of the traditional advocates and practitioners of coeducation and from those of the liberal integrationist feminists of the 1970s. They argued that females and males had different values and behaviors. They claimed that schools honor and reward male concepts of knowledge and ethics while slighting the feminine. Some saw psychic and social costs to women in coeducation and argued for the benefits of separate schools and other institutions of socialization for girls; such separate contexts could ensure that the values of females could be validated and their leadership potential stimulated. Stressing differences between the sexes, reformers of this decade believed that gender identity and social roles of women had become problematic because they had been undervalued in male-dominated institutions. (A sample of texts that make the argument for different values of males and females include Arnot, 1983; Belenky, Clinchy, Goldberger, & Tarule, 1986; Gilligan, 1982; Noddings, 1984; Tetreault & Thompson, 1986.)

These arguments continued to maintain an article of faith strongly held in the United States since the days of Horace Mann: The years of childhood and youth are formative—"as the twig is bent, so grows the tree." Those who have written about gender have taken this dictum very seriously, penning many articles and books on the importance of sex-role socialization in the early years. Implicit in much of this analysis is the notion that persons acquire a gender identity and patterns of behavior quite early and go through life enacting scripts learned as children. Psychologists have developed this paradigm; they typically focus on individuals who live out these dramas in a seamless web called "society" (Maccoby, 1990; Maccoby & Jacklin, 1974).

How do girls and boys learn different sex scripts? Research on this question has focused primarily on mainstream children of middle-class, European American families. Findings have shown for these families that boys and girls at about age three prefer same-sex play groups; this is true even among children whose handling by their parents is largely gender free. Although children may know something about the roles of the other sex, they concentrate primarily on enacting their own roles. They learn these behaviors from observations of the people around them, including reading, television, and their own relatives. This pattern of seeing the self as belonging to a specific sex and preferring to be with members of that sex persists from preschool to puberty.[1]

School-age boys working in groups behave in a dominant manner toward girl groups of the same age. Not surprisingly, girls avoid such situations—part of an understandable human tendency to avoid interacting with those with whom one cannot establish a relationship of reciprocal influence. Boys also avoid the company of girls. In fact, boys' cross-sex avoidance is probably stronger than is girls' avoidance of boys, and this predisposition maintains itself independent of adult interventions. Boys and girls develop different interactive styles, with girls being more indirect and compromise prone and with boys being more self-assertive and aggressive (Maccoby, 1990).

Mainstream children's expectations of the salience of gender and appropriate gender roles differ enormously by age and social or institutional context. Consider the different gender meanings embedded in these contexts: the dentist's office and the singles' bar, the business office and the bridge club, the Little League and the supermarket, the church service and the English class, the superhighway and the boxing ring, and the army and the old age home. There is not one gender script for these settings but there are many, each appropriate to context and often to age. How, then, if children are socialized at an early age to gender behaviors presumed to stick with them, do they learn through life so many conventional sets of gender expectations? The twig of sex socialization does not become a rigid tree but rather a flexible bush of many branches.

Young people and adults seem to learn these rules easily enough from peers or from authority figures and seem to have no great difficulty in shifting their behaviors from context to context—from classroom to playground or from workplace to family or church. Moreover, many learn to expect discrepancies in opportunities across these settings. Boys and girls in an elementary school expect to be treated fairly by the teacher; they expect uniform application of rewards and punishments, among other things. But when these same children become adults, they enter a work force that is mostly segregated and unequal in compensation. A woman who is a star in an academic setting may still find herself relegated to licking stamps in a political campaign. A relatively egalitarian setting for boys and girls in schools and other youth institutions may not lead anywhere significant for women in the future.

Decisions for Youth Organizations

What does this multiplicity of gender contexts mean for youth organizations? What does it mean that on the playground, children develop their own set of rules governing appropriate behavior for the two sexes, one that is quite different from that expected in the classroom? What does it mean that the young clearly keep on learning about gender roles as they age and move through various kinds of institutional settings that make different kinds of demands on them? And, perhaps most important, what does the mainstream belief in the early years as formative for adulthood mean for organizations that must meet the needs of young people who take up adult activities and roles at an early age?

At the end of the 20th century, young people who reach their teens have already become skilled in navigating settings in which gender has quite different meanings. They have shown they can adapt rather easily to either sex segregation or integration depending on the type of activity. Thus, in a community center sponsored by the parks and recreation division of their city, adolescents might expect both a coed dance and a boys' boxing ring. Their level of comfort with gender practices is likely to be relative to specific settings, not a function of some fixed sex-role socialization norms. It may be argued that youth organizations do not need to choose between being sex segregated or sex integrated; some activities may be open to both genders, and others may not. Such a mix may jar adults, who sometimes intellectually demand more organizational consistency than they in fact experience, but the mix would not necessarily surprise young people accustomed to mixed practices in schools, churches, and families.

Young people may quite successfully and unselfconsciously navigate a variety of differently normed gender settings. What happens in one organization insofar as gender relations are concerned appears not to influence gender relations in another. Young people are flexible, attuned to specific activities rather than to generic policies. Hence, the importance of any one experience of gender separation *or* integration for adult equality may be vastly overrated.

Young people also make their own gender norms if given the leeway to do so. These peer-generated norms often go unnoticed by adults and can be at variance with preferred adult practice. An ethnography of an open elementary school in Minneapolis illustrates this point (Cone & Perez, 1986). The school sought to eradicate sexist practices by integrating boys and girls in all activities and by avoiding gender stereotyping. The school had a progressive philosophy that promoted student initiative and sought to make young people partners in the teaching-learning process.

Maps that pupils drew of the classroom indicated that students themselves divided the classroom by gender whenever they had a chance. In three of the four classrooms, the teacher allowed the pupils to arrange their own desks where they wanted, but in the fourth, a traditional teacher assigned seating in a pattern desegregated by sex. In the first classroom, students divided space into a boys' section and a girls' section, where the desks of each sex were separated, and their maps generally showed their own side on a larger scale and in more detail. In the second room, the 16 children who had desks of their own segregated them by sex, and even in the more public spaces, boys and girls generally associated with members of the same sex. The third room had lofts for private work spaces, and these were identified as male and female territories. Only one girl placed her desk in a boys' space, and a boy complained that she was hostile to boys, refusing to permit boys to sit on or at her desk (Cone & Perez, 1986) while allowing her girlfriends that privilege. In the fourth room, where the teacher was more traditional, the teacher-enforced desegregation of the sexes in formal seating arrangements dissolved into separate-sex groupings when the students had a free choice of activities.

Then, researchers asked all the boys and girls to locate three animals—a tiger, pig, and monkey—on their maps of the classroom. In two of the rooms, the children placed the positive ones (tiger and monkey) in their own territory (except for one boy, who put the tiger in the girls' space to frighten them) but put the pig (which they thought of as smelly and undesirable) in the territory of the opposite sex.

The "open" classroom approach gave pupils more social autonomy than did the more traditional class. When they could follow their own preferences for gender interaction as they did on the playground, the children tended to segregate themselves by sex despite the nonsexist philosophy of the school. When the researchers pointed out to the teachers what was happening, two of the teachers decided to integrate the seating of boys and girls but gave it up because it produced disruption: Cone and Perez (1986) comment that teachers accepted students' wishes regarding sex segregation of space and encouraged integrated activities such as a mock trial and a business project.

The looser the structure of an organization—as in a progressive classroom in contrast to a traditional teacher-dominated one—the more the children's own preferences shape gender arrangements. Youth organizations represent a broad spectrum on this dimension of rigid/loose structure but are more on the informal side than most schools. Thus, young people's own desires about sex integration or separatism usually have more play in neighborhood-based organizations than in schools. Because children and youth are not *compelled* to take part in voluntary organizations, as they are in schools, their participation may depend in part on whether they feel more comfortable with separate-sex or mixed-sex activities. These asymmetries in gender styles do not, however, maintain themselves in mature adult relationships. Although some differences do remain, in well-established adult couples, they do not seem to imply differences in power. The explanation may be that married couples are no longer competing for resources or protecting separate turf. In a different situation, one in which joint objectives are dominant, men and women adapt their behaviors accordingly (Maccoby, 1990).

Gender Segregation Across Cultures

For young people in some cultural and socioeconomic contexts, gender-organized peer groups persist and are durable. This issue of peer influence on gender norms deserves far more attention than it has received. Much literature on gender is based, either explicitly or implicitly, on hierarchical models of socialization in which influence flows from adults to the young as a "natural" part of the maturation process. Yet some research has questioned this premise and has called attention instead to the way young people create their own attitudes and behaviors. Understanding how this takes place is important either if one wants to *adapt* organizations to the cultural patterns of the young or if one wants to alter these patterns of belief and action (Heath & McLaughlin, 1991; Thorne & Luria, 1986).

The tendency to overestimate adult influence on youth has strong historical roots, and most youth organizations led by adults have embodied such assumptions. Scouting, for instance, introduced early in the 20th century, was intended to counteract the softness of home life by a system of authoritarian control coupled with strenuous outdoor activities intended to toughen up youth. Two key assumptions shaped these boy-oriented youth groups. One was that class and religious differences were much less important than biological maturation. "Instincts" could be charted and "scientifically" used by various boys' organizations: Emulation and imitation, as well as pugnacity, could all be channeled to good effect as youngsters moved through the various ranks of organizational accomplishment (Kett, 1977).

Equally important was the belief that adolescence was the critical period for shaping the adult character. It followed that young people, regardless of social class, were in need of close and sustained adult supervision to navigate the tricky passages to adulthood. Such youth programs as the Boy's Brigades, 4-H Clubs, and Camp Fire Girls were predicated on the belief that adult-directed activities, when properly aligned with youths' maturation level, would produce socially beneficial behaviors that would persist through adulthood. The complementary belief was that unsupervised youth were prone to fall under the sway of youth gangs and that their influence was the decisive factor in producing adult criminals. (See Gilbert, 1986, on this point and on mass-culture influences in the making of delinquency.)

As the century progressed, the limitations of adult-directed youth organizations became apparent. They were failing to reach lower-class boys who valued physical prowess, spontaneity, and defiance of authority. Made up of relatively homogeneous middle-class youth who often defined themselves by their antagonism toward youth of other classes or nationalities, these organizations were not equipped to reach out to immigrant and working-class youths. The transformation of post-1920 adolescent subculture saw peer norms substituted for adult-driven standards of accomplishment. Youth raised in this more permissive postwar environment engaged "in a self-conscious grasping after the symbols of adult status and in admiration for young people who challenged adults, expressions represented as fully by reckless driving in the 1950s as by public kissing in the 1920s" (Kett, 1977, p. 269). These young people were by and large free of parental pressure to join the old type of adult-sponsored youth organizations with their emphasis on character and moral virtue.

The final decades of the 20th century witnessed another change. As moral standards relaxed, succeeded by a more laissez-faire attitude toward youth, the need even to challenge adult conventions diminished. This left adolescent subcultures, viewed simply as insulated and self-contained units, more or less autonomous. This was particularly the case for young people of color in inner cities. Their youth groups grew more and more self-contained, although specific patterns of activities and social norms varied across groups (see chapter 4). Not to attend to such differences is to repeat the naive homogenizing assumptions of 19th-century psychologists who ignored class and religion or those of the 20th century who often equated culture with socioeconomic class. For example, there is evidence that among Latino youth raised as Catholics, both religious and family values continue to cohere with adult norms. Other ethnic groups whose youth have failed to sustain affiliation with their parents' religious institutions may have lost traditional avenues of adult influence.[2]

A study of young African Americans in an inner-city neighborhood carried out over several years indicates the pervasive, largely autonomous influence of peer culture on both adolescent boys and girls (Anderson, 1990). Gone are the "old heads," both male and female, that represented important institutions of the traditional community. The role of male elders was to instruct, as well as support and encourage, young men to meet their responsibilities with regard to the work ethic, family life, the law, and decency. Described as a "kind of guidance counselor and moral cheerleader," the old head could be a minister, church deacon, local policeman, favorite teacher, athletic coach, or street corner man. Usually a churchgoing family man, he often served as a link to the more privileged classes in the black community, using moral tales, wit, exhortation, and example to help "his boys" make their way in a segregated society. Older females, often called "Mama," "Big Mama," "Mis' Lu," or "Mis' Dawson," to show deference, exerted their influence on boys and girls alike. Typically, they played the grandmother role, meting out advice, discipline, and when appropriate, even corporal punishment. They relied for their effectiveness on a network of community relations and on their reputation for living a "good life." Their responsibility was not limited to their own children; it extended to neighbors' children as well, one of the benefits of a coherent community.

The influence of male and female elders has plummeted in the face of increased mobility, segmentation, and anonymity within the African American community. The scarcity of jobs for young African American males has discredited the message of hard work; the high-risk, quick-money drug culture offers a more alluring prospect. Older females lament their diminished influence; the girls and boys they seek to influence see them as "square old ladies."

Long-term case studies of families and not just neighborhoods echo the fact that many African Americans find their old and young pulled apart in inner-city housing.[3] Young women raised in rural areas or small towns with supportive networks through their families' church membership and through their own neighborhoods now find themselves in high-rise apartments without older family members and in the midst of other young mothers, often of different linguistic and cultural backgrounds. The severe economic recession of the early 1980s broke up old neighborhoods when many adults lost their jobs and had to go on welfare for the first time. Their new locations cut them off from institutions beyond the home and from the rich traditions and support of the larger African American community. Old symbols of connection, persistence, and pride were unavailable to them; the socialization of very young mothers was left to the modeling of other young mothers often in similar states of loneliness and isolation.

Isolation is a recurrent theme of the relatively few studies that look long and closely at peer cultures or find sufficient entry into these groups to listen to the young talk of their perspectives on their situations (Kotlowitz, 1991; Lefkowitz, 1987; Sander, 1991; Vigil, 1990). Close-knit groups of "street girls" who attempt to fill the void left by family and community with new norms of being "cool" and having fun feel abandoned once babies arrive, the fathers disappear, and their former friends lose interest in the day-to-day details of child care. The young feel they have very little control over their lives; playing out what they have come to see as their "inevitable" gender roles of being single mothers seems to them their only choice.[4]

Community Organizations as Family

Some of these young people find their way to youth organizations where adults and older peers engage them in athletics, artistic events, and the routines of running a community-based organization. Groups most successful with inner-city youth attempt to provide much that matches traditional family ideals: support, expectations, discipline, and something to achieve. In these organizations, the concern that young people learn to mix well with those of different ethnicity and gender seems far less critical for the time being than the need to rediscover cross-generational channels of influence.

But this view is not yet widely shared by educators and agencies or organizations that see themselves as "serving" youth. Just as many adults tend to underestimate the influence of youth-created peer groups that seem at the end of the 20th century to have taken the place of adult-sanctioned ones, so do adults who set policies for schools and youth-serving agencies believe that the future of youth—the kind of adults they will become—is more important than what goes on in the present. In other words, the goals of those responsible for shaping many youth organizations is to offer guidance for being future citizens rather than to focus on achievement and affiliation in the short run to meet the present-mindedness of many youth cultures.

The rhetoric of justification for public schools, for example, talks a lot about preparing students for work or making the nation economically competitive. When students discuss why they go to school, however, they are apt to say that they want to hang out with their friends. People argue that girls learn more in separate-sex schools, have more opportunity to take leadership positions, and gain more self-confidence—all of which will give them as adults an equal start with men in whatever type of work they do. But when young women and men have a choice, they typically prefer to go to school with members of the opposite sex, as the vanishing breed of private single-sex schools and colleges attests. It is surely arguable that youth's intense present-mindedness will hold its own against adult concerns about whether and how they are prepared for the future.

In cultures as severely disrupted as those described in many chapters of this volume, a major transformation would be to bring youth into deeper and more sustained relationships with adults. Children who increasingly have to take on responsibilities for either younger siblings or their own babies need contact with adults capable of developing in them immediate possibilities of achievement and resulting images of their own potentiality. It is arguable that if single-sex organizations are demonstrably the most effective way of doing this, other values must temporarily give way to this pressing need.

But at the very least, young people need situations in which they can interact with adults of both sexes so that they become directly acquainted with the full and rich range of gender behaviors possible for adults. Perhaps it is time to focus more on the peer group, the present, the particular organization, and the specific activity rather than seek some universal policy about gender that will ensure a bright future. We now have a patchwork of gender and ethnic policies in youth organizations, and it may be that this very diversity is a sign of the kind of adaptability to specific circumstances that is needed. Such a patchwork is not a sign of tidy policy, to be sure, but it may be warranted if the overwhelming need at present is to provide proximate goals and more immediate satisfactions for youth who otherwise risk encapsulation in impoverished peer cultures.

Notes

[1]Maccoby (1990) describes studies that indicate this same-sex play preference and notes that "if a child has reason to believe that a given adult model is not typical of the pattern of behavior that generally prevails for that individual's sex, the child will reject this person as a model. Thus the influence of parents depends on how sex-typical they are, and seems to be a consequence, rather than a cause, of the child's sex-typed understandings." (See also Perry & Bussey, 1979.)

[2]Elijah Anderson (1990), an African American sociologist and long-time resident in inner-city Philadelphia, argues that forces such as urban renewal, gentrification of old neighborhoods, and the growth of integrated sections of the city have diminished the traditional influences of the African American church, as well as respect for the wisdom of elders. See also Heath (1990) for an illustration of how public hous-

ing policies that exclude extended families and that group highly diverse linguistic and cultural groups in the same housing units diminished the possibilities of young African American families, especially those headed by a single mother, to sustain church membership.

[3]Heath (1988, 1989, 1990) traces the lives in the late 1980s of several young women whose childhood socialization in a small southeastern town of textile mills had been documented in the 1970s. Their own roles as young mothers differed substantially from those of the women of their childhood community and churches. In particular, their status as single mothers and sense of vulnerability to "the system" often led to a sense of hopelessness for their own futures and of helplessness to mold healthy contexts of discipline for their children—especially their boys.

[4]Anderson (1990) describes this sense of inevitability as critical to the lives of the young African American inner-city youth of his study; these young people "see no future to derail—no hope for a tomorrow much different from today." (p. 66). Sexual activity may be one area where the young sense control, at least temporarily: "Status goes to the winner, and sex is prized not as a testament of love but as testimony to control of another human being" (p. 114).

References

Anderson, E. (1990). *Streetwise: Race, class, and change in an urban community.* Chicago: University of Chicago Press.

Anyon, J. (1983). Intersections of gender and class: Accommodation and resistance by working-class and affluent females to contradictory sex-role ideologies. In S. Walker & L. Barton (Eds.), *Gender, class and education* (pp. 19–37). Sussex, England: Falmer Press.

Arnot, M. (1983). A cloud over co-education: An analysis of the forms of transmission of class and gender relations. In S. Walker & L. Barton (Eds.), *Gender, class and education* (pp. 69–92). Sussex, England: Falmer Press.

Belenky, M. F., Clinchy, B. M., Goldberger, N. R., Tarule, J. M. (1986). *Women's ways of knowing: The development of self, voice, and mind.* New York: Basic Books.

Cone, C. A., & Perez, B. (1986). Peer groups and organization of classroom space. *Human Organization, 45*(Spring), 80–87.

Frazier, N., & Sadker, M. (1973). *Sexism in school and society.* New York: Harper & Row.

Gilbert, J. (1986). *A cycle of outrage: America's reaction to the juvenile delinquent in the 1950s.* New York: Oxford University Press.

Gilligan, C. (1982). *In a different voice: Psychological theory and women's development.* Cambridge, MA: Harvard University Press.

Heath, S. B. (1988). Language socialization. In D. Slaughter (Ed.), *Black children and poverty* (pp. 29–41). *A developmental perspective.* San Francisco, CA: Jossey-Bass.

Heath, S. B. (1989). Oral and literate traditions among black Americans living in poverty. *American Psychologist, 44,* 1–7.

Heath, S. B. (1990). The children of Trackton's children: Spoken and written language in social change. In J. W. Stigler, R. A. Shweder, & G. H. Herdt (Eds.), *Cultural psychology: Essays on comparative human development* (pp. 496–519). Cambridge, England: Cambridge University Press.

Heath, S. B., & McLaughlin, M. W. (1991). Community organizations as family: Endeavors that engage and support adolescent youth. *Phi Delta Kappan, 72,* 623–627.

Kett, J. F. (1977). *Rites of passage: Adolescence in America, 1790 to the present.* New York: Basic Books.

Kotlowitz, A. (1991). *There are no children here.* New York: Doubleday.

Lefkowitz, B. (1987). *Tough change: Growing up on your own in America.* New York: Free Press.

Maccoby, E. E. (1990). The sexes and their interactions: Some explanatory models. In Mellon Colloquium (Ed.), *The invisible majority* (pp. 19–37). New Orleans: Graduate School of Tulane University.

Maccoby, E. E., & Jacklin, C. N. (1974). *The psychology of sex differences.* Stanford, CA: Stanford University Press.

Maccoby, E., & Jacklin, C. (1987). Gender segregation in childhood. In H. Reese (Ed.), *Advances in child development and research* (Vol. 20). New York: Academic Press.

Noddings, N. (1984). *Caring: A feminine approach to ethics and moral education.* Berkeley, CA: University of California Press.

Perry, D. G., & Bussey, K. (1979). The social learning theory of sex differences: Imitation is alive and well. *Journal of Personality and Social Psychology, 37,* 1699–1712.

Pottker, J., & Fishel, A. (Eds.). (1977). *Sex bias in the schools: The research evidence.* Rutherford, NJ: Fairleigh Dickinson University Press.

Sander, J. (1991). *Before their time: Four generations of teenage mothers.* New York: Harcourt Brace Jovanovich.

Tetreault, M., & Thompson, K. (1986). The journey from male-defined to gender-balanced education. *Theory Into Practice, 25,* 227–234.

Thorne, B., & Luria, Z. (1986). Sexuality and gender in children's daily worlds. *Social Problems, 33,* 170–176.

Tyack, D., & Hansot, E. (1990). *Learning together: A history of co-education in American public schools.* New Haven: Yale University Press.

Vigil, J. D. (1990). Cholos and gangs: Culture change and street youth in Los Angeles. In R. Huff (Ed.), *Gangs in America: Diffusion, diversity, and public policy* (pp. 146–162). Beverly Hills, CA: Sage.

9

Casting the Self: Frames for Identity and Dilemmas for Policy

Milbrey W. McLaughlin
Shirley Brice Heath

The few who do break through the hell-crust of prevalent conditions to high ground should be crowned, extolled and emulated. This is the work of the artist. [Paint, write,] let the submerged man and the world see those who have proven stronger than the iron grip of circumstance.

Georgia Douglas Johnson
The New Negro Renaissance

Possible Selves: Different Perspectives

MRS. KNOWLTON (CIVIC ACTIVIST): There are a lot of crime problems and gangs, but I think the bottom line of youth is that they're not motivated, which can feed crime, can feed gangs. Citizens . . . and schools need to find a way to motivate these kids. [However,] there are some children you will not be able to touch regardless of what you do. It doesn't matter what you do, those children are untouchable. The parents are unmotivated, they don't care.

MRS. COBB (LEADER OF A VOLUNTEER ORGANIZATION): They [youngsters from impoverished African American neighborhoods] have to learn to grow up and improve themselves a little bit. And then let their children improve themselves. I mean, they gotta come up the ladder slowly . . . and when they see people who have more, they want more, but they don't know how to get more. You know, it's a vicious circle. They're unhappy and then they think, "I'll never get there; it'll never happen." This mind-set makes it hard to compete with the running of drugs for $500 a day rather than staying in school and working to get a degree and maybe make a little some day.

MR. MALLEN (CIVIC LEADER): Most of the youth have no motivation. It's learned at home from parents who don't work hard or work only when it is convenient for them. They come home at night and drink beer. Or maybe they don't even come home, a lot of them just carouse at bars. The kids do poorly in school. We need help to redirect the parent. Their main problem is that the parents have no respect for education.

RICKY (A GANG LEADER): The reason why a lot of kids drop out, it's a matter of a positive reception; you know, you gotta do better and if you don't do better, then you're a waste. And so, kids . . . ah, you know, it's not only pressure, it is a negative. And kids don't respond to that very well. And so, they want to go somewhere where they're accepted no matter what they do. When kids can't meet those expectations, they just get down on themselves. The only people who don't have expectations are gangbangers; they say just be yourself, do this for us, that's it.

MARCELLO (A GANGBANGER): A big reason why kids join gangs is that they are lonely . . . you're not getting enough attention in your house . . . your family's working too much or they got too many problems to pay much attention, and they forget all about you, you start feeling lonely so the only ones to hang around with is the guys on the corner. So, you start robbing your brothers and all that. Since [no one] is helping you out, you gotta help yourself out . . . you're gonna hang with someone who is gonna listen to you.

RICKY: I finally just lost it [in terms of academics]. I gave up. I just lost it because, uh, you couldn't please the teachers. You know, I tried hard to please the teachers, and you know, most of them are just beatin' you down. You know, the wear and tear of high school students, you know, you forget sometimes that some kids are really trying. . . . Kids' frustration comes from life, from the way they live. It's a buildup of negative energy. Kids are losing out. They get that frustration from school, from parents who aren't around, that's just more negative. And, just on the streets, it's just—you can feel "negative" everywhere.

ANGELA (A LEADER OF A NEIGHBORHOOD-BASED YOUTH ORGANIZATION): There is
nothing there for these kids . . . they just go until they get killed or end
up on the streets. These kids—the gangbangers, the dropouts, the criminals—they're the products of a community environment inundated with
drug trafficking, unemployment, a school system which—I've seen kids
graduate from [the local school] with a second-grade reading level and
then they are expected to function. Talk about having self-confidence,
talk about positive self-esteem, they don't know the meaning of that. No
career goals, no support from home because parents don't understand
what's going on, then you've got a school system that is so crazy. So, the
kids get involved with gangs because that gives them the support structure they need, that gives them that "Wow! You are really something."

Frames for Identity

Ricky, Marcello, Angela, Mrs. Knowlton, Mrs. Cobb, and Mr. Mallen refer to
the same reality: the barren contexts of inner-city youth, the dysfunctional
activities and attitudes young people exhibit, and the bleak futures that face
them. But their perspectives on the nature of the problem and, consequently, their thoughts about appropriate responses differ dramatically.

These youth and adults are among those we met in the course of 5 years
of study of youth-based organizations in the inner cities of three major
metropolitan areas.[1] Mrs. Knowlton and Mrs. Cobb, wealthy civic leaders
and political activists, diagnose rising school dropout rates, increasing teen
pregnancies, gang-related crime, and other destructive youth behaviors in
terms of perceived deficiencies in the families of poor, urban youngsters
and in the attitudes of youth. These women believe that insufficient motivation and willingness to work hard, compounded by parental indifference,
derail low-income minority youth from productive, socially sanctioned
lives. More incentives to achieve, such as promises of support for college
attendance, can activate youngsters to take school and their achievements
seriously. Mrs. Knowlton and Mrs. Cobb, well meaning though they are,
"blame the victim" and seek solutions that fix deficiencies or control deviant
behavior. Mr. Mallen, a community leader, echoes their indictment of the
motivations and energies of the families and communities from which the
youth come.

From Angela's, Marcello's, and Ricky's perspectives, these adults misunderstand thoroughly the sources of their alienation from so-called mainstream society, the signals and events that reinforce their low self-esteem
and pessimistic sense of the future, and the reasons why they may choose
to join a gang, to rob, to have a baby, or to drop out of school. They know

well how they are characterized in the public media: Note their repetitions of key phrases abundant in the media's presentations of inner-city life. But Marcello, Angela, and Ricky maintain that outsiders also misunderstand the kinds of activities, programs, and institutions that could meet their needs and enable them to build a positive sense of personhood and future. Whereas Mrs. Knowlton, Mrs. Cobb, and Mr. Mallen locate the problems they see in the individuals concerned, these teens and workers in organizations that young people judge as effective see the roots of negative behavior in the failures of institutions that compose their social contexts.

Together, the chapters included in this book aim to distinguish between *objective* or outsider perspectives on youth and youth policy and *subjective* or insider views of the young people themselves, the view from the street, and the views of leaders of effective youth organizations that help young people to shape their sense of themselves. Our intent has been to examine the relationships between these two frames for identity—one, an objective target for policy defined by such variables as socioeconomic status, ethnicity, gender and race, and the other, a subjective sense of personhood constructed from collaborative involvement in group endeavors and engagement with long-running tasks and teams. The disjuncture between these frames forces reconsideration of identities and experiences salient to inner-city youth and a reconceptualization of the policies and practices that can enable these youngsters to find a firm footing on the path to maturity.

A youth's sense of personhood, self, and future results from the interplay of the multiple contexts in which he or she moves: community, neighborhood, family, peer group, social institutions, and labels of ethnic membership defined by larger society. These give multiple dimensions—son, Latino, student, Baptist, younger sister, gangbanger, athlete, immigrant, mother—and situate meaning and circumstance.

Productive Environments for Inner-City Youth

Mrs. Knowlton, Mr. Mallen, and others—citizens, policymakers, and analysts—who share their assessment of the "youth problem" often wonder why young people who grow up in the desolate and hostile environments of urban, inner-city neighborhoods fail to take advantage of the many programs, interventions, and opportunities that public and private sources make available to them: tutoring programs, drug prevention efforts, skills training, remedial education, and so on. Inner-city youth behave "irrationally" when they avoid such efforts or refuse to cooperate when assigned to them.

However, from the perspective of the young people intended to benefit from these efforts, such youth policies and programs operate from a choice model that misunderstands their particular world views and circumstances. They, like their more advantaged peers, make choices based on what seems best for them at the time. Alternatives for inner-city youth are few, vision is limited, and the self-confidence necessary to "make it" is often lacking. Teens from inner-city neighborhoods, especially African American and Latino males, point to stereotypic conceptions of them as "delinquents" and "bad" as invidious forms of racism that obstruct their access to even the most menial of jobs.

Young men and women join gangs out of fear of the "nowhere jobs" and resulting social death they see in their parents or in neighborhood adults; young people join gangs to acquire the sense of legitimacy, productivity, and status denied them in an environment of high unemployment or limited opportunity as they understand it.[2] Individuals who are in gangs are not the "lowest of the low" or "just out to screw society" or interested only in easy gain, as some commentators suggest. They act out of their perceived best interest *within their context*. Young girls have babies because "that's all there is" and "to show I'm a woman" and "to have someone to love me." Teens drop out of school in search of a bonding supportive environment that will give some sort of recognition. Teens feel "all the negatives" from school and resent the almost exclusive focus on academic achievement geared toward college. They wonder at the lack of attention to "real work" in schools and point out that tracks in school are usually "college bound" and "non–college bound." The financial exigencies of their everyday lives tell teens that they must work—either before, during, or instead of college—and yet they point out readily that high schools give no positive acknowledgement of the idea of work. Some teens also face logistical problems of getting to school: "I can't cross gang boundaries. It's easier to drop out." "I can't take my baby to day care until he is 8 months old."

Social science and social policy generally have failed to understand the perspectives of individuals growing up in inner cities of the 1990s, especially the several key ways in which these perspectives differ from those of the 1960s and 1970s. As relatively few social science studies have described the inner cities since those tumultuous decades, policymakers often formulate decisions on their view of inner cities as troubled, agitated, ethnically coherent, and impoverished neighborhoods. The extent of ethnic mixing (especially in public housing projects), exploitation by outsiders (ranging from drug dealers to insurance scam artists), and poor health (particularly among children) have reshaped inner cities since the early 1970s. Yet policymakers rarely have access to close-up descriptions of these situations; they learn of them only in disembodied statistical reports and sensationalist headlines that report the failures of local institutions, such as hospitals and schools.

Policymakers have not heard young people in their contexts and have not recognized the many signs, frustrations, and fears that young people believe signal society's disregard for them and their families, that foster and support low self-esteem, and that erode personal dignity. To a great extent, social scientists have since the 1960s prized the objective view from the outside, leaving aside what they have sometimes dismissed as the biased or narrow view of insiders. By the early 1990s, however, the coming together of humanistic interests with social science began to bring some recognition of the value of the indigenous sense of history.[3]

Within the chapters of this book, we have tried to offer something of the rhythms of life in youth organizations to allow readers to hear young people and the youth organization leaders who work with them tell their own stories and give characterizations of themselves. For many of these youngsters, there is a "never for me" determination: "I'm not gonna end up like my brother, in jail with a kid he's never seen. Or like friends, blown away by gangs." This drive to survive—to construct a future—pushes them to get out of the only place they've known: the streets of the inner city. We have tried to convey the numerous ways in which both youth policymakers and those in inner-city youth organizations appropriate and misappropriate each other, which makes any kind of structural change extremely slow and highly dependent on new channels and messages of communication.

Those who find the objective perspective comforting and necessary as a means to stability will charge that the subjective view is too relativistic and that it asserts the equal validity of all norms and values, making moral judgments and cultural progress impossible. In the praises of youth and their leaders for local autonomy and contextualized responses, objectivists will hear a call for an end to all generalized, top-down schemes for the reform of inner-city youth.

Those who urge a more subjective view would respond that the essence of relativism lies in its plea for a fundamental respect for cultural differences among groups and for a recognition of the far-reaching and often unexpected results of top-down bureaucratic and political attempts to "shape up" inner-city families. Subjectivists would ask for ways of learning that center on communication within and between cultures and that challenge the need for youth policies to affirm universal values, usually from the mainstream, middle-class, nuclear family vantage point. Essential in this request is the need to recognize that the public ideal of leisured and paced mainstream middle-class childhood, adolescence, young adulthood, and adulthood, often portrayed in the media, lies outside the realm of possibility for those who grow up in inner cities anywhere in the world at the end of the 20th century.

Thus, policies framed on this ideal view of stage development with accompanying varying levels and types of support will not work for urban youth—or, quite possibly, for other segments of American youth. Closely linked to the need to see that adult responsibilities and realities push themselves on youngsters at an early age in inner cities is the recognition that academic achievement and advanced education must not be set out as the single measure of success for young people: jobs as bus drivers, warehouse managers, plumbers, electricians, and postal workers should stand as worthy of aspiration as either short-term, along-the-way, or long-term occupations. These jobs require decision making, technical skills, an ability to deal with the public, and commitment to accuracy and attention on the job.

The public's perceptions, like those of Mrs. Knowlton and Mr. Mallen, that inner-city youth "resist" social reform programs must be revised in light of the need for eminently pragmatic solutions that involve young people in their contexts. The public's perception that it is "too late" to intervene positively in the lives of youngsters once they are beyond the early elementary years must take into account the amount of responsibility and survival knowledge these young people must have by the age of eight or nine. If enrolled as part of the process and the planning, many of these young people can and will use opportunities to reshape their self-expectations and sense of the future. These same young people will indeed resist programs that try to control their behavior, that label them as deviant or deficient, that ignore their culture and context, that offer them little in the way of personal accomplishment and skill, or that hold them to low levels of expectation and accomplishment. They will resist youth organizations that attempt to herd them into ethnic membership as the single or primary key to self-identification. They will resent naive messages regarding safe sex and appropriate norms of gender behavior that disregard the actions of their local and media heroes and heroines. They will say quickly that when they assume adult responsibilities, take on decision-making, and handle financial and child-care tasks, they receive no recognition or support; ironically, especially for young women, their only hope for some support and recognition often comes only when they become mothers.[4]

An organization must add up to something for youth, must have significance for its members, and must allow them to reach out to other aspects of society than those they have known in the inner city. Travel, consistent sponsorship, and extended exposure to work situations of a wide variety enable young people to compare, critique, and contemplate choices available beyond their own streets. Such institutions are hard to franchise and hard to specify from outside the local setting in which they operate. The environments that support and engage inner-city youth—the organizations with which they choose to affiliate—are palpably local and are responsive to needs as defined by youth and to their context. Environments that succor and support youth are familylike organizations with productive, goal-directed activities. They differ in crucial elements of design and orientation from organizations that set out to serve youth. We distinguish between *youth-serving* and *youth-based* organizations—the latter being groups ever responsive to changing local needs and insistent on the importance of youngsters' input to the organizations.

Youth-based organizations share a conception of youth as a resource to be developed rather than a problem to be managed. Their conception of youth generates program activities that respect the views and abilities youngsters bring with them, that remain attuned to developmental needs and cultural differences, and that strive to provide the supports that mesh with their unmet needs. These organizations admit that the youngster who is one day responsible for getting a sick baby sister to the doctor and caring for her through the night may the next day fly into a temper tantrum to match that of a 2-year-old. Leaders of these groups talk of the need to expect rapid fluctuations among the young who carry many responsibilities and worries that would wear down their elders.

Activities in youth-based organizations embrace the whole person, not just a single issue or component such as ethnicity, pregnancy, substance abuse, or school success. Thus, although a single focus such as basketball, tutoring, or tumbling defines the organization, these activities are instrumental in helping attend to the fuller emotional, social, educational, and economic needs of participants. The basketball team holds regular study halls and homework sessions; the director of the tumbling team serves as employment counselor, emergency banker, and even emergency babysitter. The tutoring project takes field trips, finds money-making activities for youth, and often assists youths' families with crisis management in terms of social services or city bureaucracies. The community center becomes not only a place for basketball practice, homework tutoring, and puppet shows, but also a center where adults can come to prepare for taking the test for their General Education Diploma (GED), learn about jobs, and meet with attorneys who specialize in poverty law.

Youth-based organizations walk a thin line between heavy personalization of all who join their group and strict adherence to rules that apply to everyone. The janitor of the Girls Club may greet each group of girls as they enter between 6:30 and 7:00 each morning to get their breakfast, finish homework, and wait for a bus to take them to school, but he also insists each child sign in and turn in permission slips for the afternoon field trip. Those who fail to do so receive stern warnings and no club privileges until they adhere to the rules. The tumbling team member who is told to meet the van on a certain corner at a particular time but fails to show up on time is left behind; the basketball team member told to be in front of his apart-

ment complex at 4:30 A.M. for a ride to the airport for a 6 A.M. flight knows
if he is not there at the appointed minute, he will miss the team trip to the
West Coast for tournament play. At the same time, leaders also allow older
youth leeway in some of the organization's rules as a sign of respect and
acknowledgement of tenure with the group. For example, a Boys and Girls
Club that strictly enforces a requirement that youth carry their membership
card at all times in the club excuse older members from doing so. But the
rules that bind and advance youth and their activities are upheld with
"tough love."

Activities driven by a conception of youth as a resource to be developed
thus invest a significant measure of responsibility for maturation in the
youth. All leaders believe that the rules of their organizations match those
of the world of work and bureaucracy: If you don't do things on time, do
them right, and fill out the paperwork, you'll lose out in the end. Entrusting
plays a critical role in the group norms of social control; any latecomer
knows not to expect sympathy from teammates as much as he or she knows
nothing will be gained by pleading the case with the leader. The unflinching sense of responsibility and strict adherence to rules of youth-based
organizations come wrapped in fairness, equity, consistent concern, and
high expectations (as echoed by Ianni's [1989] formula for effective schools
as firm, fair, and consistent). Again and again, those who complain about
the rules describe their leaders as "fair," "sure," "certain," "making us work
hard," and "making us believe we can do it." The discipline lies centrally in
the expectations.

Their activities in these organizations suggest the sense of ownership
these young people gain is a shared one—a sense of "being in this together"
with the team, the center, or the troupe. Although each individual must be
able to hold up his or her responsibilities, each does so with a view of connection and linkage. Letting down on the part of one person weakens the
entire enterprise; thus, the youngsters work hard to keep each other up and
to bring recalcitrants in line. A program attractive to teenagers is a program
that is "theirs." A program attractive to adolescent youth empowers them,
underscores their competence, and bolsters their sense of social worth.

Diversity within the group ensures access to a wide variety of types of
expertise. Newcomers find themselves tested for what they know and can
do within their first few visits to the Boys Club or the girls' softball team.
The fact that becoming a member of a drama or dance group may call upon
not only one's singing talents but also know-how with stereo equipment,
access to a church auditorium, and ability to illustrate posters never leaves
the mind of some of the old-timers in the group. Newcomers with diverse
talents can help relieve others of some of the onerous tasks they have had
to carry out. During the summer at a community center, new young people

enrolled in day programs know that their leaders will be eyeing them with a view to whether they might be hired for some of the many jobs in the center that come up through the year. Adherence to daily sign-ins, cleanup rules, and safety regulations, as well as showing responsibility in helping younger participants to find their way through the maze of rooms, are the unspoken achievements that can win one notice as a possible junior employee at the center.

Important, too, is neighborhood investment, because it links the adults in a young person's life to the organization. For example, the director of a neighborhood Boys and Girls Club tells of the debilitating falloff of community volunteers and board members when the Club's financial authority was centralized "downtown." Youth-serving organizations that are vital and effective from the community's perspective have their roots deep in the community and so can draw on the local environment for political, financial, and instrumental support. Local investment can take the form of staff from the neighborhood, not just dollars. This local knowledge also enables program staff to understand the young people with whom they work in terms of family and neighborhood contexts and lets them interact with these young people as individuals. Local youth leaders face a dilemma of accessing the resources downtown without alienating or excising the resources of the neighborhood.

Knowing communities and families often adds up to not asking questions and not making ingenuous assumptions that each youngster has parents or guardians who are reliable, safe, and trustworthy. Youth leaders know that many of the youngsters in their groups have parents who rarely show up and are abusive and cruel when they do. Moreover, they know that young people every day see adults walk right back into situations that have previously harmed them; they hear too often from abused mothers that "there's nowhere else to go. I don't want to be alone." Some youngsters take their resentments out on parents, schools, and any form of authority, resisting any fencing in that might make them vulnerable to unfair and unpredictable treatment like that which they have known at home or in school.

Yet another important feature of successful programs for inner-city youth is responsiveness to "local ecology," or the resources and unmet needs of the community. Generic program models or standardized service menus, especially those created at some remove, risk redundancy or irrelevance. Not all neighborhoods have the same configuration of resources in terms of schools, recreational activities, social services, family coherence, political clout, economic outlets, or cultural opportunities. Not all youth programs need the same offerings of sports, education, social supports, or training. Efforts that have effectively engaged and sustained the participation of youth are efforts that have defined their emphases and offerings in terms of the local topography and "fit" with the neighborhood, its resources, and its culture.[5]

Youth-based organizations attract young people by the safe, supportive, and personal environment they provide. Even within these organizations, however, teenagers present special emotional and social needs, difficult to meet in the context of general-purpose institutions intended to provide a broad range of activities and program to youth of all ages and interests. Even the most effective of these organizations often experiences a membership dropoff as youngsters enter their late teens; the organizations that met their needs in earlier years apparently do not continue to do so as they enter adolescence. Teens cite the absence of a space just for them, of program or activities relevant to their interests, or of signs or symbols to mark their "elder" status as reasons why they believe the organizations they enjoyed earlier are now "just for kids."

One key to retaining adolescents' interest and involvement is the ability to employ these older youngsters within the youth-based organizations. In the relatively few situations in which this is possible, these young people serve as assistant coaches, apprentice electricians or custodians, assistant education directors for tutoring programs, and so on. Their continued role in the youth-based organizations offers these young members a sense of continuity and builds a financial base and sense of stability that often help them to translate future goals into attendance in vocational programs or a return to school.

Organizations in the inner cities that engender the commitment and engagement of young people beyond the age of 14 offer not only financial opportunities but also environments of small cohesive groups engaged in intense, demanding, goal-focused, and rewarding work. Long waiting lists of youth exist for activities that provide teenagers with involvement in a socially cohesive, distinctive group—evidence that youth will choose a positive identity or affiliation if such a choice is available. In even the most desperate inner-city neighborhoods, vibrant youth groups absorbed with such activities as theater, dance, basketball, or tumbling came by the early 1990s to have long waiting lists—sometimes of as many as 3,000 youngsters who wanted a chance to prove themselves and become part of a particular team or troupe. The similarity of these groups to the gangs that involve most of the neighborhood's adolescents are apparent: strong social identity, interdependence of members, and clear and stable relationships and roles.

These productive youth groups possess something difficult to create within the context of larger organizations: the group cohesiveness necessary to frame and sustain social identity in terms of group norms, values, and goals. In Lakeside, membership in the Liberty Theatre group (as discussed in chapter 3) provides definite and positive social identity, member-ship by itself sufficient to escape pressures from gangs ("Who do you fly with?" "What do you be?") and to furnish a positive connection with status in mainstream society. So, too, is involvement with a winning, tournament-trekking basketball team a source of station, acknowledged identity, and positive comment on contribution and competence.

Involvement in such tightly structured, goal-focused, cohesive groups enables inner-city adolescents to reclassify the group to which they belong from "deviant" and "destructive" to "positive" and "productive" (Turner, 1987). Involvement in such groups shifts the ground for casting self and constructing social identity: It provides buffers from the fierce communion of the streets and the attractions of gangs and offers evidence of compe-tence and worth. Cohesive, predictable groups license trusting relationships and mutual dependence, dimensions of human relations generally missing for most inner-city youth. One teen told us, "I don't have trust or faith in no one, nobody. We can't depend on someone to help us, protect us. You've got to protect yourself, help yourself. You are the only one you can trust." Learning to trust and to depend on others counts among the most important learning that occurs in inner-city youth-based organizations of the sort we describe here.

Ethnicity and gender figure in this construction in highly varying ways. Social self-concept, part of an individual's mental structural field, draws from the social groups with which an individual affiliates *together with* other emotional or personal associations—for example, male, Lakesider, sister, Latino, Hungarian, project-dweller, Catholic. Activities, products, perfor-mances, and even winning seasons form the core context from which youngsters build a sense of accomplishment and pride in their future and into which they can fit a sense of racial or ethnic pride.

Some groups focus on ethnicity and culture for some explicitly instru-mental purpose: to provide the pride of heritage necessary to participate confidently in the broader culture. "When children's (or communities') iden-tities become shrouded in shame, they lose the power to control their own lives in situations in which they interact with members of the dominant group."[6] But more often in the 1990s, youth organizations try to center pride in the actual spatial territory of community and the people there. When a youth organization originally founded in the 1960s to instill pride in being Puerto Rican tried to maintain that focus in a neighborhood of young peo-ple from mixed-ethnic families, as well as families from Mexico, South America, and Puerto Rico, young people balked. They admitted their irrita-tion that one of the youth leaders was "always talkin' about Puerto Rican, Puerto Rican, Puerto Rican. . . ." This outburst provoked a discussion of the need to acknowledge other origins:

ALICIA: We don't like this, you know, 'cause she's always talkin' about Puerto
   Ricans. We're not even Puerto Ricans. We're Mexican and Peruvian.
RAOUL: I'm half Puerto Rican.

These young people and many of their peers see notions of "ethnic
purity" or "cultural identity" as anachronistic symbols of another generation
and political agenda.[7] In the hybrid demographics of urban institutions, ethnicity is reinterpreted and reinvented within the multicultural contexts of
schools, housing projects, community organizations, and social life. Advocates
of exclusionary, militant ethnic organizations generally represent *their* perspectives on ethnic identification, products of earlier eras of ethnic enclaves,
not young people's conception of self.[8] For today's youth, ethnicity comprises
not the primary identity but an additional "layer" of identity that youth—especially youth from minority cultures—can adopt as a matter of pride. Effective
youth organizations assume this view of ethnicity as an aspect of multidimen-
sional identity and thus celebrate ethnicities and accept differences.

Most of the successful groups and organizations we encountered viewed
individual characteristics of ethnicity or race as instrumental to building a
positive social identity and as part of the new ethnicity that equips individuals to have multiple perspectives on an issue or experience (Novak, 1980,
elaborates the concept of "new ethnicity." See also McLaughlin, chapter 2,
this volume). Ethnic identity became most important when an individual had
built a sense of immediate and primary team membership through sustained
involvement in group activities. Beyond this foundation, a sense of ethnic
membership helped enable these individuals to move confidently into larger
society with a sense of linkage to a larger group with an identifiable proud
history. Community-based organizations are in a unique position to provide
links to the mainstream *and* to celebrate ethnic identities (Cahill, 1991). Key
to ethnic identities within the contemporary urban context is recognition that
youth inhabit multiple realities and that expressions of self represent multiple repertoires. In this embedded context, ethnicity signals only one part of
a broader social identity, an aspect of self in which youth must take pride but
which in and of itself is an insufficient social brief or inadequate guide for
organization. In contemporary America, youth's ethnicity obtains meaning in
the larger culture and is reinterpreted in each locale and by each generation.

Pride in gender identity further challenges the imagination and structure
of many youth organizations. Even though Congress passed an amendment
in 1974 that exempted voluntary youth organizations from the effects of
Title IX of the Education Act Amendments of 1972, such groups have still
felt pressure for increasing sex equity. In 1990, the Boys Clubs of America
changed its name to Boys and Girls Clubs of America, largely as a result of
the club's loss of a California court case concerning gender equity. With this

change, the Girls Clubs of America, whose leaders felt that many particular needs and interests of girls would not be well served by a coeducational facility and program, reaffirmed their commitment to young women and changed the name of the Girls Clubs of America to Girls Incorporated. There, they could provide programs, schedules, personnel, and projects that catered to what they viewed as the needs of young women: birth control and child-care classes and cooking and tutoring programs. In recent years, Girls Clubs/Girls Incorporated have also developed major program components for girls on leadership skills, career development, basic sports skills, and math and science (Nicholson, 1987; Wahl, 1988) in recognition of the changing role of women in society and the uneven support that girls receive in developing confidence or expertise in these areas.[9] Little League and other sports teams occasionally felt public pressure to open membership to girls and boys, but most of these demands came in middle- and upper-class neighborhoods and not in inner cities.

Community centers, church youth groups, and artistic groups that foster dance, music, and theater consistently have included both boys and girls, although many such groups provide separate activities, places of meeting, and competitions for each. Rationales for such separations center around matters of identity and the need to have a safe, intimate place to talk about issues in which both adults and young believe the other gender has either no competence or interest. For young women, particularly, such occasions are most important for the opportunity they offer to talk about matters of sexuality and their confusion about the mixed signals they often receive from gangs and from adult women about relations with men. When adults fail them, girls cling together and often become appendages to gangs of young men. The desire for sexual favors from one male often fosters a competitive spirit among girls in gangs, which keeps them from talking among their gang peers. Yet our experience with such young women in community organizations indicates that they worry about how to meet the demands of a man while realizing that, by their own estimate, about 80% of males leave pregnant girls stranded and never help out with the baby.[10] In a supportive group in a community organization, girl gang members can confess that most of the girls "don't like to have babies. Like these chicks that I hang around with, if they're pregnant or anything and they see us cruising and everything . . . they go 'man, I can't wait till I get this thing out of my stomach.'" Some inner-city parents—male and female—have been gang members in their youth, and their children thus have to reconcile any admonitions their parents may give to them with what they know and see of their parents' behavior and with public and school admonitions against gang membership.

Having women within community organizations to direct activities, listen to girls, and understand the contradictions and dilemmas of their backgrounds is critically important. Yet finding women to direct such groups is difficult, and on the whole, most youth organizations that include boys and girls have male leaders. Short-term female volunteers who find the realities of the lives of inner-city youngsters too harsh and overwhelming do not last long in inner-city youth organizations. The few women who stay on in these groups tend to be those who share similar backgrounds with the youngsters or those whose personal or religious ideologies enable them to listen without judging and to accept without condition. These women play specialized roles for particular small groups within the organization. In our research, only a handful of organizations for teens were headed by women, and men far outnumbered women in youth organizations of all types—ranging from athletic to artistic.

However, contrary perhaps to public expectations, males within coeducational organizations tended to be highly sensitive to the needs of young women for support. For example, when a 13-year-old girl who had been a regular and exemplary member of a community center was hired to work as a junior leader for the next summer and became pregnant in the interim year, the male director accepted her dual roles of child and expectant mother. She participated in all the recreational opportunities of other junior leaders, but the center also arranged for her to have prenatal counseling. Plenty of time for small-group talk sessions, viewing of films, planning of puppet shows, and cross-age tutoring allowed males and females to talk about problems they had in common of resisting the dangers of both street and home life. Yet ample opportunity for private "girl talks" also ensured that young women's gender-specific concerns received attention. Cross-age groupings for females tended to center on personal and social concerns far more than did such occasions for males. Such conversations, especially in mixed-ethnic groupings, offered opportunities for young women to consider how parental expectations differed across cultures and how only certain norms and institutions could reinforce strong self-identities, counter to the generalized media image of young man or woman, young minority or majority ethnic member, and rich or poor.

Dilemmas for Policy

The matter of where norms and institutions might come from and what role youth policy should play in upholding these highlights the first of many dilemmas for youth policy. Often, youth leaders heard youngsters offering testimonies to their peers of how their church or their very traditional, old-fashioned grandmother kept them out of trouble. In many cases, youngsters able to stay in school and out of trouble also attended strict religious institutions. Community youth organizations funded either partially or fully by public sources or foundations could not endorse in public ways these institutions or their teachings, although they might wholeheartedly endorse the effects of the church on the lives of young people. These and other dilemmas highlight the fact that sensitive youth leaders often see both the inside and outside perspectives of the lives of youngsters and find themselves caught in the middle.

Policymakers and social scientists frequently give quiet nods to the importance of understanding and basing youth policy on the perspectives and actualities of young people—the subjective view that captures the multiple pressures, competing demands, and special rationality of young people's inner-city, urban context. But mere head nods usually do not lead to a serious grappling with contradictions and dilemmas. Economic demands for "efficiency," bureaucratic mandates for organizational control and accountability, and political calls for "equity" and neutrality with respect to religion deflect serious attention from the messy, noisy, undisciplined, and particular realities of urban youth.

Placed side by side, these two perspectives—that of the outsider and that of the insider—generate essential and uncompromising dilemmas for policymakers. The policy responses to these tough questions—the extent to which policy reflects Mrs. Knowlton's diagnosis of the "problem" and framework for "solution," or Ricky's and Angela's perspectives—has everything to do with whether urban youth will react as policymakers hope or whether youth policy initiatives aimed at benefiting both youth and society will again disappoint.

The dilemmas for youth policy run deep in our country's traditions of pluralism and democracy and of age-appropriate sexual behaviors and preparation for child rearing. These values underlie the procedures developed to assure taxpayers and foundation boards that their dollars are spent responsibly and fairly. The insiders' perspectives lead to a policy model and policy approaches that differ in critical, elemental ways from those in place today. We lay out here several examples of the tough interrelated choices we found among the 60 youth organization sites involving 24,000 youngsters in three major metropolitan areas.

"Value Neutral" Programs Versus Programs with Specific Religious or Moral Orientation

Few if any youth organizations could be called value free.[11] Most seek and hold a strong value base that they strive to inculcate in the young people who take part in their activities. For example, both the YWCA and Girls Incorporated have serious commitments to gender equality. The "One

Imperative" of the YWCA—to eliminate racism by whatever means necessary—and the strong, proactive affirmative action position of the Girl Scouts signal strong organizational value positions about race and equity. The values on which the Boys Scouts organization builds—achievement, patriotism, community service, and religiosity—are everywhere evident in their program and protocols.

The policy dilemma involves not support for organizations that pursue these general philosophical positions but public backing of institutions that advocate specific religious or ideological positions (such as a specific religious denomination or a moral position on an aspect of private life). Tradition and constitutional law separate church from state in America; public norms resist the use of public dollars to support activities characterized by particular ideological perspectives. Yet organizations of such a "missionary" stripe are often among the more important resources for inner-city youth. Young people growing up in the oppressive contexts of depressed urban neighborhoods desperately need a clear, coherent value system—a secure, positive belief system in which to cast self and imagine futures. The significance of a cohesive, explicit value orientation (most often Christian) and its importance for young people were apparent in many of the effective youth organizations we observed. A number of youth told us personal stories similar to Jerrold's:

> When I got saved [as part of the church youth program], my whole attitude started to change. You know, that's when I started learning about God and started seeking for my own life. So, I finally gave in to all of that anger that I had built up from gangs and from my home life and, uh, just vented it on sports [that were part of the Christian youth group].

The insiders' perspective on such groups is that they offer to youngsters—often in the most difficult of circumstances—reliable, supportive, and firm environments for learning that do not exist in either families or schools. Moreover, certain types of youngsters can be reached by these groups when nothing else can offer them a way to achieve a sense of control over their destiny. Thus, the sweep of youth organizations available within inner-city communities should include churches or religious groups that are youth centered, strictly disciplined, and strongly demanding of loyalty and obedience. Yet the specific religious or moral teaching of such organizations raises fundamental questions as to their eligibility for public support.

Standardized Programs Versus Locally Constructed Practices

Ease of management and notions of equity promote standardized, "uniform" program approaches.[12] Policymakers, as well as leaders of national organizations, worry that decentralized programming could result in organizational chaos, defy management and control, and possibly support unequal programs and opportunities across sites. The insiders' perspective, however, suggests that whatever disorganization or inefficiency that may result would be far less costly in the long term than the expense of program dollars spent ineffectively. Programs that are irrelevant to local needs, incongruent with the local ecology, and insensitive to neighborhood cultures are bound to fall short. For example, one national organization's guidelines for facilities resulted in a well-equipped downtown athletic facility that is empty of youth, while glass-strewn parks in their neighborhoods are filled to capacity with young African American males unable or unwilling to travel downtown.

The dilemma for policy is to strike an effective balance between control or direction from the top and autonomy at the bottom, or the community level. Most national youth organizations recognize that rigid specification of standardized practices and insistence on uniformity or "program replication" are only apparent efficiencies and likely portend wasted dollars and energy at the level of youth. For example, a nationally sponsored educational program that proceeded on a centrally determined formula for collaboration among youth-based organizations succeeded in River City because the school partners that it collaborated with were strong and able to work with community agencies; however, it accomplished little in Lakeside, where the schools are notoriously weak and where deep animosity exists between schools and target neighborhoods. Neighborhood leaders could have designed and carried out a program to the same end, using other community resources, but were unable to do so because of national guidelines.

"What works" for inner-city youth conforms to the contexts in which an activity is embedded and to the subjective realities of the youth it intends to advance, not to distant bureaucratic directives. There are significant differences among national youth organizations on this dimension: Boy Scouts, Girl Scouts, and Camp Fire adhere to a top-down model of program development but permit and reward local innovation. Other organizations, such as Boys and Girls Clubs, Girls Incorporated, the YWCA, and the YMCA, follow a different model that stresses local autonomy in program development, within national guidelines. However, the trend within these organizations is more centralized development of program models as a strategy for reducing costly program development and incorporating proven notions of effective program strategies. These nationally developed models are not required of local affiliates and offer considerable flexibility. The challenge for national organizations is to find ways to integrate local knowledge, commitment, and realities with national models. As resources for youth programs shrink, the temptation to achieve economies of scale and efficiency by moving responsibility for program definition away from the local level becomes great, with the apparent benefit of being able to redirect dollars from program development to the maintenance of services and activities.

"Ethnic Blind" or Nondiscriminatory Policies Versus Policies That Acknowledge Ethnicity, Gender, and Race

Democratic values of fair play and nondiscrimination are the American way. Nonetheless, when important differences in design and implementation related to culture or gender are overlooked, programs often fall short of expectations. For example, ignorance of culture caused a well-intended effort backed by the business community to fail in Big Valley. A fund to disperse up to $10,000 to any teenage mother willing to return to school went largely unspent. Sponsors overlooked the cultural norms of this largely Latino target group, which require Latinas to stay home and raise their children. The "benefit" attached to the program ran counter to cultural values and expectations.

Failure on the part of Boy Scouts to modify sufficiently their programming, based on European American, middle-class norms and values, continues to frustrate urban scouting efforts aimed at African American, Latino, and Asian American inner-city youth. The assimilation/accommodation debate that fired discussions of youth policy 100 years ago rages today (see chapter 7). A Boys and Girls Club facility that offered exactly the same locker room and shower facilities to boys and girls ignored girls' different needs of privacy and stirred resentment that the leaders were not "really" willing to have girls in their facility.

Policies that disregard cultural differences exhibit other public attitudes toward diversity—mind-sets that have little to do with fairness and much to do with comfort. The public's fear of digging down past the fluff of "cultural awareness"—past food and festivals—to confront the meaning of cultural differences in terms of such everyday factors as speech, conceptions of time, and views about child-rearing keeps policy intended to accommodate diversity at a superficial level. Furthermore, the unwillingness of the general public to address the implications of deeply seated cultural differences finds support in the cries of middle-class African Americans or Latinos of "stereotypes." Policymakers and the public often wrap themselves in the banner of "nondiscriminatory practices" to slide over the set of extremely sensitive, highly charged issues of ethnicity, race, or gender that are constantly subject to local demographics, youth perceptions, and economic possibilities.

Responsiveness to Constituents Versus Responsiveness to the Powerless

A tour of any urban center's park facilities, public schools, recreational buildings, hospitals, or other public services reveals profound disparities between what is available in wealthy parts of town and what is available in inner-city neighborhoods.[13] For the most part, city officials acknowledge these inequalities but defend them in terms of relative political voice and influence. Asked to explain the incongruities between the country club parks maintained in Lakeside's affluent neighborhoods and the barren, dangerous park facilities allocated to housing project neighborhoods, an official shrugged and said "the voters wouldn't stand for it" were it otherwise. The well-known political calculus that provides more and better resources to the affluent than to poverty-stricken neighborhoods not only denies equal treatment to poor neighborhoods but also deprives them of the very resources they need to construct a positive environment for youth: good schools; clean, well-equipped, and supervised recreation; responsive medical care; and other social services (Littell & Wynn, 1989, p. 66). City politics being what they are, the old adage holds: Those who have, get; those who don't, don't.

These wealth-based inequities are only one way in which urban youth are disadvantaged by local political processes. Only a small portion of voters in urban areas have a direct interest in the services available to youth; for example, in the cities we studied, only between 12% and 17% of voters had children in the public schools. The common responses across sites— that "there is really not much here for youth" and that there "is nothing to do," for teens especially—are not surprising. The remarks of the president of a neighborhood association in Big Valley are typical:

> We have a multipurpose center in our area, but beside that, there really is nothing. When the neighborhood association set priorities, youth probably ranked around third or fourth. And with the little funding we have to work with, that is a low priority. We focus more on public services such as road and drainage problems, then on senior services, and then youth. But there is never much left when we get to that.

Communities are concerned about the "youth problem," but demands from more powerful constituencies shove programs and resources for youth far down the priority list.

Professionalism Versus Local Knowledge

Issues of public safety, as well as assurances of program quality, drive demands for certification and the professionalization of youth programs. But a clear message from the effective youth organizations we observed is that the knowledge that matters most is local knowledge and sensitivity to neighborhood, families, and school contexts for young people. Many of the leaders of the organizations we studied had formerly been schoolteachers, and they had found their way to youth organizations to escape what they saw as schools' insensitive responses to urban youth needs. Others were committed locals or trained professionals with a strong commitment to place. The expertise gained through formal education had little to do with forging ties to the local context, which is so necessary for effective programs.

Local youth leaders resented the fact that city youth policy boards and administrators often included youth professionals whose career interests and mobility worked against these critical neighborhood connections. These professionals' commitment often was to the profession or to advancement within the national organization rather than to the neighborhood or a particular group of young people.

Beyond perpetual problems of funding, sustaining a healthy organization in an environment that thwarts its purpose and saps vitality from all institutions requires local knowledge, local ties, and local commitment to the community and its young people. Honor for local knowledge also signals respect for the community and its people. A Lakeside youth worker put it this way: "Residents of low-income communities are rarely heard—their voices are drowned out by 'those in the know,' those who really have no idea what it is like to live in the community."

Accountability Versus Adaptability

The demand from public and private funders for "accountability" tops youth workers' list as an impediment to the flexible, responsive programming associated with effective youth programs. Complaints are not about evaluation per se, but rather about the types of evidence demanded. Requirements to specify "treatments" and outcomes in advance lock in program and constrain program staff to identity "outputs" that can be easily measured, counted, and demonstrated. The "softer" outcomes, such as an improved self-concept, an expanded sense of possible futures, a connection with a coherent system of values and beliefs, and a sense of personal and emotional safety, elude typical evaluation instruments and so do not "count." Yet these are the outcomes that matter most to youth and to their productive futures. In addition, evaluations often call for a show of outcomes over very short periods of time. Insiders know that bringing about substantive change in young people whose lives have been and will in all likelihood continue to be buffeted by violence, poverty, abuse, and unpredictability takes time.

Furthermore, youth workers complain that their "success" is too often evaluated against bureaucratic criteria rather than in terms of what they accomplish for young people. In this view, rule-based accountability schemes reward the wrong things and lead to a "body count" or "audit" mentality that diverts organizational attention from youngsters' needs, that drives program decision making to focus on numbers and balance sheets, and that constrains adaptability.[14]

Enlightened Futures Versus Feasible Goals

Policies and programs aimed at the horizon and futures of inner-city youth through education and support for achievement—for example, programs that award scholarships to college-bound youngsters, that award honor roll status, or that bring professionals to inner-city schools as part of a career fair—may indeed motivate a small portion of inner-city youngsters. But for many young people, these programs further erode their sense of value and dignity because the expectations established are beyond them and the "options" given distinction are largely professional, white-collar positions. Absent is honor for the unexceptional, for the "average Joe"; absent is support and encouragement for simply finding balance in a productive social role. Ironically, many well-intended educational programs serve only to further disadvantage vulnerable inner-city youth.

Relaxation and Recreation Versus Remediation and "Work"

Youth workers and program planners confront choices of focus, message, and environment as activities are developed and programs designed for inner-city youth. It seems there is too much to attend to at once. Young people need to be able simply to relax in a supportive environment at safe remove from the endless succession of dangers, stresses, and challenges that characterize daily life in many inner-city neighborhoods. But they must also be able to find assistance, structure, and opportunity to acquire the basic skills and information essential for success in school and for the development of healthy, personally positive responses to invitations for involvement in drugs, unsafe sexual activity, crime, or other destructive behaviors.

Finding a balance between these objectives stretches slim resources and often countermands the directions of funders or public officials. Inner-city adolescents generally spurn programs that are purely recreational without concrete purpose or product. Such activities, in their view, are a waste of time because they do not add up to anything practical. Further, inner-city youth often see "fun" programs as demeaning because they fail to recognize the adult roles and responsibilities that many of these young people have carried since their early years. Programs based on organizations that have traditionally served European American, middle-class youth often err in this direction in program design and in their assumptions about the preferences and perspectives of the inner-city youth they hope to involve.

But adolescents, who can no longer be commanded by a parent or youth worker to show up for a tutoring session or counseling activity, also reject programs whose sole focus is on remediating, "fixing," or otherwise managing their behavior. Programs that focus on single issues, such as academic performance, substance abuse, sexual behavior, and parenting skills, frequently disappoint funders and planners, because young people fail to attend or to respond consistently.

The dilemma for policy, then, is to strike the appropriate balance between relaxation and serious work, between "time off" or recreational activities and a focused effort on developing the skills and attitudes necessary to negotiate successfully through inner-city environments to positive adulthood.[15] Many youth organizations have been unsuccessful in striking this balance and have defined themselves in terms of one or the other focus, as required by their institutional identity or policy mandate. And consequently, most youth organizations report a falloff in young people's participation once they reach teen years and can "vote with their feet." Yet conclusions that adolescents "won't participate in organized activities [outside gangs]" or are "uninterested in youth organizations" are unjustified. The exceptions to this general pattern are found in the organizations described here, whose activities derive from a conception of youth as a resource to be developed. These organizations link recreation and improvement together in a programmatic frame that expressly values and empowers young people. Moreover, these organizations do not define themselves as "after" or "out of" with respect to schools; they existed for young people and for the projects, performances, and participation they could create. The dilemma for policy involves moving from a programmatic stance that revolves around society's goals (e.g., reduction in crime, lowered rates of teen pregnancy and substance abuse, and lowered rates of school dropouts) or around particular institutional (often national) identities to organizations and activities that derive from the needs and perspectives expressed by youth. Unfortunately, this youth-centered position is not popular in state legislatures, foundation board rooms, or national organizations, whose conception of the problem, of solutions, and of ways to allocate scarce resources drive programs.

Professional or Bureaucratic Boundaries Versus Comprehensive Needs

Anyone who has lived, worked, or spent time in high-poverty, depressed inner-city neighborhoods knows that the problems of families and youths who live there come not in neat packages labeled "medical," "educational," "economic welfare," and so on, but in disorderly, complex bundles that mirror an individual's context and personal condition. Successful programs and their staff recognize the impossibility of meeting the needs of inner-city youth without crossing the boundaries of profession and agency. Successful programs take their substance, shape, and rhythm from the needs and nature of those they serve rather than from the precepts, strictures, or boundaries erected by professions or bureaucracies.

The fundamental disjunction between the traditional requirements of government agencies, bureaucracies, and professionalism and the needs of inner-city youth helps to explain the paucity of effective programs and the prevalence of disappointing initiatives. At root is perspective; how the problem is understood, where it is located, and the conception of promising responses compose the frame that drives policy.

The very small number of effective programs for inner-city adolescents also reflects a constraining myth: It is "too late" to do much with adolescents; they are a lost cause and thus an inefficient target for policy investment. Our extended fieldwork in youth-based organizations of inner-city neighborhoods provides abundant evidence to the contrary. Teens connected with groups or organizations such as those described in this book have recast their identity and purpose in ways that enable them not only to "duck the bullet" of early pregnancy, school failure, gangbanging, or death, but to move on to legitimate and productive futures as workers, parents, and citizens.

They may not do as policymakers would ideally wish them to do. They may become pregnant in their early teens, drop out of school, and go on welfare, but many sustain their connections with youth organizations, find their way to night school, and end up working for youth groups or serving as aides in their children's school. They may father several children, have scrapes with the law, and leave school, but if they emerge from these experiences through the athletic program of a youth organization and find their way to a vocational education program, they have some hope of supporting themselves and their families and of participating in larger society.

For such struggles to be seen as victories, institutions must give the clear message that such paths—unconventional from a purely academic or professional career orientation—warrant respect and support. Youth organizations often include leaders and workers whose lives have followed such directions, and they therefore offer clear and realistic models of hope and dignity for young people. Beyond the personnel of these youth organizations, their frame and ethos must fit the youth population in which their existence is based. Mrs. Knowlton and others who attempt to diagnose and prescribe from the outside, who derive policy goals primarily from society's needs rather than those of youth, and who place the burden of change on youth and their families rather than on the institutions that serve them must reframe policy responses to reflect the insiders' view and the rationality of inner-city neighborhoods.

The culture of the programs that "work" with inner-city youth supports the trust, social cohesion, and respectful relationships that enable young people to leave behind the cynicism, defeatism, disregard, and low self-esteem that generate the problems that concern society. Their work is artistry—helping young people to release themselves from the "iron grip of circumstance." Their programs must support and go beyond simplistic, single-identity labels of ethnicity, race, and gender to impart a positive social identity, broadly conceived; they seek not to control or remediate youth but to develop and nurture their spirit and their strength to negotiate success-fully the cumulative entrapment—"the hell crust"—of the inner city. Estab-lishment-defined, top-down policies that retain control of program design and implementation are bound to disappoint in the absence of knowledge-able, independent, and innovative local leadership because they usually reflect scant understanding of the socioeconomic milieu in which youth construct their sense of self and because they permit little ownership or social investment of the neighborhood or its youth in the program.

Frames for Identity and Principles for Policy

Frames for identity that enable inner-city youth to move to healthy, pro-ductive adulthood and that provide connections to society and the future derive from programs that are youth based. And from the youth's perspec-tive, the principles fundamental to programs that "work"—activities and institutions that can support them along positive paths to maturity—are sim-ple and few.

Most important are the motivations and goals that drive programs or policies for youth. Youth avoid programs defined in terms of society's goals of "social control"—for example, reduction of teen pregnancies, dropout rates, involvement in dangerous or illegal activities. Youth do not elect to participate in programs that label them as deviant, "at risk," or in some way deficient or negative. Inner-city youth, like youth in more advantaged cir-cumstances, want to be involved with activities that take a positive view of them and their development. They choose activities that convey respect rather than condemnation for who they are and hope rather than fear for what they can become.

Positive programs and policies for inner-city teens avoid labels that sort youngsters into categories of more or less socially desirable behaviors or problems. Organizations in which inner-city adolescents get involved expressly challenge the many myths held by the general public about the value and potential of youth growing up in inner-city neighborhoods. These myths claim that youth:

- have little to offer the community
- cannot be trusted with responsibility
- have no interest in organizations
- are beyond redemption
- are lazy—just want to hang out or have fun
- have neither the interests nor abilities necessary to accomplish much

These myths constrain positive strategies for youth while they convey disrespect and preclude the empowering strategies essential to youth's productive development.

Inner-city youth and the adults who work with them point to the irony and waste of policy decisions that retain and reinforce social control objectives while abandoning developmental efforts. Recreation efforts scaled back to support beefed-up park security, jobs programs axed while drug prevention programs multiply, peer gang intervention programs dropped while "Green Beret" enforcement squads expand—policy choices such as these opt for fixing and controlling rather than developing and supporting. Dollars spent on development, the insiders agree, yield a higher return than those allocated to problem management and social control, and efforts to "fix" have a greater chance of success when located in a nurturing, positive context than in a punitive framework.

Youth quickly decide whether a program or an organization is attractive to them on other grounds as well. Their assessments of program appropriateness are conveyed in comments such as "it's just for kids," "there's nothing happening there," "the folks there just don't get it," or "it's too much like school."

Adolescents are unusually sensitive to whether activities or organizations are "developmentally appropriate." Programs that attract teens and sustain their interest and commitment are programs that exploit adolescents' needs in positive ways. Such programs provide a safe place in which peers can achieve a sense of belonging and of valued membership; here, youth both have mentors and can mentor others. Effective youth programs ensure that every member can come to feel he or she is an "expert" in something that others who are novices need to know. Such programs empower and entrust youth as young adults and give them meaningful roles within the organization. Programs that are developmentally appropriate for teens develop concrete competencies that are valued within the group and by the larger society. And appropriate programs for youth develop those competencies in a gratifying, not a punitive, way. "Good for you" activities are also fun and meet adolescents' social and psychological needs at the same time. The most powerful "treatments" craft coherent communities of youth and adults joined in enjoyable, productive purposes.

Young people also have clear but diverse preferences for the kinds of activities they enjoy and want to pursue. The effective organizations portrayed within these chapters run the gamut from basketball teams, to dance groups, to baseball teams, to scout troops, to social organizations, to academic support groups. Each has its own clientele and its own niche within the community. Youth well served by one would likely be uninterested in another. Effective policies for youth attend to what the young people both want to do and see as needed for them and their community.

Inner-city youth, who live in the shadows of the so-called "helping institutions" as problems to be managed, want most of all for the public and policymakers to understand who they are and the resources they need. They want chances to communicate their views about what works for them. Both youth and the adults who work with them compare successful youth organizations to two seemingly disparate institutions: families and gangs. In the words of one youth leader:

> What teenagers need most is structured attention. And if you have something, it may not be the most sophisticated and it may not be in the most glamorous setting, but if you got some caring folks that want to give some time and attention, you're going to be able to help some kids. . . . gangs are those kinds of organizations, they provide the kinds of things we should be providing. They provide a family, they provide career opportunity. If you work hard, you can advance. They give you a sense of family. You don't have to be anything to join; you can come as you are. You can find a niche and some funk that's gonna be your homies. I mean, you got a group, you've got support.

Inner-city youth have too much time on their hands, too little to do, and too few places to go. They flock to activities that protect them, nurture them, and respond positively to their needs and interests. Programs and policies based on the perspectives of youth acknowledge youth as fearful, vulnerable, cynical, and lonely but also frame them as capable, worthy young people eager to grow up to a healthy and productive future.

Acknowledgments

The close reading and comments of Arnetha Ball, Juliet Langman, and Jane Quinn enhanced and clarified this chapter; we thank them. The work reported here was supported by a grant from the Spencer Foundation to Shirley Brice Heath and Milbrey W. McLaughlin for a 5-year research project entitled "Language, Socialization, and Neighborhood-Based Organizations."

Notes

[1]River City, Lakeside, and Big Valley are pseudonyms, as are all names of the organizations, neighborhoods, and individuals mentioned in this chapter. Except where otherwise noted, all quoted comments were made by respondents in the course of our fieldwork. To preserve the confidentiality of sites and individuals, we identify respondents only in terms of their community role.

[2]See Jankowski,1991, for elaboration of the isolation and diminished hopes of inner city youngsters.

[3]Such works include Anderson (1990), Ianni (1989), Kotlowitz (1991), and Lefkowitz (1987). These works include not only extensive descriptive materials, but also some portrayal of the lives of the inner city by insiders—young and old.

[4]Compare, for example, the cases in Lefkowitz (1987) that recount in youngsters' own words their reasons for running away from home and taking to the streets.

[5]Based on an extensive literature review, researchers at the Chapin Hall Center for Children at the University of Chicago concluded that youngsters' affective, cognitive, and moral-social development is enhanced and enabled when they are linked explicitly to dimensions of their everyday life. Community-based organizations, with their strong ties to the neighborhood and normative congruity with the local setting, are in the best position to promote young people's positive growth (Wynn et al., cited in Cahill, 1991, p. 2).

[6]Jim Cummins, 1989, *Empowering Minority Students,* as quoted in Cahill (1991, p. 4).

[7]See Gomez-Pena (1988) for elaboration of the generational aspects of ethnicity and the distortions of ethnicity introduced by the "folkloric prism of Hollywood" (p. 132) and the ideological distortions of the media. Other scholars with this perspective include Nelson and Tienda (1989) and Sollors (1989).

[8]Young people, as well as adults, resent the ignorant homogenizing wrought by labels like *Hispanic,* which obscure important differences. See Gomez-Pena (1988) for an example.

[9]See, for example, descriptions of Operation SMART (Science, math and relevant technology), a Girls Clubs of America project, in Nicholson (1987) and Wahl (1988).

[10]Researchers who studied girl gangs note that the women's movement has had the effect of moving girl gang members out of a totally passive role into some kind of independence and has caused a change in girls' roles in gang life (Campbell, 1991).

[11]Jane Quinn's critique substantively improved this section by clarifying the important distinction between an organization's general philosophical or ideological position as seen in the Boy Scouts or the YMCA and its advocacy of specific religious or moral positions.

[12]Jane Quinn provided important correction and detail to this section, most par-

ticularly in noting that many national youth organizations have worked diligently to avoid an autocratic, top-down approach to programs and activities at the local level.

[13]Julia Littell and Joan Wynn detail these intra and inter-city discrepancies in their 1989 study of the availability and use of community resources in a major metropolitan area.

[14]See chapter 6 for elaboration of the conflicts that youth workers in various organizations experience as demands for "body counts" collide with assessments of programmatic responses appropriate for participating youth. The tension between bureaucratic requirements and the needs of youth derailed efforts at collaboration and eroded trust among organizations in all of the communities we studied.

[15]Robert Halpern (1992) develops this point in his analysis of "after-school" programs for inner-city children aged 6 to 12 and concludes that programs that seem "too much like school" create inhospitable environments for urban youth.

References

Anderson, E. (1990). *Streetwise: Race, class, and change in an urban community.* Chicago: University of Chicago Press.

Cahill, M. (1991). *Community youth programs—bridging gaps in personal, cultural, and public identity: Ethnicity, race and gender in youth organizations.* Stanford University, Stanford, CA.

Campbell, A. (1991). *The girls in the gang* (2nd ed.). Cambridge, MA: Basil Blackwell.

Gómez-Peña, G. (1988). Documented/undocumented. In R. Simonson & S. Walker (Eds.), *The graywolf annual five: Multi-cultural literacy* (pp. 127–134). Saint Paul, MN: Graywolf Press.

Halpern, R. (1992). The role of after-school programs in the lives of inner-city children: A study of the "Urban Youth Network." *Child Welfare, 7*(3), 215–230.

Ianni, F. A. J. (1989). *The search for structure.* New York: Free Press.

Jankowski, M. (1991). *Islands in the street.* Berkeley, CA: University of California Press.

Kleinfeld, J., & Shinkwin, A. (1982). *Youth organizations as a third educational environment particularly for minority group youth: Final report to the National Institute of Education* (ERIC no. ED240194). Washington, DC: National Institute of Education.

Kotlowitz, A. (1991). *There are no children here.* New York: Doubleday.

Lefkowitz, B. (1987). *Tough change.* New York: Doubleday.

Littell, J., & Wynn, J. (1989). The availability and use of community resources for young adolescents in an inner-city and suburban community. Chicago: The Chapin Hall Center for Children at the University of Chicago.

Nelson, C., & Tienda, M. (1989). The structuring of Hispanic ethnicity: Historical and contemporary perspectives. In R. D. Alba (Ed.), *Ethnicity and race in the U.S.A.* (pp. 49–74). New York: Routledge.

Nicholson, H. J. (1987, July). *Operation SMART: From research to program—and back* (ERIC no. ED302403). Presented at the International Conference of Girls and Technology.

Novak, M. (1980). Pluralism in humanistic perspective. *Concepts of ethnicity* (pp. 27–56). Cambridge, MA: Belknap Press of Harvard University Press.

Sollors, W. (1989). Introduction: The invention of ethnicity. In W. Sollors (Ed.), *The invention of ethnicity.* (pp. ix–xx). New York: Oxford University Press.

Turner, J. C. (1987). *Rediscovering the social group: A self-categorization theory.* New York: Basil Blackwell.

Wahl, E. (1988, April). *Girls and technology: Stories of tools and power* (ERIC no. ED302402). Presented at the annual meeting of the American Educational Research Association, New Orleans, LA.

Index

Abortion, 25
Abreu, J., 141
Addams, J., 177, 179, 180
Affirmative action, 18, 19, 33$n4$, 226
Anderson, E., 34, 44, 51, 205, 208, 237
Anderson, J., 182
Anyon, J., 198
Arnot, M., 199
Arts, performing, 8, 69–91
  communication in, 86, 87, 88, 90
  cultural, 78–82
  in public projects, 73–78
  schools of, 93$n8$
  therapeutic value of, 92$n7$
Asher, S., 136
Auletta, K., 40
Authority
  acceptance of, 7
  crisis of, 132
  defiance of, 204
  expansion of public, 179
  peer competition with, 103

Bales, R., 136
Ball, A., 69–91
Behavior
  altruistic, 130
  culturally specific, 183
  destructive, 54
  dominance, 136
  gender-related, 6, 25–26
  patterns of, 200
  social, 27
Behaviorism, 123
Belenky, M., 199
Belief
  in social control processes, 106
  systems, 62, 108–109, 164–165
Bennett, J., 141
Berger, P., 143
Bing, L., 117
Bogardus, E., 96
Bourjaily, V., 131
Boyle, G., 114
Brady, M., 139
Brenzel, B., 183
Bronner, S., 136, 140
Brooks-Gunn, J., 34

Burgess, E. W., 117
Bussey, K., 208

Cahill, M., 222, 237
Campbell, A., 237
Cartwright, D., 107, 116
Cavallo, D., 128
Children
  "at risk," 121, 131
  bias toward individualism in, 125
  culture of, 120–143
  emphasis on fun, 124
  feeling toward discipline of, 133
  historical images of, 122–126
  reform movements for, 128, 143, 177–182
  social interaction of, 122
Choloization, 97, 98, 106, 109
Churches, 18
  community-building function of, 50
  decline of African American, 51, 208$n2$
  support for youth groups, 79, 87, 114–115
Clinchy, B., 199
Cloward, R. A., 117
Coeducation, 10, 13, 137, 197–198
Cohen, A., 106
Coles, R., 142
Collaboration
  administration in, 168–169
  communication in, 169, 171
  communitywide, 154–156
  conflict resolution in, 169–170
  consensus in, 172
  in coordination of services, 150
  costs of, 157–158, 173
  day-to-day operations in, 168–170
  factors affecting, 156–173
  formalized relations in, 168
  as funding requisite, 150
  goals in, 170–171
  joint planning in, 150
  local context in, 166–167
  and localized options, 150–156
  in organizations, 147–174
  positive aspects, 149–150
  problem solving in, 169–170
  with professional organizations, 152–154
  sharing of services and resources in, 150
  successful, 166–167

About the Contributors

Arnetha Ball is assistant professor of education at the University of Michigan. Her research centers on the oral and written language uses of culturally and linguistically diverse populations in community learning settings and schools. When she was a 1991–1992 postdoctoral fellow at Stanford University, her research focused on the language of inner-city African American females in a neighborhood-based youth dance program. She has published articles in *Written Communication* and other journals in language education.

Gary Alan Fine is professor and head of the department of sociology at the University of Georgia. His book, *With the Boys: Little League Baseball and Preadolescent Culture* (1987), won the Opie Prize of the American Folklore Society. He is completing an ethnographic study of the world of high school debaters that focuses on the socialization of argumentation and public discourse.

Elisabeth Hansot is a senior lecturer in the political science department of Stanford University. She is coauthor with David Tyack of *Learning Together: A History of Co-education in American Public Schools* (1990), *Managers of Virtue: A History of Leadership in American Public Schools* (1982), and *Public Schools in Hard Times: The Great Depression and Recent Years* (1984). Her research interests include gender issues in public education, utopias (she is the author of *Perfection and Progress: Two Modes of Utopian Thought* [1977]), and women in organizations.

Shirley Brice Heath is professor of English and linguistics at Stanford University. She is an anthropological linguist whose primary interests are language socialization and the sociocultural contexts of language use by young people of diverse cultures. She is author of *Ways with Words: Language, Life, and Work in Communities and Classrooms* (1983) and coauthor with Shelby Anne Wolf of *The Braid of Literature: Children's Worlds of Reading* (1992).

Thomas James is associate professor of education and public policy at Brown University. A historian of education and author of *Exile Within: The Schooling of Japanese Americans, 1942–1945* (1987), he is working on a study that focuses on the movement of social science ideas and constructs into American education during the first half of the 20th century, from which the perspectives in this book are drawn.

Juliet Langman is a visiting teacher at the Linguistics Institute, National Academy of Sciences, Budapest, Hungary. Her research interests center on the role of ethnic and community organizations in the development of individual and group identity. Her work also explores the manner in which voluntary organizations affect social and educational policy for minority youth both in and out of school. She has studied Yugoslav guest workers in the Netherlands, as well as European American and African American urban minority groups in the United States.

Milbrey W. McLaughlin is professor of education and public policy at Stanford University and director of the Center for Research on the Context of Secondary School Teaching. Her interests focus on policy implementation, contexts for teaching and learning, and educational settings for nontraditional youth. Her recent books include *Contexts of Secondary School Teaching* (1990), coauthored with Joan Talbert and Nina Bascia; *Teachers' Cultures: Individual and Collective Identities* (forthcoming), coauthored with Judith Little; and *Teaching for Understanding: Challenges to Research, Practice and Policy* (forthcoming), coauthored with David K. Cohen and Joan Talbert.

Jay Mechling is professor of American studies at the University of California, Davis. He edited *Western Folklore,* the quarterly journal of the California Folklore Society, for 5 years and is now president of that society. He is completing a book on the Boy Scouts of America and is at work on a book on the animal rights debate.

James Diego Vigil, professor of anthropology at the University of Southern California, is an urban anthropologist whose work focuses on Mexican Americans. He has conducted research on ethnohistory, education, acculturation, and adolescent and youth issues, especially street gangs. He is the author of *From Indians to Chicanos: The Dynamics of Mexican American Culture* (1984) and *Barrio Gangs* (1988). He is also the author of articles in journals such as *Hispanic Journal of the Behavioral Sciences, Human Organization,* and *Aztlan.*